THE BENNETS OF TRESILLIAN

Tresillian House: drawn by C.J. Greenwood, 1845

THE BENNETS OF TRESILLIAN

R. G. Kerswell

The Pentland Press Limited
Edinburgh • Cambridge • Durham

First published in 1994 by
The Pentland Press Ltd.
1 Hutton Close
South Church
Bishop Auckland
Durham

ISBN 1 85821 155 7

Typeset by CBS, Felixstowe, Suffolk
Printed and bound by Antony Rowe Ltd., Chippenham

To Armenell, Jennifer,
Rosemary and Jeanette,
the last Bennets of Tresillian.

ACKNOWLEDGEMENT

The editor wishes to express sincere gratitude for access to deeds, letters, diaries and papers belonging to the Bennet family.

CONTENTS

PREFACE

The County of Cornwall, lashed by the wild Atlantic and soothed by the more gentle English Channel was civilized by the Phoenecians who came to trade in tin many years B.C. Following the christianization of Ireland, Irish missionaries turned to the conversion of Cornwall during the first century A.D. Towns and villages abound in the names of Celtic saints. The county has a long history of loyalty to the Monarch and the Old Religion but it did not escape the excesses of King Henry VIII; sadly churches, convents, monasteries and abbeys fell to pillage and plunder.

This is a chronicle, extending over seven generations, of a family who lived at and farmed Tresillian. The story begins and ends within the Parishes of St. Columb, St. Enoder, St. Gwinear and St. Newlyn. The Manor of Tresillian was built in the thirteenth Century and came into the hands of the Gully Bennets during the closing years of the seventeenth Century.

The diaries, letters and papers of the families of Gully, Bennet, Basset, Hosken, Wallis and Palmer tell their story lasting nearly three centuries. Drama mixed with disappointment, sorrow, failure and success of this family is absorbing. Their journeys take them throughout the continent of Europe, to Asia Minor, India, Hong Kong, China, Japan, New Zealand, Australia, America, Canada and South Africa.

Cornwall, though, provides the warp and the woof of this rich tapestry.

ILLUSTRATIONS

PART ONE

CHAPTER 1

Robert, Count of Mortain, was the biggest landowner in England after his half-brother King William and Cornwall was above all his Province. There he was Lord of many more manors than the King Himself. The manors tended to be small. The County was divided into seven Hundreds. Cornwall's maritime importance did not assert itself until well after the Norman Conquest – Penzance is not mentioned until the middle of the 14th Century and Bude is first mentioned in 1400.

The Domesday Book

In 1806 King George III of England was in the forty-sixth year of his reign. Lord Grenville became Prime Minister in succession to William Pitt who died on 23 January. The Holy Roman Empire ended following Napoleon's reorganization of Germany. Admiral Nelson's great victory at Trafalgar on 21 October 1805 was fresh in mind and blunted Napoleon's declaration that Great Britain was in a state of blockade. The British went about their business.

The 2nd December 1806 was a cold and windy day. Cornwall was covered by dark cloud and lashed with squalls of rain.

In the darkening afternoon at Newton's Hotel in Camborne some thirty persons gathered in the main parlour to attend a public auction of the Lease and Tythes of the Parish of Gwinear. To almost all those present the auction was no different from other sales of leasehold land within the county. The *Royal Cornwall Gazette* had carried advertisements of the sale for three successive weeks. A written notice proclaiming the auction had been posted on the main door of the Church and for the past three weeks the Rector had announced the sale from his pulpit at the principal Sunday service.

While the bidding progressed, the seller, Joseph Norway, solicitor of St Columb Major, sat before a fire in the proprietor's sitting room drinking tea with his wife and her sister. Thomas Rosewarne, one of the tenants of Gwinear, together with his brother Richard, visited the sitting room and remarked to Norway: 'The bidding has gone far beyond our mark. We

3

cannot afford to give anything more.' The bidding continued without the Rosewarnes and eventually James Vivian emerged as the highest bidder with a price of £1,430. The Lease and Tythes of Gwinear were sold to him.

On the surface there was nothing significant or strange about the auction. The sale was well attended, bidding was brisk and, thereafter, there was no occasion for anyone to be further concerned. But in 1811 rumours, gentle at first, more colourful with the telling, persisted and with varying degrees of hostility accused Joseph Norway of fraudulently rigging the sale five years earlier. It seemed as if the entire gentry of Cornwall and half of Devon were gripped with the rumours and the personalities involved.

Inevitably there was recourse to law and so began a suit which was to occupy the parties, their lawyers, and the High Court in Chancery for the next eight years. The litigation was between members of the same family. Their relationships became soured and their pockets impoverished. It was something of a *cause célèbre* throughout Cornwall and the adjoining County of Devon.

Before expanding on this affair it is necessary to explain something of the background of the parties to the suit.

CHAPTER 2

Here lies a most beautiful lady,
Light of step and heart was she:
I think she was the most beautiful lady
That ever was in the West Country,
But beauty vanishes; beauty passes;
However rare, rare it be;
And when I crumble, who will remember
This lady of the West Country?

Walter De La Mare: *Epitaph*

On the 23rd July 1694 Dame Martha Cary of Stone in the Parish of Parkham in the County of Devon sold and conveyed to Samuel Gully of Leigh in the Parish of Rickington in the County of Devon the manor house, farm and lands called Tresillian in the Parish of Newlyn in the County of Cornwall together with the nearby farm of Trewarthen. Following the death of Samuel Gully of Leigh, the Manor of Tresillian and Trewarthen passed to his son Samuel Gully of Tresillian who in 1738 married Philippa Prater who bore him five children. Samuel, William, and Anne died in their infancy. Philippa and Richard survived. Samuel Gully prospered and increased his estates within the Parish of Newlyn and the neighbouring Parishes of St Enoder, St Eval and St Columb Major.

In 1764 Philippa Gully married the Reverend John Bennet, Vicar of Gwinear (son of the Reverend Thomas Bennet, Vicar of St Enoder from 1735 to his death in 1767) and bore him eight children, of which the names of John born in 1765, Patty in 1777 and William in 1778 will recur.

The Parish of St Enoder lies some two miles east of the Manor of Tresillian just off the main highway linking Truro and Bodwin. The Church and Manor of St Enoder, dedicated to St Enodrus, antedated the Norman Conquest and belonged to the monks of Bodwin. Later the lands fell into lay

5

hands and in 1268 they were given to Glasney College, a place of learning established for clergy by Bishop Bronscombe at Penryn. To that College the benefice was appropriated in 1270, becoming a vicarage. The present church is a spacious fifteenth century building of Norman style. The tower was rebuilt in 1686. It is set on rising ground surrounded and protected by many tall trees. The Reverend Thomas Bennet's tenure as Vicar for thirty two years is commemorated by a tablet within the church. Another tablet is in memory of his much respected great great grandson, Richard Gully Bennet and his wife Mary Jean Bennet who were married for sixty years.

The Parish of St Gwinear is a mile or two south of the main road between Camborne and Hayle with magnificent views northwards to St Ives Bay. Mines in the Parish produced copper, tin and silver for several centuries but the district is now largely agricultural land. The present church, of large proportions, with some Norman remains, dates back to the fifteenth century and incorporates fourteenth century remains of the chancel window. The advowson of Gwinear belonged to the Manor of Drannack. In 1311 the Earl of Gloucester and Hertford at the instance of the Bishop of Exeter gave it to Sir Richard de Stapleton in aid of and for the maintenance of twelve scholars

Parish Church of Saint Enoder

at the University of Oxford. On 21st October, 1318 Sir Richard conveyed the deed to the Dean and Chapter of Exeter and the Bishop of Exeter bestowed the great tithes of the Parish of Gwinear upon Exeter College, Oxford, which he had founded. The Reverend John Bennet, son of Thomas Bennet Vicar of St Enoder was appointed Vicar of Gwinear on 2nd March 1768 and served that Parish until his death on Sunday 13th February 1785. He was buried in his own chancel on Thursday 17th February 1785.

On the 17th February 1774 at the Church of St James, London, Philippa's younger brother Richard Gully married Ann Carr shortly after he had inherited Tresillian and his father's estates in Cornwall. Ann was the only child and heir of Lieutenant General Edward Carr of the Parish of St. George, Hanover Square in the County of Middlesex. Subsequently Richard established a home in Portland Place, London. By letters patent granted by King George III Richard was appointed High Sheriff of Cornwall on the 31st January 1776. Until his death fifteen years later he stayed only occasionally in his London home, in the main devoting his energies to his estates in Cornwall and the duties of High Sheriff.

Richard and Ann Gully's marriage was childless and their interest in young people became concentrated on their nephews and nieces, the children of Richard's elder sister Philippa and her husband John Bennet, the Vicar of Gwinear. Philippa Bennet died in 1784 and her husband the Reverend John Bennet survived her for only a year leaving some of their children still minors. This sad situation prompted Richard Gully to make his will on the 6th August 1786 in which he provided for the whole of his estate to be held in trust by Thomas Prater Solicitor of St Columb and Charles Rashleigh of St Austell for the benefit of his wife Ann in her lifetime and to pass to his nephews and nieces upon her death save for two minor legacies and two annuities. Ann Gully died on the 27th July 1791 and four months later her husband Richard died while staying in his London house on the 22nd November 1791.

The deceased's nephew John Bennet, aged twenty-six years, was then Curate of Antony in Cornwall and not two months wedded to Elizabeth Wallis daughter of the Reverend Mydhope Wallis formerly of Trethill in the Parish of Sheviock, Cornwall. The Reverend John Bennet took charge of his uncle's funeral arrangements and all was done to ensure that Richard Gully would be buried in the soil of his native Cornwall.

The services of Messrs Walbank and Smith, Undertakers of 4 John Street Oxford Street London were engaged and their account reveals that no expense was spared to ensure that Richard Gully was accorded that atmosphere of dignity and degree of mourning befitting a gentleman of his rank. The funeral bill, prepared with minute detail, presents a colourful account of such a melancholy event and deserves inclusion.

	£	s.	d.
Men with a board and going to lay out the corpse.	0 –	5 –	0
A strong elm coffin the inside lined with a quilt lining and fine ruffle.	2 –	2 –	0
A superfine shroud, sheet, cap and pillow.	2 –	15 –	0
A superfine mattress.	0 –	18 –	0
A strong cast lead coffin well soldered compleat.	5 –	10 –	0
Tolling the bell at St Mary le Bone.	0 –	5 –	0
Men bearing in the coffin and stand.	0 –	12 –	0
A Lead Plate for inscription on lead coffin.	0 –	7 –	6
Soldering up lead coffin.	0 –	7 –	6
A strong outside elm case covered with a superfine black cloth drove with double rows all round of best brass gilt nails four large bags cherubim handles with enchased grips and finished with rich enchased ornaments all brass double gilt.	8 –	10 –	0
A large brass square engraved plate with the inscription double gilt.	1 –	11 –	6
Men bearing in the case and moving downstairs into Parlour.	0 –	15 –	0
Best velvet pall – 20 days.	5 –	5 –	0
Lead adorned with plumes of the best black ostrich feathers – 20 days.	5 –	5 –	0
Man with plumes of best black ostrich feather – 20 days.	5 –	0 –	0
Head screws for enclosing of case.	0 –	2 –	6
8 gentlemen's cloaks for journey – 20 days.	8 –	0 –	0
7 gentlemen's hat bands of crepe.	1 –	15 –	0
13 rich allamode hat bands.	5 –	17 –	0
16 allamode hat bands for tenants at 7s. 6d.	6 –	0 –	0
8 3/4 rich amozine scarves for gentlemen.	16 –	16 –	0
2 3/4 amozine scarves and hoods to Housekeeper and Servant.	3 –	18 –	0
6 rich allamode scarves to gentlemen in country.	9 –	9 –	0

26 pairs black and grey silk gloves to gentlemen and ladies in town and country.	6 – 10 – 0
19 pairs black kid gloves to tenants and servants.	2 – 7 – 6
2 conductors on horseback – 20 days.	24 – 0 – 0
The porters silk dresses – 20 days.	2 – 2 – 0
Hearse and 6 horses – 20 days.	63 – 0 – 0
Coach and 6 horses – 20 days.	63 – 0 – 0
The best black ostrich feathers and velvet the coach and horses for journey.	5 – 5 – 0
4 pages to attend coach.	0 – 12 – 0
4 velvet for Gully Esquire coach horses.	0 – 12 – 0
4 cloaks for coachmen and postillion – 20 days.	4 – 0 – 0
18 allamode hat bands to Coachmen Postillions Coach Pages and Porters and Feathermen and men in country.	5 – 17 – 0
28 pairs of gloves for above and Hearse Pages.	2 – 2 – 0
A large attachment with the Arms properly covered and backboards covered with fine black cloth.	4 – 15 – 0
Wall hooks and assistance.	0 – 15 – 0
Attending the funeral on horseback – 20 days.	15 – 0 – 0
Cash expended on the journey Turnpikes.	9 – 14 – 3
Bills on the Journey at the different Inns.	16 – 2 – 0
Expenses for rooms to receive the corpse on the journey.	3 – 17 – 0
Allowance for 4 coachmen the two porters and Feathermen for 20 days.	35 – 0 – 0
Chambermaids and Waiters at the Inns.	3 – 16 – 0
Expenses self home by desire of Mr Bennet.	3 – 15 – 0
Paid men at different inns on the journey taking the corpse out and putting it into Hearse in the mornings.	3 – 0 – 0
Man sitting up each night on the road with corpse.	1 – 5 – 0
Turnpikes and bait tenant's horses.	0 – 9 – 0
The bell tolling at Bodmin.	0 – 11 – 0
Paid Minister for Affidavit.	0 – 2 – 6
Gave Feathermen and Coachmen by order of Mr Bennet.	1 – 11 – 6

After twenty solemn days the funeral procession finally wound its way into the Churchyard of the twelfth Century Parish Church at St Newlyn East and the High Sheriff of Cornwall, Richard Gully, was laid to rest on the 14th December 1791 aged fifty-two years.

Bennet Tablet: Parish Church of Saint Newlyn

October 31st 1820 – January 11th 1910
In memoriam
Richard Gully son of
Richard Gully Bennet
and Loveday his wife
of Tresillian House
J.P. for Cornwall 1843-1910
Keep innocency and take
heed unto the things that
is right for this shall bring
a man peace at the last.

May 31st 1821 – June 2nd 1906
In memoriam
Mary Jean
wife of
Richard Gully Bennet of
Tresillian House
daughter of Richard and Ann Hosken
of Carevick Cubert
The Master is come and
calleth for thee;
As soon as she heard that
she arose quickly and
came unto him.

St Newlyn East takes its name not from New Lyn (or New Town) like Newlyn West by Penzance but from a Celtic Saint, St Newlyna. The Church, dedicated to St Newlyna was begun in the twelfth century and some rebuilding took place in 1258. Bishop Bronscombe of Exeter rededicated the Church on the 25th September 1259. The tower was added in the fifteenth Century. On the vestry wall is a list of the names of Vicars from the thirteenth century together with portraits of latter-day incumbents. The Reverend Edward Dix, Vicar from 1839 to 1856 was a close friend of the Bennet family. Records of baptisms, marriages and burials are well preserved from 1559. The Parish boundaries extend for some two and a half miles on every side of the Church and encompass Tresillian Manor. The last record in Newlyn Church of the Bennets of Tresillian is an imposing tablet on the wall of the north transept close to the Lady Chapel. Erected to the memory of Richard Gully Bennet and his wife Mary Jean Bennet it was blessed at a service of dedication on Ascension Day 1911.

By June 1792 an account of Richard Gully's estate had been prepared and his nephew, the Reverend John Bennet, newly married as mentioned, inherited the greater part of a substantial fortune. In the Parish of Newlyn he became the owner of the Manor of Tresillian with its farm, Tresillian Wicket and Trelight and the farm of Trewarthen in the Parish of St Enoder, tenements called Goenhoskyn, Chingweal, Trewinnion, the Manor of Retyn with several lands and tenements belonging, Bonallack Farm, Bonallack Strap Farm, Trevillack Farm and Trevorrick Farm passed to him.

In the Parish of St Columb Major the real estate consisted of Well Close or Well Park part of Bospolvans, the Barn Meadow and Stitch, the Parsonage Meadow and Moor, the Rock Close, the Mowhay and Town Place in Bospolvans, the Trevargan Tenement comprising the Meadow under the Orchard, the Meadow under the Mowhay and the Meadow under that, the Two Higher Parks, the Oak Park and a third part of The Downs adjoining, a tenement called Trevarren Martha and a plot of land on the south side of Trevarren Down to depasture cattle thereon. In the Parish of St Eval there were several messuages and lands in Treviscarr Vean and a tenement and two closes of land being a parcel of Treviscarr Vean Tenement.

In all the lands in Fee situate within Cornwall amounted to some 1,225 acres. In addition to the real estate mentioned there were two leaseholds under leases from Lord Arundel for ninety-nine years dated 1746 and 1754 of Hodges Tenement in Tresillian and several tenements called Tregonning, all in the Parish of Newlyn which John Bennet inherited for the remainder of the terms. John's brother William, younger by three years, inherited £1,500 together with two houses on the east side of Bond Street in the Parish of St George Hanover Square in the County of Middlesex under lease from the Mayor and Citizens of the City of London at a yearly rent of £11 and a fine of £77 payable every fourteen years with the perpetual right of renewal on paying the fine. Both houses were well let to two very good tenants and returned a handsome income.

Government stock exceeding £12,000 was sold to pay estate debts and legacies. Richard Gully's seven nieces each received a legacy of £500 and after providing for some annuities the residue of the estate comprising money, plate, jewels, furniture and other effects passed to the Reverend John Bennet.

John and Elizabeth Bennet took up residence in the Manor House of Tresillian. John settled in to running his new estates and Elizabeth bore him four children. The eldest was Elizabeth born on the 25th September 1792. Their first son and heir, Richard Gully named after his father's uncle, was born on the 13th November 1793. Their second son, Mydhope Wallis, named after his mother's father, was born on the 13th January 1795 and their second daughter Ann was born on the 3rd December 1796.

The Reverend John Bennet's father who had died in 1767 when Vicar of Gwinear had in his lifetime purchased from the Rector and Scholars of Exeter College at the University of Oxford the Lease of the Gwinear Tythes which he had renewed every three years under the rent of £60. When John Bennet inherited his uncle Richard Gully's estate he was the owner of those same leaseholds previously enjoyed by his late father and thus the Great Tythes of Gwinear had been part and parcel of his own estate in Cornwall from 1767.

The Reverend John Bennet died at Tresillian on the 31st December 1804 at the early age of thirty-nine. By his will executed only thirteen days earlier he bequeathed £3,000 to his wife Elizabeth together with 'my Mansion House Offices and Gardens at Tresillian with the use of furniture, linen, plate and books until my beloved son Richard Gully Bennet shall arrive at the age of twenty-one years.' His freehold and leasehold lands and cottages in the Parish of St Enoder were devised to his second son Mydhope Wallis Bennet together with the sum of £500. The will continued: 'I give and bequeath unto my beloved daughters Elizabeth and Ann the sum of £1,800 each to be severally paid to them when and as they shall respectively attain the age of twenty-one years or sooner at such time as my Trustees shall think proper with interest at the rate of five pounds per centum per annum from my death to be applied to their maintenance and education'. To Richard

Gully Bennet he gave and devised: 'all and every my freehold and leasehold lands and premises lying and being in the Parish of Newlyn and also my freehold lands and premises of Goenhoskyn, Chingweal with the cottages thereto and belonging and lying in the Parish of St. Enoder'. His wife Elizabeth, his brother, Captain William Bennet, and his brother-in-law Joseph Norway, husband of Patty formerly Bennet, solicitor of St Columb Major were appointed Executors and Administrators to whom passed all other lands and premises lying in the Parishes of St Columb Major and St Enoder and all other real and personal estate not specially given or disposed to hold upon trust for Richard Gully Bennet. The same three Executors were appointed Trustees and Guardians of the estates of all four children during their minorities.

The Prerogative Court of the Archbishop of Canterbury granted Probate to John Bennet's Will on the 27th May 1805 but within three months Elizabeth Bennet died in August 1805 leaving her four orphans aged thirteen, twelve, ten and nine years.

Elizabeth Bennet's will had been executed on the 3rd April 1805. Her brothers-in-law William Bennet, Captain in the Royal Cornwall Militia, and

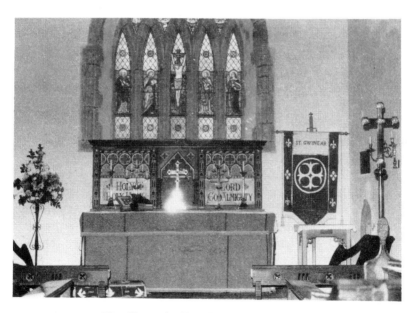

The Chancel: Church of Saint Gwinear.
Burial place of the Reverend John Bennet, Vicar.

13

Joseph Norway, solicitor of St Columb Major were appointed Executors and Trustees. The tuition and custody of Elizabeth and Ann during their minorities were entrusted to their mother's sister Ann Roberts. The tuition and custody of Richard Gully Bennet and Mydhope Wallis Bennet during their minorities were entrusted to their two uncles, Captain William Bennet and Joseph Norway. In addition to the inheritances from their father's estate Richard Gully Bennet, Elizabeth Bennet and Ann Bennet inherited from their mother the sum of £50 each secured by Deed Poll on the Liskeard Turnpike Road. To Mydhope Wallis Bennet his mother devised those freehold and leasehold lands which had been subject of her marriage settlement in August 1791 consisting of one moiety of lands and tenements called Penhale in the Parish of St Martins in the County of Cornwall, one moiety of a plot of ground being Trethill in the Parish of Sheviock also in the County of Cornwall together with eight other lands and tenements situate in the Parishes of Sheviock and St Germans. All these estates had been inherited by Elizabeth Bennet from her late father the Reverend Mydhope Wallis of Trethill in the County of Cornwall who, save for a few legacies to his servants and the poor of Sheviock, gave, devised and bequeathed his entire estate to his two daughters Ann, wife of the Reverend Doctor Bryan Roberts, Rector of Drewsteignton in the County of Devon and Elizabeth Bennet in equal shares.

After their mother's death in August 1805 the four infants were taken from Tresillian which to begin with was looked after by a servant and then let for the benefit of the Trust Estate. Richard Gully and Mydhope were sent to the Reverend Johns at Tiverton in Devon who boarded them and provided tuition until the Summer of 1809 when, aged sixteen and fourteen years, they were sent to the Reverend William Hutchinson in Exeter where they boarded during terms and received tuition from him until the end of the Summer term of 1811 when Richard Gully, aged eighteen years, went up to Pembroke College, Oxford.

Mydhope then moved to the Reverend H. Nicholls of Barnstaple in North Devon with whose family he boarded and by whom he was taught until September 1813 when he joined his brother at Pembroke.

Elizabeth and Ann had boarded for tuition throughout the school terms from 1806 to 1810 with a Mrs Louis and then until December 1812 when Ann celebrated her sixteenth birthday she received tuition from a Mrs Broadhurst with whom she boarded.

Throughout the years from August 1805 to 1812 Mr and Mrs Joseph Norway took overall responsibility for the children but Mrs Ann Roberts, a maternal aunt, had Elizabeth and Ann with her at Drewsteignton during holidays when they were frequently joined by their brothers. In 1808 Dr Bryan Roberts died after a short illness. Richard Gully, then fifteen years, wrote to his Aunt from Tiverton:

> My dear Aunt
> We received your letter this morning acquainting us of the melancholy event that has taken place at Drewsteignton. It quite astonished us.
> I suppose we shall not spend our holidays at Drewsteignton since the melancholy event has taken place there. I shall write to my sisters next Saturday for I suppose they are in great trouble too. When you write please put down the directions to Uncle Major Bennet's for he desired me to write to him.
> Master Darke desires to be remembered to his friends and he hopes that they will write to him soon dont forget to tell them of it.
> I suppose my sister will not return to school yet as this melancholy event has taken place.
> Brother joins with me in duty to Uncles and Aunts and love to sisters and cousins. I and my brother desire to be remembered to all the House.
> I remain your ever dutiful nephew   R Gully Bennet.

The children also spent a good deal of time with their Aunt Patty and Uncle Joseph Norway at St Columb Major. Mr Norway's books of account, subsequently called into question, demonstrate that all the children were expensively and well educated. Their pocket money was generous, there were many outings and journeys during school holidays. Much thought and care were devoted to their upbringing which reflected their parents' standing within the county.

CHAPTER 3

Scattered about, in various holes and corners of the Temple, are certain dark and dirty chambers, in and out of which, all the morning in vacation, and half the evening too in term time, there may be seen constantly hurrying with bundles of papers under their arms, and protruding from their pockets, an almost uninterrupted succession of Lawyers' Clerks. These sequestered nooks are the public offices of the legal profession, where writs are issued, judgments signed, declarations filed, and numerous other ingenious machines put in motion for the torture and torment of His Majesty's liege subjects, and the comfort and emolument of the practitioners of the law.

Charles Dickens. *Pickwick Papers.*

During his first term at Oxford Richard Gully Bennet consulted his close friend and kinsman William Prater of St Columb Major with a view to taking legal action against his two Uncles Joseph Norway and Major William Bennet. He wanted to obtain a full disclosure of their trusteeship, the appointment of a Receiver and an order to set aside the sale of the Lease and Tythes of Gwinear. Letters were exchanged between William Prater and Joseph Norway. On the 30th May 1812 Joseph Norway wrote to William Prater and informed him that he had been persuaded to conduct the cause for himself and Major Bennet. The letter also revealed that in his zeal to prepare for the case the young undergraduate had not returned to Oxford at the beginning of the first term. Norway wrote: 'he should return to Oxford at once and not lose the benefit of studying there for a term'.

By the following month Norway had engaged Messrs Shepherd, Adlington and Gregory, Solicitors of Bedford Row London, to act as his correspondents and William Prater had engaged Messrs Vanheythuysen to act for him. Both sides had set in motion the legal proceedings from which neither would withdraw and the case of Elizabeth Bennet, Richard Gully Bennet, Mydhope Wallis Bennet and Ann Bennet, infants under the age of twenty-one years, represented by William Prater, their next friend, Complainants, versus Joseph

Norway and William Bennet, Defendants, was launched in the Chancery Division of the High Court.

In five letters written between the 17th June and the 11th August 1812 Messrs Shepherd, Adlington and Gregory advised Mr Norway of events at the High Court.

Bedford Row
June 17 1812

Dear Sir

Bennet v Bennet

No application has yet been made for an order for a Receiver and if any such were made we should recommend to oppose it. We think it very probable the Chancellor would reject the application. You had better in all events be preparing to put in your answer.

I remain Dear Sir
Yours truly
J N Adlington.

Bedford Row
July 2nd 1812

Dear Sir

Bennet v Bennet

We cannot recommend you to let so hostile an application pass without opposition but if you should so determine and an order be made then we must before the Master carry in a proposal for Mr Coode to be Receiver and which proposal must be accompanied with the names and descriptions of two sufficient housekeepers as his sureties.

I remain Dear Sir
Yours truly
J N Adlington.

Bedford Row
7th July 1812

Dear Sir

Bennet against Norway

This motion came on again this morning when the Chancellor at Mr Leach's request gave us further time to the 16th instant to file affidavits to oppose the motion. The Plaintiffs are willing to waive the whole of their motion except the appointment of a Receiver and probably as you may not consider it prudent to enter into a full discussion at this period and upon affidavit you will not oppose that part of the motion. Please to let us know your determination by return and if you do oppose the motion send us up affidavits as long before the 16th instant as possible.

I remain Dear Sir

Yours truly

John S Gregory.

Bedford Row

6th August 1812

Dear Sir

Bennet against Norway

We attended the Master again today upon these proposals. The Master is strongly disposed to listen to their proposals in preference to ours as he considers them to be the parties principally interested in the appointment unless therefore we receive a very strong affidavit by Tuesday's post at the latest we fear the proposal of Mr Paynter will be acceded to. Perhaps as the lands in question lie contiguous to those of Mr Buller or Sir W Lemon for whom Mr Paynter is concerned there may be some interference with each other or there may some circumstances which may make it improper to appoint Mr Paynter.

I remain Dear Sir

Yours truly

John S Gregory

Bedford Row

11th August 1812

Dear Sir

Bennet against Norway

We attended the Master this morning and I am sorry to say in spite of all our objections he has appointed Mr Paynter the Receiver. An affidavit of Richard Gully Bennet was produced which stated he had been informed by one Cook that you had said even if Coode was appointed the management of the property would be chiefly left to you and although we objected to the reading of this affidavit in which the Master concurred I should not be surprised if it had had its effect on the Master's mind.

I remain Dear Sir

Yours truly

John S Gregory

In the same month of August 1812 a newspaper published in Exeter carried a statement of the complaint which someone unknown ringed in black ink to draw attention and dispatched it, anonymously, to numerous people, including Joseph Norway's clients, living in Devon and Cornwall.

Mr Norway reacted angrily. By then Francis Camborne Paynter, a solicitor of St Columb had been appointed Receiver. In the course of a long and indignant letter Joseph Norway wrote:

> From the hostility I have for years experienced from Mr Paynter and his sons and particularly as the promoters of this suit I have fair reason to assume that they or their minion Richard George were the authors of that statement and the persons who caused it to be published, none other could have been guilty of so base an action.
>
> I know not a single act that has not been done for the benefit of the Trust Estate since the Testator's death and I challenge my opponents to show a single favour improperly granted to any of the tenants nor have I derived any advantage from personally undertaking the management of the Trust which I did at Mr Bennet's request. I might have drawn several leases had I looked to my own emoluments which I will venture to say has in no instance since I have been in the profession seventeen years been the case. My wish and endeavour has always been to practice absolutely with the interest of my client in view and I flatter myself that I may confidently refer my conduct to the profession and gentlemen of the County who are best able to appreciate my character to those clients who personally know me and have an opportunity of themselves learning whence the hostility proceeds. I have nothing to apprehend from this attack of the Paynters.
>
> Gentlemen of the neighbourhood have long witnessed our conduct to the infants; their last parent died in 1805 since which time they have known no other home and we have often received them two boys and two girls to our great inconvenience. Mrs

19

Norway has been in every respect a mother to them and from me they have experienced a no less parental care. I can safely say that in the management of their concerns placing them at school we have for the last eight years occupied scarcely less than a tenth part of my time. I have done this without remuneration and I feel it hard to have not only my motives questioned but great endeavours made to traduce my character. Mrs Norway and I have both lost some near and dear relatives however poignant our feelings have been at the time nothing ever so truly distressed me as the conduct of our nephews and nieces whom we have sheltered when no other house was open to them and when we regarded and acted towards as children of our own to meet with such ingratitude. I will venture to affirm that the children will sink considerably in the estimation of the world and will fail to be taken that notice of which from their station they are entitled to.

You will naturally ask how come it that they should take such a step against their nearest relatives. To explain it briefly I must state that Mr Paynter's eldest son paid his addresses to Mr Bennet and on his asking my consent I declined interfering on account of their hostile conduct to me and referred him to Major Bennet who in the discharge of his duty and from well knowing the unfavourable opinion which his brother and Mrs Bennet had of the Paynters and what would have been their decision which did his addresses. The young lady however being determined to encourage his addresses it became necessary to remove her from Saint Columb and then it was whilst I was in town in the spring of the year that the business broke out.

The first intimation that Major Bennet had was a most insulting and threatening letter from his nephew, not from the style of its writing of his declaration and I was wholly unapprised of any intention of a suit till the Bill was filed and I was served in two days after with a subpoena. If the infants had any reason to be dissatisfied with our management of the Trust why had they not spoken of it to us or have applied to some friend of their parents to have looked into the business but that would not have answered the purposes of those who level in mischief and wished to devide a united family.

I have lately put in my answer annexing thereto my Trust Account which is very long, the receipts amount to near £15000 and the payments to a little more leaving a balance of £46 in my favour.

Major Bennet has ever evinced the utmost solicitude for the welfare of his nephews and nieces and having no children of his own, none were so dear to him, he never could have thought that in giving £5 more than was offered by any local bidder in the sale for Gwinear Tythes and paying the money for the benefit of the Estate three months sooner than the stipulated time at the auction for which there were many competition and a great price at the time bid that he should be charged with defrauding his nephew.

The Paynters would not stick at trifles. They have declared that they will ruin me if they can and I have no business that they would not try to take from me because I stand in the way of their overbearing disposition and have foiled them in every attack they have hitherto made upon me. I have professionally resisted with success several actions in which they have been concerned, some of them personally, in one of which the second son James was severely reprimanded by Mr Justice Bayley for his conduct towards my client, a poor widow, which joined with other things, drew down upon him the censure of the profession at our Society Meeting and he was for a while refused admittance. It not infrequently happens that the evil which persons project for others recoils upon themselves and I shall in this instance be mistaken if they don't fail in their main object that of endeavouring to lessen me in the esteem of the County.

There are few, if any, I believe, who think that the suit has been instituted for the benefit of the infants who are made the tools of private spite and malice. The children without such advisers never could have acted as they have done. Was it probable that they would have ransacked my office papers as they did one day during my absence or have broke open the desk at Tresillian Mansion of which I had the key where there were many of the Trust papers without such abettors.

I thank God I have done no one act that I am ashamed to disavow. I rather wish every transaction of the Trust to be investigated that the true management of it may be known as soon as the Accounts are passed. I intended to request some independent gentleman to examine them with every circumstance relative to the Trust. I feel and know that I have been unfairly dealt with, in time the matter will be seen in its true lights.

To the Motion upon which the Estate Statement in the papers was made we opposed not the appointment of a Receiver or a Guardian. We were in fact not Guardians to the children though we exercised the unthankful office of being Executors and Trustees of the property and the Trust in Kindred. The personal Guardianship was given by the Testator to Mrs Bennet alone with whom it ceased on her death. It has been and is our wish to submit ourselves entirely to the direction of the Court and to make a finish of the suit as soon as possible. This is the first Trust that I ever personally undertook and I hope it will be the last that I shall ever be required to other than in a professional view.

I will conclude with the assurance that everything has been done openly and with the best intention for the interest and welfare of those concerned in the property confided to us.

The strained relationship between the Paynter family and Joseph Norway is reflected in a letter from St Columb written by James Paynter to Richard Gully Bennet and addressed to him at Pembroke College.

St Columb
25th November 1812

My dear Gully

I enclose the desired remittance of Fifty Pounds herewith of which I will thank you to acknowledge.

My brother, I believe, informed you that your friend Symons had taken Little Tresillian. Bospolvans is let in three lots. Retyn is taken by Glanville and Trewinion by Richards. Bonallack and Bonallack Strap are let to two responsible tenants.

The Chevalier is gone from home for two days a fortnight. I consider he is in London for the purpose of being fully advised as to his Answer.

You must not calculate on so liberal allowance of £500 per annum as the Master before he grants such allowance as that will require an affidavit that that amount is absolutely necessary.

Mr Dampior has given his opinion as to vacating the leases of such farms as are let at inadequate rents. The opinion is that ejectments may be maintained in all cases where it can be clearly shown that the lands devised to you and your brother are let at less rents than any reasonable man would have thought of accepting.

The legal estate in the real property being vested in your friend, the Chevalier feels that no ejectment can be maintained so to that estate the Chevalier has omitted to say whether Varco's lease can be set aside.

I write in much haste.

I am, Dear Gully

Yours very truly

J Paynter.

The term Chevalier was frequently used in the Complainants' correspondence when referring to Mr Norway. Mr Paynter was quite correct in his surmise that Joseph Norway was busy in London for two days a fortnight preparing his Answer to the Complainants' Notice of Motion by the Bill filed. Indeed Mr Norway was very busy in the preparation of a meticulous reply. The Answer, a prodigious document, was finally engrossed consisting of nine parchments to which financial schedules occupied another thirty-four parchments, and filed in the Court of Chancery on the 17th February 1813.

Joseph Norway, answering for both Defendants, dealt first with the Complainants' allegations concerning the sale of the Lease and Tythes of the Parish of Gwinear.

And this Defendant also admits that the said Testator was possessed of the Rectory or Parsonage of Gwinear in the Bill mentioned and as this Defendant believed of all the Tythes of Corn and Grain yearly arising within the Parish of Gwinear under a Lease thereof from the Master and Scholars of Exeter College Oxford bearing date on or about the first of May 1803 for the term of ten years from Ladyday when last passed.

And this Defendant saith that in managing the property and estates given and bequeathed to his said nephew and nieces by the said Wills he this Defendant acted in the best manner he was able and best calculated according to his judgment and belief for their respective benefits and took great pains and trouble therein and spent a great portion of his time in attending to the bringing up of the family of the said Testator and in managing and looking after the said estates and concerns and seeing that the same were used and managed in as proper and husbandlike manner by the respective tenants thereof. And this Defendant verily believed that owing to the good and husbandlike manner in which the said estates have been farmed and managed the same has very greatly increased in value since the death of the said Testator and Testatrix respectively. And this Defendant further answering saith he admits it to be true that the Freehold and Leasehold Estates of which the said Testator died seized or possessed or the greatest part of them were or was let by him to good and solvent tenants at large yearly rents.

And this Defendant further answering saith that the said Testator at the time of his death was possessed of the great and praedial Tythes of the Parish of Gwinear aforesaid under the Lease thereof hereinbeforementioned. But this Defendant saith that such Lease did not contain any clause or condition that the same should be renewable every three years or at any other time or times whatsoever. And this Defendant verily believed that such renewal and the terms thereof were wholly at the discretion or will of the Master and Scholars of the said College. And this Defendant saith that on or about the 9th July 1806 and not in the month of June as in the Bill indicated this Defendant and the said William Bennet surrendered the said Lease which had been granted to the said Testator from the said Master and Scholars of Exeter College and as such Trustees aforesaid and this Defendant and the said William Bennet therefrom took a new Lease of the said Rectory and Tythes for such time as in the Bill is mentioned save that the same is not renewable every three years or at any other time as in the Bill is alleged nor was it part of the terms of such new Lease that the same should be renewable at any time or times whatsoever. And this Defendant saith that the said Lease was dated the said 9th day of July 1806 and was made between the said Master and Scholars of Exeter College Oxford of the one part and the said William Bennet and this Defendant of the other part by which Lease the said Master and Scholars in consideration of the sum of £240:15:6 to them paid by the said William Bennet and this Defendant granted the said Rectory or Parsonage of Gwinear and the great and praedial Tythes of the Parish of Gwinear to the said William Bennet and this Defendant their executors administrators and assigns for the term of ten years from Ladyday then last passed at the yearly rent of £60.

And this Defendant further answering saith he denies it to be true that this Defendant and the said William Bennet did at any time form any plan for appropriating to themselves or either of them the benefit to be derived from the said Lease or that any agreement was entered into between them for that purpose or for the sale or assignment of the said Lease to the said William Bennet. On the contrary this Defendant saith that he found it necessary to sell some part of the said Testator's estate for the payment of his debts and having caused an auction to be held for the sale of the Real Estates devised for that purpose by the will of the said Testator at which sale no adequate price being bid for the same and a small part only being thereupon sold as hereinbeforementioned this Defendant was of opinion that it would be most advantageous to dispose of the said Leasehold Estate and conceiving that it would be likely to sell with more advantage if the said Lease was renewed this Defendant and the said William Bennet did accordingly with the sole view and object of making the most of the said Testator's Estate obtain such renewal thereof as is hereinbeforementioned and which was so obtained with the intention to proceed to an immediate sale thereof but this Defendant being seized with a severe fit of illness which continued for several months the sale was necessarily postponed for a short time that is to say till the December following when the same took place as hereinafter indicated.

And this Defendant further answering saith that he admits that the said Lease hath been sold and assigned to or in trust for the said William Bennet for the price and consideration and under the circumstances hereinaftermentioned. And this Defendant saith he doth not know nor can set forth as to his information or belief whether the price or consideration for the same was inferior to the value thereof but this Defendant positively saith that at the time the same was sold to the said William Bennet this Defendant conceived that the price he paid for the same was very large and the utmost value thereof and that no larger sum could be obtained for the same.

And this Defendant admits it to be true that the said William Bennet after the said Lease had been assigned to him and in or about the month of July 1809 surrendered the said Lease and took a new Lease of the said Rectory Tythes and Premises from the said Master and Scholars of Exeter College aforesaid in his own name and which was so taken by him in his own name as this Defendant believes because he considered himself the owner thereof.

Turning then to the general allegations made of underselling and underletting assets by the Trustees, Joseph Norway continued:

And this Defendant further saith he denies it to be true that he and the said William Bennet or either of them have or has sold any parts of the said Testator's or Testatrixes Estate except the said Lease of the said Rectory and Tythes and also except a freehold field called the Parsonage Meadow and Moor situate in St Columb Major aforesaid which this Defendant admits was sold by him by private contract in or about the month of July or August 1805. But this Defendant saith that the same together with other parts of the said Testator's estate devised by him UPON TRUST to be sold for the payment of his debts were a few days previous to such sale or some short time before at the particular desire of the said Elizabeth Bennet who was then living and very anxious that the Testator's debts should be discharged put up to sale by public auction but no parts of such estates were sold at such auction because this Defendant did not conceive that an adequate price was bid for the same states or either of them and the sum of £326 which was considerably more than had been bid for the said Parsonage Meadow and Moor at such auction being afterwards offered for the said Parsonage Meadow and Moor the Defendant on the part of himself and his Co-Trustees agreed to sell the same for such sum to this Defendant having been advised that the same was the full value thereof. And this Defendant verily believed that the same was in fact the full value thereof. And this Defendant positively denies that he was ever informed nor were or was his said Co-Trustee or either of them to this Defendant's knowledge or belief ever informed that by selling the same estates by private contract they were injuring the estate of the said Testator or those entitled thereunto as untruly alleged by the said Bill or that any such or the like information or declaration as in the Bill is alleged or to any such or the like effect was made or given to this Defendant to this Defendant's knowledge or belief to the said other Defendant the said William Bennet.

And this Defendant further answering saith he admits it to be true that he does carry on the business of an Attorney at St Columb Major and also of a Banker at the same place he being one of the partners of a certain Bank called the Pyder Bank. But this Defendant saith he hath only carried on such business of a Bank since the month of April 1810 and that he did not at any time carry on the trade of a Banker either as a partner in the said concern called the Pyder Bank or in any other manner previous to such time. And this Defendant saith he admits it to be true that he and the said Defendant William Bennet have granted various leases of parts of the estates devised to them as aforesaid. And this Defendant saith that previously to letting the same this Defendant and the said Elizabeth Bennet deceased or one of them caused the said estates except the estate called Tredinnick to be valued part thereof by John Stephens and the other part thereof by William Paynter both eminent Land Surveyors and the same were let at sums equally or exceeding such valuation except the farm called Trevarton which had been valued by the said William Paynter as worth the yearly rent of £187:11:0 but George Hawke the tenant thereof refused to give such rent alleging that the same had been greatly overvalued. And this Defendant after making enquiries of other persons and examining himself personally the said farm was of opinion that the sum of £187:11:0 was too high a rent and the said George Hawke being a good farmer and responsible man and having been much in the esteem and confidence of the said Testator and Testatrix in his and her lifetime this Defendant did not think himself warranted in turning him out of the estate and at length agreed to let and afterwards demised by lease the said estate to said George Hawke at the rent of £167:5:6 being in this Defendant's judgment and belief a full and fair rent for the same and being an advance of £45 upon the rent he had before paid.

And this Defendant saith that with respect to the said farm called Tredinnick the same was in hand at the time of the said Testator's death by reason of some litigation with the former tenant thereof and the same got into a bad or irregular state of cultivation. And this Defendant thereof let the same to John

Whitford at the rent of £110 for the first year and £120 for the second year and afterwards at the yearly rent of £150 which rent this Defendant considered to be the full value of the said farm having been shortly before the Testator's death valued for him by the said John Stephens to be worth the rent of £122:15:0.

And this Defendant further saith that the estate called Treviscar and Tregone which had been let at £48:7:6 was valued by the said William Paynter at the rent of £80 and the old tenant giving up the said farm this Defendant let the same to Johnson Paynter at the said rate of £80. And this Defendant further saith that not being able to procure a tenant for the mansion house called Tresillian in which the Testator lived this Defendant permitted Temperance Jane an old servant of the said Testator residing with him at his death and who afterwards married William Arthur to occupy part of the said mansion house in order to take care thereof and this Defendant afterwards let to the said William Arthur as tenant from year to year a garden and some small pieces of land adjoining the said mansion house and which had been usually occupied therewith at the yearly rent of £21.

And this Defendant saith that except as aforesaid he doth not believe that the rents which have been reserved by the said leases or any of them are inferior to the rent which would have been reasonably gotten for the same from good and unexceptionable tenants but this Defendant saith that in case any of such leases are granted at rents under the real value thereof but which this Defendant doth not admit or believe this Defendant positively saith that at the time of granting such leases respectively he verily believed as well from the valuations aforesaid as from the advice and information he obtained thereon it was most for the benefit of the estate and of the persons entitled thereto to let the said estates at the rents and upon the terms and to the persons to whom the same were so respectively let and that the same were let at the fair value thereof under all the circumstances taken together.

And this Defendant further answering saith that at the time of the death of the said Testator he this Defendant was tenant to the said Testator from year to year of two fields situate in St Columb Major covering three acres and a half of land or thereabouts and no more at the yearly rent of £14 with premises this Defendant hath greatly improved by draining and manuring the same at his own expense. And this Defendant admits that he has ever since been in the possession of the said fields and in his Accounts of the said Testator's Estate he had debited himself with the said annual sum of £14 and this Defendant at Michaelmas 1811 entered into the possession as tenant of certain other fields or parcels of pasture land containing four acres or thereabouts situate in St Columb Major aforesaid. And this Defendant has in the Accounts which this Defendant has set forth in the Second Schedule to this Defendant's Answer which he prays may be taken as a part thereof debited himself with the annual sum of £20 being an advance of £2:3:0 above the rent occupied therewith at the yearly rent of £21. And this Defendant saith he believed the same might be worth a greater rent but he took into consideration the time of the said William Arthur and his wife having charge and taking care of the said mansion house and the furniture and goods therein. And this Defendant further saith that all the leases which have been so granted by this Defendant and his said Co-Trustees or either of them except those to the said John Whitford Johnson Paynter and William Arthur as hereinbeforementioned have been granted to persons who were tenants of the said Testator at the time of his death or their representatives or assigns and who were respectively in possession of the estates of which leases were so granted to them at the time of the granting thereof.

In rebuttal of allegations that he had improperly used his profession and his position as Trustee to the detriment of the Trust's beneficiaries Joseph Norway answered:

And this Defendant further saith that he had not to the best of his remembrance and belief transacted business as an Attorney for any of the persons to whom leases have been granted as aforesaid nor were any of such persons customers of the Defendant as a Banker previous to the time of entering into agreements for the granting of such leases except some very inconsiderable conveyancing for one or two of the said persons not amounting in the whole to the sum of £20. And this Defendant positively denies that such leases or any of them were granted with a view of benefitting the lessees as being the clients or customers of this Defendant or that such or any of the leases granted by this

Defendant and his said Co-Trustees were granted by this Defendant with any corrupt or improper view whatever. And this Defendant further answering saith that the said William Bennet concurred in the granting or agreeing to grant all the said leases.

And this Defendant saith that except as aforesaid he doth not believe that the rents which have been reserved by the said leases or any of them are inferior to the rent which would have been reasonably gotten for the same from good and unexceptionable tenants but this Defendant saith that in case any of such leases are granted at rents under the real value thereof but which this Defendant doth not admit or believe this Defendant positively saith that at the time of granting such leases respectively he verily believed as well from the valuations aforesaid as from the advice and information he obtained thereon it was most for the benefit of the estate and of the persons entitled thereto to let the said estates at the rents and upon the terms and to the persons to whom the same were so respectively let and that the same were let at the fair value thereof under all the circumstances taken together.'

'And this Defendant further answering saith that at the time of the death of the said Testator he this Defendant was tenant to the said Testator from year to year of two fields situate in St. Columb Major covering three acres and a half of land or thereabouts and no more at the yearly rent of £14 with premises this Defendant hath greatly improved by draining and manuring the same at his own expense. And this Defendant admits that he has ever since been in the possession of the said fields and in his Accounts of the said Testator's Estate he had debited himself with the said annual sum of £14 and this Defendant at Michaelmas 1811 entered into the possession as tenant of certain other fields or parcels of pasture land containing four acres or thereabouts situate in St. Columb Major aforesaid. And this Defendant has in the Accounts which this Defendant has set forth in the Second Schedule to this Defendant's Answer which he prays may be taken as part thereof debited himself with the annual sum of £20 being an advance of £2:3:0 above the rent at which the same was let by the said Testator in the same year in which he died and except as aforesaid this Defendant has not taken possession of any part of the said Estate as tenant thereof nor are the sums of money which this Defendant hath debited himself with far inferior to the real value of the lands occupied by him. And this Defendant hath hereinbefore set forth a description of the lands occupied by him and the rents which he pays for the same.

Canvassing the complaint about the Trustee's administration of Mydhope Wallis Bennet's inheritance Joseph Norway continued his Answer:

And this Defendant hath from time to time let out at interest at the rate of £5 per cent per annum all sums of money which have been received by this Defendant on account of the Rents and Profits of the Estates given and devised to the said Complainant Mydhope Wallis Bennet as soon as this Defendant was able after the same had been received in order that the same might accumulate for the benefit of the said Mydhope Wallis Bennet. And this Defendant saith he denies it to be true that he hath kept in his hands or hath deposited in any Bank House in which this Defendant is a partner nor hath the said other Defendant William Bennet to this Defendant's knowledge or belief kept in his hands or deposited in any such Bank House any sum or sums of money whatsoever being part of the said Testator's or Testatrixes Personal Estate and Effects or of the Rents and Profits of his or her Freehold or Leasehold Estates or any sum or sums of money which have arisen from the sale or any of the said Freehold or Leasehold Estates save and except for a very short time and for safe custody only until the same could be applied by him in manner aforesaid and also except such balance as aforesaid and which were kept by him in his own hands or paid into the said Pyder Bank to answer the current expenses or the said Trust and Executorship.

Joseph Norway then traversed the Complainants' allegation that there had been sufficient funds in the two Estates to meet funeral expenses debts and other expenses necessary to the execution of the Trust. His Answer continued:

And this Defendant saith he denies it to be true that the personal estate of the said Testator died possessed exclusive of the said Rectory and Tythes of Gwinear were more than sufficient for the payment of the Testator's debts and funeral expenses but on the contrary thereof this Defendant saith that such personal estate was not specifically bequeathed including the said Rectory and Tythes were not nearly sufficient for the payment thereof. And this Defendant saith that the whole thereof have been exhausted in payment of the Testator's debts and funeral expenses and the necessary purposes of carrying into execution the trusts of the said will.

And this Defendant saith that the only savings which have arisen from the Testator's or Testatrixes Real or Personal Estates have arisen from the rents and profits of the Real Estate given and devised to the said Complainant Mydhope Wallis Bennet which this Defendant has from time to time let out at interest as aforesaid which savings together with such interest thereof now amounts to the sum of £1,200 or thereabouts.

And this Defendant further answering saith it was necessary to sell the Lease of the Rectory and Tythes of Gwinear for the reasons hereinbeforementioned and that the same Tythes were accordingly put up to sale by public auction on the 2nd day of December 1806 at Newton's Hotel in Camborne in the said County of Cornwall which is near adjoining to the same Parish of Gwinear and that such intended sale was on three successive days previous thereto that is to say on the 15th, 22nd and 29th days of November 1806 advertised in the *Royal Cornwall Gazette* and this Defendant directed notice to be published in the Churchyard of the said Parish of Gwinear in the usual manner immediately after service on a Sunday a short time before such auction was held and a written notice thereof was posted on the door of the said Church for some time previous. And this Defendant believed it to be true that there were various persons in the neighbourhood who were likely to become purchasers of the said Tythes and this Defendant believed that by the means aforesaid such intended sale was generally known in the neighbourhood and in the County of Cornwall. And accordingly various persons attended at such auction and there were present thereat to the best of this Defendant's remembrance and belief between twenty and thirty persons. And this Defendant admits it to be true that James Vivian in the Bill mentioned attended as the Agent of this Defendant and his said Co-Trustee but this Defendant denies that any other of the persons who attended at such sale was the Agent of this Defendant and his Co-Trustee or either of them nor were any of such persons to the best of this Defendant's remembrance and belief the tenants of this Defendant or the said William Bennet or either of them except Richard Rosewarne John Rosewarne and John Foster in the Bill named who were the tenants of the said Rectory and Tythes to this Defendant and the said William Bennet as such Trustees as aforesaid. And this Defendant denies it to be true that he did nor did the said Defendant William Bennet to this Defendant's knowledge or belief require any persons to attend at the said sale who had no intention or were not likely to become the purchasers thereof. And this Defendant saith that there were many bidders at such sale as this Defendant recollects and believes not fewer than nine of them except the said James Vivian and who were as this Defendant believed bona fide bidders for the same and meant and intended to have purchased if they could have obtained the same for what they considered to be the value thereof. And this Defendant further answering saith that the said Thomas Rosewarne and not Richard Rosewarne as in the Bill mentioned bid the sum of £1270 and not the sum of £1300 for the said Rectory and Tythes and after he had bid such sum he together with the said Richard Rosewarne came into the room where this Defendant together with his wife and her sister had retired to tea and they or one of them thereupon said to this Defendant that the bidding had gone beyond their mark and that they could not afford to give anything more, that the price was too great, and that they had done or to such purport or effect and thereupon this Defendant admits that he might have said to them or one of them that he thought the said Lease would be bought in for the Testators' family. But this Defendant doth not recollect or believe that he at any time declared to them or either of them that it was no use for them to bid or to the like effect nor did this Defendant say anything as to the probability of the same being bought in till after they had declared that the biddings were gone beyond their mark and had as this Defendant verily believed given up all idea of bidding any further for the same. And he is the more satisfied thereof because he had previously to the sale limited the said James Vivian in bidding to a sum not exceeding £1400 which this Defendant considered a full price to be obtained for the said Tythes and this Defendant positively denies that he made any such declaration to the said Peter Pender or to any such or the like effect as in the Bill is mentioned nor did the said Peter Pender as this Defendant verily believed nor at any time before the said biddings were closed that the said James Vivian was bidding on behalf of this Defendant and the said William Bennet as such Trustees as aforesaid or that there was any probability of the said Lease being bought in and this Defendant positively denies that the said Peter Pender was deterred further continuing the said biddings in consequence of any such information as in the Bill is mentioned or as this Defendant believed of any information whatever given to him by this Defendant. And this Defendant also denies it to be true to the best of his knowledge and belief that the said John Rosewarne and Richard Rosewarne and Peter Pender or either of them were or was deterred from continuing the said biddings in consideration of any information or declaration given or made by this Defendant to any persons whatever. And this Defendant saith he believed that they respectively bid to the utmost extent of what they thought the Leasehold including the said Rectory and Tythes was worth and shortly after such biddings were concluded the said Peter Pender declared that he had bid £100 more than he had previously intended to give for the same. And the persons in the said auction room or part of them declared that the price at which the same was knocked down was much larger than the real value thereof. And this Defendant further answering saith he admits it to be true that the said James Vivian bid the sum of £1,430 for the said Leaseholds and that he was declared the best bidder for the same and that the same was bought in by the said James Vivian at such sum as the Agent and on behalf of this Defendant and the said William Bennet as such Trustees as aforesaid.

And this Defendant saith that the said William Bennet was absent from Cornwall on duty with his Regiment for a considerable time previous to and at the time of such sale which was entirely under the direction of this Defendant. And this Defendant saith that his reason and motive for employing the said James Vivian to bid at the said sale was to prevent the said Tythes from being sold at less than the full value and according to the best of this Defendant's recollection and belief he, this Defendant, by signs caused the said James Vivian to bid higher than he originally intended which he was induced to do perceiving the biddings to be made with spirit and thinking that possibly a greater advance might be obtained. And this Defendant saith that the said William Bennet having afterwards offered to give the sum of £1,430 for the said Lease and which this Defendant conceived was the utmost price for the same no person having offered to give any larger price the said Lease was shortly after the said auction was held that is to say on or about the 15th day of the same month of December agreed to be assigned to the said William Bennet in consideration of the said sum of £1,430 the whole of which sum the said William Bennet agreed to pay at Christmas 1806 instead of Ladyday 1807 at which time only by the terms of the said conditions of sale a part of the said purchase money was to have been paid. And the said William Bennet accordingly on the 23rd day of December 1806 paid the said sum of £1,430 to Messrs Biddulph Cocks & Co of Charing Cross, London, the Bankers of this Defendant and also the Bankers of the said Testator at the time of his death on the account of this Defendant and this Defendant very shortly afterwards applied the whole thereof in payment of the Testator's debts.

And this Defendant saith that at the time the same was agreed to be sold to the said William Bennet this Defendant conceived the same was a very large price and the utmost that could be gotten for the same. And this Defendant further answering saith he admits it to be true that no valuation was taken of the said Rectory and Tythes on the behalf of this Defendant and the said William Bennet or by any agent employed on behalf of the persons entitled to the said Rectory and Tythes because this Defendant saith the same would not have been valued with a survey and valuation being made of the whole of the Parish out of which such Tythes were payable which was always considered a very objectionable measure by the farmers and tenants of the land out of which Tythes were payable who were averse to have their lands valued and it would have been very difficult for any surveyor to have ascertained the true value thereof without the consent of such tenants and farmers. And this Defendant saith he admits it to be true that the said Rectory and Tythes were in or about the month of August 1804 let by the said Testator John Bennet to the said John Rosewarne Richard Rosewarne and John Jocken for seven years at the annual rent of £210 as aforesaid. And this

Defendant saith that the same were so let and under the advice of Messrs Grylls Borlase & Scott who acted as the Attorneys and Agents of the said Testator and who lived in the neighbourhood of the said Parish of Gwinear and the amount of such Tythes were at the time the same were so let raised from the sum of £195 to the sum of £210. And this Defendant conceived that the same was the full and fair rent for the same. And this Defendant admits that conceiving the same was a full and fair rent no notice was given to determine the said Lease at the end of two years from the commencement of the said term according to the powers reserved in the said Lease.

And this Defendant conceived and believed that the said rent of £210 was a full and fair rent for the same and this Defendant doth not believe that the same could have been let for the sum of £700 as alleged by the said Bill nor doth this Defendant believe that the said rent of £522 could have been gotten for the same if the farmers holding the lands out of which the said Tythes were payable had not agreed to take the respective Tythes thereof.

Concluding his long Answer Joseph Norway said:

And this Defendant further answering saith that he hath hereinbefore and in the Second Third Fourth and Fifth Schedules to this his Answer annexed and which this Defendant prays may be taken as part thereof set forth according to the best of his knowledge remembrance information and belief a full true and just account of all and every sum and sums of money which have been from time to time received by him and by any person or persons by his order or for his use from the sale of any part of the Testator's Freehold or Leasehold Estates or of his Personal Estate or for or in respect of the Rents or Profits of the said Testator's Freehold and Leasehold Estates or for or in respect of the Rents Profits and Produce of the Freehold Leasehold and Personal Estate of the said Testator or any part thereof especially and by whom and from whom and for what all and every such sums of money were received. And this Defendant hath therein distinguished which of each sums were respectively received on account of the Estates given or devised or appointed to the said Complainant Mydhope Wallis Bennet and the several sums which have been received for or on account of the said Complainants Elizabeth Bennet and Ann Bennet respectively and this Defendant denies it to be true that he has nor has the said Defendant William Bennet to this Defendant's knowledge or belief employed any part of those moneys in any business or trade except as hereinbefore mentioned nor has this Defendant nor the said William Bennet to this Defendant's knowledge made any profit or advantage therefrom whatsoever other than as hereinmentioned and credited in the Schedules hereunto annexed.

And this Defendant further answering saith that he hath hereinbefore and in the Sixth Seventh Eighth and Ninth Schedules to this his Answer annexed and which this Defendant prays may be taken as part thereof set forth according to the best of his knowledge remembrance information and belief a just and true account of all and every sum and sums of money which have been from time to time actually paid or disbursed or allowed by him for and in respect of the debts due and owing by the said Testator and the said Testatrix at their respective deaths or for or in respect of repairs or otherwise on account of the Real and Leasehold Estates of the said Testator and Testatrix and in execution of the Trusts and Executorship of their said Wills or for the maintenance and education of the said several Complainants and by whom and whom and for what all and every such sums were respectively paid disbursed or allowed and how and in what manner all and every the sums of money which have been received by him in any manner on account of the Freehold Leasehold and Personal Estates of the said Testator and said Testatrix respectively have been applied and disposed of and to whom the savings of the Rents and Profits of the Estates and property given and bequeathed or appointed to the said Complainant Mydhope Wallis Bennet or of the interest which have arisen therefrom have been lent and what interest has been made therefrom.

And this Defendant saith that he hath in the Tenth Schedule to this his Answer annexed which he also prays may be taken as part thereof set forth according to the best of his knowledge remembrance information and belief a full true and just inventory and account of all and singular the Personal Estate and Effects whatsoever which the said Testator was possessed of interested in or entitled to at the time of his death remaining unsold and not disposed of and the true and real value thereof. And this Defendant further saith that all such other Personal Estate and Effects of which the Testator died possessed except his Leasehold Estates especially bequeathed have been sold and the particulars and full produce thereof mentioned and accounted for by this Defendant in the Sixth Schedule hereunto annexed. And this Defendant denies that he hath any balance in his hands on the whole of his Trust Accounts relating to the Testator's and Testatrixes Estate. On the contrary thereof he believes that there is due to him for money laid out for the said Complainants or some or one of them on the balance of such Accounts the sum of £46:2:6½ as will appear by the Schedules hereunto annexed. And this Defendant denies all unlawful Combination or Confederacy wherewith he is charged.

Joseph Norway, the Defendant, was duly sworn to the truth of his Answer in the Borough of Truro on the 17th day of February in the fifty-third year of the reign of His Majesty King George the Third in the Year of Our Lord Eighteen Thirteen.

The Plaintiffs filed a Reply setting out their observations upon the Defendants' Answer and on the 13th August 1814 the Vice-Chancellor delivered a decree. In terse language he summarily set aside the sale of the Rectory and Tythes of Gwinear in the following words:

> And let the said Master declare the sale of the Rectory and Tythes of Gwinear in the pleadings mentioned is void and that the Defendant William Bennet holds the same upon the Trusts declared by the Will of the Testator concerning the same. And let the said Master take an account of the Rents and Profits thereof received by the said Defendant William Bennet or by any other person or persons by his order or for his use. And let the said Master also take an Account of what is due to the said Defendant William Bennet on account of the sum of £1430 paid by him as also all fines costs and expenses on renewing the Lease of the said Tythes and let the said Master compute interest on all sums he shall find to have been so paid after the rate of £4 per cent per annum from the time such sums were respectively paid.

It has always been a golden principle of the law of England that a Trustee must observe proper diligence and good faith and must never put himself in a position where his interest conflicts with his duty. Major William Bennet as Co-Trustee had breached that principle by selling to himself an asset of the Trust no matter how financially advantageous to the beneficiaries such sale was pleaded. By his decree the Vice-Chancellor thus disposed of the controversial issue which had been at the root of the proceedings but all the other questions remained in issue. As to them the Vice-Chancellor ruled:

> Our Decree that it be referred to Mr Cocks one of the Masters of this Court to whom several references in this Cause have been made to take an account of the Personal Estate of the Reverend John Bennet the Testator in the pleadings named come to the hands of the Defendants Joseph Norway and William Bennet his executors or either of them or the hands of any other person or persons by their or either of their order or for their or either of their use. And let the said Master take an account of the said Testator's debts funeral expenses and legacies and compute interest on such of the debts as carry interest after the rate the same respectively carry interest and on the legacies from the end of one year after the said Testator's death after the rate of £4 per cent per

Parish Church of Saint Gwinear

annum unless any other time of payment or rate of interest is limited by the Will and in that case according to the Will. And let the said Master cause an advertisement to be published in the *London Gazette* and such public papers as he shall think fit for the creditors of the said Testator to come in before him and prove their debts and he is to fix a peremptory day for that purpose and in default of their coming in to prove their debts by the time so to be appointed they are to be excluded from the benefit of this Decree and let the said Testator's Personal Estate be applied in payment of his debts and funeral expenses in a course of administration.

Identical provisions were made in respect of the personal estate of the late Elizabeth Bennet. The Decree then continued:

And let the said Master take an account of the Rents and Profits of the Real Estates in question accrued since the respective deaths of the said Testator and Testatrix received by the Defendants or either of them or by any other person or persons by their or any of their order or for their or any of their use and let the said Master enquire what sums of money have been properly expended by the said Defendants in the maintenance and education of the Plaintiffs the Infants and let such sums as the said Master shall find to have been properly expended by them in such maintenance and education be allowed to the said Defendants in taking the Accounts before mentioned. And let the said Master enquire what part of the said Testator's Real Estates have been sold since his death and let him take an account of the money arisen by sale thereof and of the application of the money arising by such sale.

And it appearing by the Answer of the Defendant Joseph Norway that he hath held part of the Real Estates of the Testator in his own hands let the said Master set a value thereon by way of Rent during the time he was in possession thereof and let him be charged therewith in taking the Accounts before directed. And let the said Defendant Joseph Norway on or before the first day of Michaelmas Term next pay into the Bank with the Privity of the Accountant General of this Court In Trust in this Cause the sum of £1600 directed to be paid in by him on or before the first day of Easter Term last by an Order made in this Cause bearing date the 9th day of December 1813. And let the Receiver appointed in this Cause be continued and pass his Accounts before the said Master and for better taking the Accounts and discovery of the matters aforesaid the parties are to produce before the said Master upon Oath all deeds papers and writings in their custody or power relating thereto and are to be examined upon entries as the said Master shall direct who in taking the said Accounts is to make unto the parties all just allowances and reserve the question of the Costs of this Suit and of all further directions until after the said Master shall have made his report. And let any of the parties be at liberty to apply to this Court as they shall be advised and refer to the said Mr Cocks one of the Masters of this Court.

Mr Cocks appointed William Foot, Solicitor of Plymouth Dock in the County of Devon to investigate all the allegations, counter-allegations, denials and rebuttals of the parties set out in the pleadings. Mr Prater and Mr Norway were invited to appear before him and argue the matter. They did so for three days.

On the 30th March 1816 Joseph Norway wrote from St Columb to Mr Foot:

My dear Sir

Since my return from Dock I have been looking through these long accounts again with a desire to correct any errors and I am inclined to think that the £4:1:1 charged to Gully Bennet (Schedule 6) 11th November 1809, does not belong to him notwithstanding the entry in my Cash Book at the time, but should be £4:1:7 and charged to Mydhope (Schedule 7), same date, instead of £1:16:4.

In Schedule 8 Elizabeth Bennet is debited 5th March 1807 with £2:2:0. I observe the same item forming part of her Aunt's charge £6:3:5½ immediately preceeding it, and therefore I conclude that it is wrong. And the £5:9:8 charged to her on 11th November 1809 I think also belongs and is charged to her sister (Schedule 9) August 1809. And that in this last Schedule Miss Ann Bennet is debited 11th November £4:18:3 when that sum is charged and belongs to Gully Bennet. I have been looking at the particulars of these things with Mrs Norway and such is the impression on our minds but her sister Miss A Bennet is not with us at present and I cannot refer to her through whose hands these things chiefly passed.

Several other corrections were made in the minutest detail and then Mr Norway concluded:

> I have also been at some pains since I saw you to take out the receipts and payments in each year as they stand in the Account on the 1st January which I also send you and by which you will observe that in no one year had I more money in hand than was necessary to carry me through the year for current expenses. Some of the balances appear large but on referring to the payments large sums were immediately paid off and I was always in advance to Mrs Roberts and the workmen who had their money long before the times stated in the Account when receipts were taken and the fact is that I never had any material balance in my hands beyond the sum on which interest is charged.
>
> I do not know that I have done myself justice in charging so much interest against me as I have done, but I was willing there should be no cause for complaint notwithstanding I have made no charge for my trouble and I am satisfied the sums charged for Board Postages etc is very much less than the actual costs out of pocket. The few professional charges I have made are, I believe, not unreasonable. I have looked through the Tythe Account also and I believe you will find that to be correct.

Mr William Foot, Solicitor of Plymouth Dock, representing the Master in Chancery, was no less punctilious than Joseph Norway. On the 17th July 1816 he wrote his report to the Master:

> I have perused the Bill and Answer with the numerous Schedules, the Decree of the Vice-Chancellor, and all the Papers submitted to me by the parties in this Cause. I have heard the allegations of Messrs Prater and Norway, and carefully investigated the Accounts of the latter as exhibited in the different Schedules, and it is known to those gentlemen that three whole days were occupied in the investigation and in comparing the items with the vouchers. I have bestowed much attention on them since that time, and if the view I have taken of the whole should be the

means of saving a further expense and litigation before the Master, my humble opinions may be so far useful.

Observations on First Schedule

The First Schedule to the Answer contains An Account of the Freehold and Leasehold Estates of which the Testator John Bennet died seized or possessed and to whom and for what Rents the same are and have been let.

I am not aware that it is incumbent on me by the terms of reference to say anything respecting the Items of this Schedule. Indeed not knowing the condition of the Estates or any other particulars about them, or their occupiers at the time of the new letting of them by the Defendants, I am incapable of judging whether they did or did not in the particular instances enumerated exercise their discretion wisely by letting them (as they appear in most instances to have done) by private contract. Perhaps a public survey or letting is the surest way of getting the most Rent in all cases but many inconveniences are known to result from Surveys, and it is not always wise to get the utmost Rent that may be offered and to turn out a good responsible old tenant who offers a fair price, and run the risk of a bad one who may offer more.

When Estates belonging to Infants are let by their Trustees by private contract, it is, however, usual to have a previous valuation by a Surveyor. This appears to have been done in some though not all the instances that occurred, but I should add that in the cases where it has been omitted, nothing has appeared before me to lead to the belief that the omission was otherwise than accidental. Being nearly allied to the Infants it might not have occurred to the Trustees to be so particular as they would have been if acting for strangers.

The Decree of the Vice-Chancellor having directed the Master to set a value on the fields which were in Mr Norways' occupation at £14 per annum rent, before and after Mr Bennet's death, it may perhaps be wished by the parties to the suit that I should set such value but it does not appear by my notes on the papers left with me that I have the means of doing so by reference to an Ex Parte affidavit left by me with Mr Prater it is stated as the opinion of the

43

Deponents therein that the said fields were in 1811 worth to be let from year to year £46:10:0 per annum and by another statement that they have since let for £28:0:0 per annum. I should think therefore that £14:0:0 was an insufficient rent. But generally on the sufficiency or insufficiency of the Rents paid by the respective tenants and appearing in this Schedule I have no means of forming a correct judgment.

Observations on Second Schedule

The Second Schedule contains An Account of all sums of money received by this Defendant from the sale of Freehold Leasehold and Personal Estates of the Testator and also of the Rents and Profits of the Freehold and Leasehold Estates of the Testator devised by him to or for the benefit of the Complainant Richard Gully Bennet, and also of the interest or produce of the Personal Estate of the Testatrix bequeathed by her to the said Complainant Richard Gully Bennet.

Mr Norway has produced a large mass of papers documents memorandums accounts of disbursements for taxes and allowances to the several tenants in support of the items in this Schedule and it is known to Mr Prater that they were very minutely examined by him and by me during the three long days sitting for that purpose at Plymouth Dock. Declaring therefore again my incompetency to decide on the sufficiency or insufficiency of the Rents paid by Mr Norway and the other tenants I have to observe that 'with the single exception mentioned underneath' every item in this account appears to me to be just and right and to be established by the documents and papers that have been laid before me. Exception alluded to: Johnson Paynter years rent to Michaelmas 1810 £80:0:0 less Property Tax £7:14:9 less Repairs £4:18:0 – £67:7:3. Now the sum of £4:18:0 allowed for Repairs is the same as in the preceding year and no voucher for it is produced. I imagine therefore that is must be the same. If so, Mr Norway will be charged with the amount (see extract of Mr Norway's letter herewith sent relative to this and several other small errors).

Observations on Third Schedule

The Third Schedule contains An account of all sums of money

received by this Defendant for or on account of the Rents and Profits of the Real Estate devised by the Testator to the Complainant Mydhope Wallis Bennet and also for or on account of the Rents and Profits of the Freehold and Leasehold Estates of the Testatrix and of such part of her Personal Estate as is given or appointed by her Will to or for the benefit of the Complainant Mydhope Wallis Bennet.

The same language that I have adopted in my observations on the Second Schedule is applicable to this Third Schedule and generally all the items in this have been satisfactorily established by Mr Norway.

Observations on Fourth Schedule
The Fourth Schedule contains An account of all sums of money received by this Defendant for or on account of the Interest and Produce of the several Legacies given and bequeathed or appointed by the Wills of the Testator and Testatrix respectively to the Complainant Elizabeth Bennet.

With respect to this Schedule, no objection was made by Mr Prater nor do I see occasion to say more than it appears to be perfectly correct.

Observations on Fifth Schedule
The Fifth Schedule contains An account of all sums of money received by this Defendant for or on account of the Interest and Produce of the several Legacies given and bequeathed or appointed by the Wills of the Testator and Testatrix respectively to the Complainant Ann Bennet.

The same observation as was made on the Fourth Schedule applies in every respect to this.

Observations on Sixth Schedule
The Sixth Schedule contains An account of all sums of money paid by this Defendant on account of the debts due and owing from the Testator at the time of his death or for or on account of the Personal Estate of the said Testator or for repairs or otherwise

on account of the Freehold and Leasehold Estates of the said Testator devised to and for the benefit of the Complainant Richard Gully Bennet and in the execution of the Trusts and Executorship of his Will and in the maintenance and education or otherwise on account of the said Richard Gully Bennet and how and in what manner all such sums have been applied and disposed of.

There follows a list of forty-three items about which Mr Foot entertained doubt. For the most part they referred to material bought and labour paid for work on buildings and repairs on the various farms forming part of the Estate. Mr Foot then added these comments:

It must be acknowledged that the bills paid for materials, labour and work bestowed and done on the buildings of the different estates are to a very large amount but that such sums have been paid there can be no doubt; Mr Norway having produced a voucher for almost every one of them. On the one hand it is alleged by Mr Norway that the new buildings and repairs were absolutely necessary and that the work was well done and in proof of it he has produced a certificate from Mr Best, a Surveyor, who surveyed for Mr Bennet in his life and after his death by the order of Mr Norway, who states as follows

Sir I beg to signify that I was employed by the late Reverend John Bennet of Tresillian House, to set and superintend the building of a new farmhouse on Tresillian and occasionally to look at the repairs of other of his farm buildings; and that I was so employed after his death by Mr Joseph Norway. And I do hereby testify that I surveyed the buildings on the several Farms of Goenhoskyn and Bonallack in St Enoder, Trevarton, Tredinnick, and Tregoning in Newlyn – that in my judgment and opinion it was necessary and advisable to erect new barns and farm buildings on Trevarton, Tredinnick and Bonallack and to make an addition to the Barn on Tregoning and to repair the dwelling houses on Goenhoskyn, Tredinnick and Trevarton, and to build new pigs houses on the last mentioned Estate in the manner and according to the plans on which the same has been done. That all the work has been completed in a proper and substantial manner

46

at as little expense as the same could be accomplished in a workmanlike manner.

I am Sir   Your obedient servant

John Best

On the other hand it is contended by Mr Prater on behalf of Mr R G Bennet that the expenditure has been enormous and in many cases useless improvident and without a due regard to economy. If I had seen or know the estates (which I never did) it would be impossible for me to form a competent judgment on the necessity of such an expenditure. I know that estates in the Counties of Devon and Cornwall are in general encumbered with more buildings than are absolutely necessary and still it is difficult to lessen them and imprudent to let them go to ruin. If therefore Mr Richard Gully Bennet continues to question, and Mr Norway to maintain, the necessity and propriety of such expensive buildings and repairs, the Parties must make out their respective cases before the Master and have his decision on them but it must be remembered that all the materials bought and all the work done cannot be unnecessary and that when Trustees act bona fide according to the best judgment they can form, without any view to their own emolument, and where they are borne out in the necessity of the expenditure by the testimony of others, the Court will not scrutinise their acts too nicely, but make every liberal allowance to them. I do therefore think that the several disbursements should be allowed.

In this Sixth Schedule there are various payments such as Pocket Money, Travelling Expenses etc of Mrs Roberts, Mrs Norway etc, for which no legal vouchers were produced nor was it possible that Mr Norway could have them but he showed Memorandums Letters etc in confirmation of most of them and I have no doubt of the whole being correct.

I must add also that the very few professional charges of Mr Norway in this Schedule are exceedingly reasonable; so is the charge for Board and Lodging of Mr R G Bennet during the time of his residence with him; and as to the great trouble, time and attention which the management of this Trust must have occasioned, there is no charge whatever made from the beginning to the end.

If therefore it should appear that the balances in hand were at times rather more than absolutely necessary, it must be recollected as a setoff that there is no charge for trouble, time and attention, and that Mr Norway has charged himself with considerable sums as the Interest of balances in hand (see his letter on this subject).

The Personal Estate of the Testatrix and for repairs or otherwise on account of the Freehold and Leasehold Estates of the Testatrix and for such of the Real Estates of the Testator as are devised to the Complainant Mydhope Wallis Bennet and in the execution of the Trusts or Executorship of her Will and also in the maintenance and education or otherwise on account of the said Mydhope Wallis Bennet and how and in what manner all such sums have been applied and disposed of.

The chief objections that were made to this account by Mr Prater in the investigation of its items, and in comparing them with the vouchers, arose from the largeness of the payments for materials and labour in erecting a barn on the estate of Bonallack.

Mr Foot then set out the various sums subject to the objections made and continued thus:

I do not think that £142:0:0 is an extravagant sum for building a good barn considering the times when this was erected timber being then at the dearest price. But the doubts entertained on these articles are whether it was prudent and proper on an Estate let for £56:0:0 a year only to lay out two years and one half rent in erecting it. That an Estate having no Barn must be much benefitted by such an addition, cannot be doubted. And it has been stated by Mr Norway in proof of it with respect to this Estate that it has since been let for £92:0:0 per annum. But perhaps much of them increase of Rent arose from the great rise which estates had experienced during the preceding term and not wholly from the advantages of a Barn. I observe that Mr Best, the Surveyor, says the Barn was absolutely necessary, that he surveyed the work which was well and with as much economy as possible.

If this be so, and other persons can bear satisfactory testimony to the same effect, I have no doubt of the Master's allowing these items of expenditure because Receivers of Infants' Estates appointed by the Court are often authorised to make large expenditures of this kind where the necessity or probable advantage of such buildings and estimates of the expense are first submitted to the Master from whom they derive their authority. And it must be recollected that in this instance Mr Norway had no such authority as that of a Master to refer to. I have thus stated my opinion pro and con on these disputed items but if Mr Mydhope Wallis Bennet is not satisfied of the necessity and advantage of such erections or thinks the money lavishly expended they must form a part of those items which the Master is to decide on.

There are some items of expenditure in this Schedule for which no vouchers are produced – for those that consist of pocket money and travelling expenses no regular vouchers could be expected; but in most of those cases memorandums in pocket books and account books have been produced by Mr Norway and I have no doubt of their correctness.

The payments for which no vouchers have been produced or about which doubts seem to have arisen in the investigation of this Schedule are few, three only. The charges for Board and Lodging, for expenses of receiving Rents, inspecting Estates, for Postages, Bill and Receipt Stamps etc towards the end of the Schedule are very reasonable. The £1600 in the hands of the Defendant William Bennet will be set against the Purchase Money of the Tythes which he is to receive. And as to the last item of £300 to Mary Bennet and £500 to Thomas Bittick I understand those sums have been paid into Court.

Observations on Eighth Schedule
This Schedule contains An account of all sums of money paid and laid out for and in the maintenance and education or otherwise on account of the Complainant Elizabeth Bennet and how and in what manner all such sums have been applied and disposed of.

I am satisfied of the correctness of these charges and have no doubt that Miss Bennet is of the same opinion. Regular bills and receipts for most of the items have been produced by Mr Norway but it cannot be expected that a strictly legal voucher for all of them should be produced by a Trustee who was a near relation of the party interested and who might not have had in contemplation the passing an account in a strict way before the Master. The charges for Board and Lodging and for Stamps etc are very moderate.

Observations on Ninth Schedule
This Schedule contains An account of all sums of money paid and laid out for or in the maintenance and education or otherwise on account of the Complainant Ann Bennet and how and in what manner all such sums have been applied and disposed of.

I cannot see objection to these charges which are nearly similar to those in the preceding Schedule. The charges for Board and Lodging and for Stamps etc are free from exception.

Finally William Foot wrote:

The Account which has been handed to me respecting the Purchase Money of the Gwinear Tythes, and the Rents that have since been received, must be decided on by the Master as they arise out of the Decree which sets aside the sale of them made to the Defendant William Bennet. I much doubt whether all the items at the end of the above account of Purchase Money etc of Gwinear Tythes (amounting to £66:1:6) will be allowed, the Chancellor being of opinion that a sale to the Defendant Mr Bennet should not have taken place, it is not likely that the Master will approve of any charge without conveying the Tythes to him.

On the 4th October 1816 William Prater and Joseph Norway signed a Memorandum which reflected a compromise by the parties. The Memorandum filed in the Court of Chancery read:

The Accounts of the Defendant Joseph Norway annexed to his Answer to the Bill of Complaint filed in this Cause, having been referred to William Foot of Plymouth Dock Esquire and minutely examined by him, and also by me, the undersigned William Prater on behalf of the Complainants; it is ascertained admitted and agreed by us as follows, that is to say:
As to the Defendant Joseph Norway:
That the Receipts of the said Defendant Joseph Norway on behalf of the said Complainant R. G. Bennet amount to the sum

of £9784:12:1 and that the payments of the said Defendant for the same Complainant amount to the sum of £9750:18:11½ and will leave a balance of £33:13:1½ due by the said Defendant Joseph Norway to the said Complainant R. G. Bennet.

Also that the Receipts of the said Defendant Joseph Norway on behalf of the said Complainant M.W. Bennet amount to the sum of £4015:13:4 and that the payments of the said Defendant for the same Complainant amount to the sum of £3884:9:11½ and will leave a balance of £131:3:4½ due by the said Defendant Joseph Norway to the said Complainant M. W. Bennet.

Also that the Receipts of the said Defendant Joseph Norway on behalf of the said Complainant Elizabeth Bennet amount to £628:0:6 and that the payments of the said Defendant for the same Complainant amount to £779:7:4 and will leave a balance due by her to the said Defendant Joseph Norway of the sum of £151:6:10.

Also that the Receipts of the said Defendant Joseph Norway on behalf of the said Complainant Ann Bennet amount to £628:0:6 and that the payments for the same Complainant amount to £631:1:5½ and will leave a balance of £3:0:11½ due by her to the said Defendant Joseph Norway.

As to the Defendant William Bennet:

That there is due to the Defendant William Bennet by the Complainant R. G. Bennet the sum of £1895:1:0 for Principal Money and Interest thereon calculated up to the first day of February next, and for Fines and Expenses paid on the Renewals of the Great Tythes of Gwinear, after allowing for Rents received of the Tenants of the same Tythes and otherwise, which Tythes are to be assigned to the said Complainant R. G. Bennet or held by the said Defendants as Trustees for Sale and Executor named in the Will of the Reverend John Bennet the Testator for the purposes mentioned in the said Will.

Also that there is due by the said Defendant William Bennet to the said Complainant M. W. Bennet the Principal Sum of £1600:0:0 and for Interest of the same from the first day of May 1812 to the first day of February 1817 the sum of £348:0:0 making together the sum of £1948:0:0.

It is also agreed to by us that the costs of all Parties in this Cause shall be referred to and ascertained by Thomas Adlington of Bedford Row Gentleman and Richard Vanheythuysen of John Street Bedford Row Gentleman the respective Agents in this Cause and if they cannot agree thereon then to such person or persons as they shall by writing under their hands appoint who shall respectively have power to determine by and to whom and out of what Fund and in what manner the same shall be paid.

And we do also agree that this Agreement shall and may be made a Rule of the High Court of Chancery in the said Cause or otherwise as that Honourable Court shall think fit.

Witness our hands the fourth day of October 1816.

Costs of the individual parties were ascertained by the two London solicitors and in the autumn of 1818 it was agreed that the costs as determined would be in favour of the Defendants payable by the Plaintiffs.

As the curtain came down on the family drama twelve years after the fateful auction Richard Gully Bennet was twenty-five years old, down from Oxford and residing in the family manor, Tresillian.

Mydhope Wallis Bennet had graduated as a Bachelor of Arts and on Sunday the 6th September 1818 in the Chapel of The Blessed Virgin Mary at the Palace of Exeter, George, Bishop of Exeter, ordained him Deacon. On the same day the Reverend Mydhope Bennet was granted faculties to perform the office of Curate in the Parish Church of Talland in the County of Cornwall at a yearly stipend of £50 payable by the Vicar of Talland with a house at Looe about one mile from Talland.

Ann, aged twenty-two, went to live with Mydhope in Looe. The eldest child Elizabeth had married Francis Camborne Paynter, son of Francis Paynter the Receiver appointed to the Trusts, and was living in St Columb Major. Major William Bennet had died a year earlier on the 20th April 1817.

CHAPTER 4

There is one panacea which heals every sore in litigation, and that is costs.

L.J. Bowen (1835 – 94)

By a Deed of Indenture dated 24th December 1818 Joseph Norway, the sole surviving Executor and Trustee of the Reverend John Bennet's Will released and conveyed the freehold estates in the Parishes of St Columb Major and St Eval to Richard Gully upon discharge of the monies due to Elizabeth, Mydhope and Ann. Only the final accounting of costs awarded between the brothers and sisters remained.

In a letter dated 28th September 1819 Solicitor William Prater wrote to Mydhope Wallis Bennet:

> My dear Cousin Myd
>
> I have not been able to get the documents till now but I send you the extracts of the Receiver's Costs and also the draft settlement the contents of which I have not had time to look into. Pray preserve them for me until a future time. I am glad Richard Vanheythuyson's letter was so explanatory. The final accounts were as I expected.
>
> I had only one day's shoot at St Austell, three brace and about fourteen brace since my return here.
>
> Adieu, the Coach is waiting.
>
> Let me know if you have any observations to make.

William Prater wrote to Richard Gully Bennet on the 1st May 1820:

> My dear Gully
>
> Having received an answer about the costs I now send you a copy of it which I think is clear and satisfactory upon the question of the Tythes Money although certainly I did not comprehend it

altogether before.

You will see that £142:9:6 went for the costs of the last application and which you will find on referring to the Petition were provided to be paid out of the Tythes Money as well as the balance due to the Defendants for the costs of suit awarded to them. It would appear therefore that the sum in question was paid to Adlington as Referee independently of the Defendants.

Eight years after the Bill of Complaint was first launched by Richard Gully Bennet and four years after the Complaint was settled by the parties with an order of costs made against the infant complainants it seemed as if the matter had come to an end. But it was not to be so. The costs payable by the four complainants to their two uncles were substantial. The vexed question of costs and in particular the accounts between the two brothers were to dominate their thinking and occupy the space of many letters for a long time to come. Moreover a question mark cast in doubt and suspicion hovered over the accounting of Mr Paynter, the Receiver. This became the cause of acute embarrassment to both Richard Gully and his brother Mydhope because by then their elder sister, Elizabeth, had married Francis Camborne Paynter, son of the Receiver. It would seem that Mr Joseph Norway's reservations about the Paynter family had not been misplaced after all. It will be remembered that in an angry letter written in 1812, immediately after service of the Bill of Complaint, Mr Norway alluded to the hostility of the Paynter family and the persistent attention of Mr Paynter's son towards Elizabeth, whose hand in marriage he won before the case of the Gwinear Tythes had been settled.

Nevertheless there were some signs of normal country life for the family despite the lingering doubt, suspicion and lack of reconciliation. On the 11th December 1819 the following notice was published:

> Whereas divers persons have lately made a practice of destroying the Game on the lands of Richard Gully Bennet Esquire situate in the several parishes of Newlyn and St Enoder Notice is hereby given that all persons trespassing on any of the said lands for the purpose of destroying the Game after this public notice will be prosecuted according to the statutes in such cases made and provided.
> Dated at Tresillian House 11th day of December 1819.

By the 17th September 1821 Mydhope was to be joined with his brother as the following notice reveals:

> Notice is hereby given that if any person or persons shall be detected in hunting shooting or coursing over Trevarton, Tresillian, Goonhoskyn, Tregoning, Retyn, Benallack, or any other the Lands of Richard Gully Bennet Esquire and the Reverend M.W. Bennet situate in the several parishes of Newlyn and Saint Enoder after this public notice will be prosecuted with the utmost severity of the Law.
>
> Dated this 17th September 1821.

Wightwick Roberts, son of the late Dr Roberts, a cousin three years senior to Mydhope was practising as a barrister in London. He wrote to Mydhope about Mr Paynter's accounts during the early part of 1818.

Hills Court
23rd January 1818.

M W Bennet Esquire
My dear Cousin

As I did not exactly know where to put my hand on Mr Paynter's letters and when they were found the accounts not being very clear, will I hope, plead a sufficient excuse for my delay in writing.

You will observe by the statement on the other side that Mr Paynter has only accounted to my mother for £43:4:8 for the timber sold on Trethill and I should observe that in his letter in December 1816 he said that the accounts were completely made up.

Not being very well satisfied with Mr Paynter's accounts (while staying with my cousin) I went to Mr Little of Hessenford, a surveyor who attended the auction and he gave me an account which I have now in my possession stating to whom and for what each Lot was sold. By his account the timber sold for £126. I am sure my mother has never received from Mr Paynter more than is specified on the other side and therefore how he made such a mistake I cannot conceive. I have in vain asked my mother for permission to write to Mr Paynter for an explanation, nor can I even get her to do it. I observe in Mr Little's document that two of the Lots were sold to Mr Hawkins for £13, but on looking into Mr Paynter's account I cannot find this sum accounted for or even Mr Hawkins' name mentioned. Will you ask him if he paid Mr Paynter because if he did not he must account for it to my mother.

My mother has now consented to pay half of your estimate (I believe £59) towards the repairs at Trethill and she hopes this will be the utmost it will cost. Could you get the Carpenter and Mason to contract for this sum? For if you cannot it strikes me that you must either let Mr Hawkins have the entire direction of the business or you must tell the Mason and Carpenter what each is to do and desire Mr Hawkins to overlook or keep an account against them. Perhaps you are aware of some better way of managing it but should you be driven to a choice of the two plans I have mentioned I should think the latter the most preferable. As Mr Hawkins now owes my mother near a year's rent of course he will advance the sum required.

I saw William Prater yesterday when I delivered your message. My mother, Ann and John unite in kindest love to Cousin Ann and yourself.

I am my dear Mydhope
    Yours sincerely
       Wightwick Roberts.

But the letters from Mydhope to his brother Richard Gully about the accounts were to continue for several years.

> Red Lion Inn
> St Columb.
> Friday evening 6 o'clock
> 1st December 1819.

My dear Brother
    I arrived here without getting wet tho' it rained incessantly and I was prevented from taking my dinner at this place till four o'clock by one thing and another. I shall not start till tomorrow morning when I hope to breakfast with Mr Nelson at Fowey and proceed to Looe to dinner. The first step I took on reaching this place was to call on Mr Mountsteven whom I fortunately found at home and who, on my informing him of the purpose of my visit

accompanied me to the office where we met Francis Paynter. This gentleman, son of F.C.P. immediately retracted what had been said of my sending a verbal message to him by Mr Mountsteven and Mr Mountsteven declared twice or three times in the presence of Mr F. Paynter that he had neither heard me mention even the name of my sister and Mr Francis Paynter on the day mentioned nor had he communicated such a thing to Mr F. C. Paynter's wife. Such is the explanation I give you and I make no further comments than expressing the hope that if anyone should eventually succeed in separating us I shall have the consolation amidst such separation that both my sayings and my actions have proceeded from a disinterested friendship for my brother's welfare.

On my accounts with Mr Paynter I have this day received in sundry bills £112:16:8 and there is a balance of £40:17:7 due to me in my account with you but which was not paid to me because the account has not been shewn to you but which when you have inspected it you will I dare say see that at no distant period the money is forwarded to me.

Mr F.C. Paynter and Mr Whitford persevere in saying that this

Red Lion Hotel: Saint Columb Major

last sum is due from you and I confess to you that I do not understand it. If you are to pay this said sum of £40:17:7 I should imagine you ought to be no loser by having a greater sum credited in the accounts passed before the Court of Chancery which accounts so passed before the Court as they end at Ladyday 1814 must, I should think, be blended with your general accounts with Messrs Paynter & Son about that time and for not knowing which I am at a loss to explain it. Mr F.C. Paynter however said that he would speak to you on the subject and I trust this will be satisfactory. As I have received this sum of money I shall not be particular about your sending to me William Gilbert's rent except you should have a good opportunity for so doing. If you will write at any time I shall be glad to hear.

    I am,
> Your faithful Brother
> M.W. Bennet.

Mydhope's letter brought forth an immediate reply from his elder brother.

> Tresillian House
> December 11th 1819

My dear Brother

    Many thanks for your letter from St Columb, for it affords me increased pleasure to find that you had succeeded in taking Mr Mountsteven with you to the office and then proved what had been stated to me as facts, to be totally false and unfounded. Fear not that any circumstance will annihilate that fraternal affection that has ever subsisted between us without an open and candid explanation. I have almost entirely withdrawn myself from the world, well convinced that their motives are so truly selfish that they would not scruple to separate by false insinuations the nearest and dearest relatives. Four or five years since no family were more united or lived in greater harmony than our own but by some untoward occurrences discord has stepped in with all her attendant horrors and made matrimony the cause of disaffection and separation. We, my dear Mydhope, have seen these afflicting circumstances and I most ardently hope that whenever the period arrives that we are to bring home the objects of our choice it will tend rather to increase our intercourse than to make us feel the loss of our two soon departed parents. In the full conviction that nothing of a trivial nature will interrupt our mutual Brotherly affection I subscribe myself as ever,

Your most sincerely attached Brother

R. G. Bennet.

East Looe
December 30th 1819

My dear Brother

I received your letter on the Tuesday after my return from St Columb and you will I am sure be glad to hear that Nanny[1] is safely delivered of a fine girl and that both the Mother and Child were doing well when James[2] wrote. It is perhaps rather singular that the young stranger appeared on the morning of Christmas day about a quarter after five o'clock. It is but justice I think to tell you that after writing to you on the Friday evening from St Columb I received a note from Elizabeth assuring me that Mr Mountsteven did say something of the sort attributed to him tho' not in the form of a message. It is right I think to mention this circumstance though the denial of it by Mr Mountsteven quite exonerates me and as I stand this clear it will make no part of my business to discover who the inventor was. Elizabeth by her note seemed hurt that I should have taken Mr Mountsteven to the office but you I am sure will agree with me that such a step was necessary to be taken after everything that had been said and I can declare it was done by me only in self-defence.

You no doubt recollect my shewing to you when I was at Tresillian a copy of the accounts passed before the Court of Chancery drawn out by Messrs Paynter & Son at my request. This copy as far as regards your estates and the payments and allowances made thereon I have since compared with the original and find it to be perfectly correct. Instead therefore of putting you to any expense you can have this copy, which, when you have done with, you may return to me again. You will observe that the

---

1   *Nanny is the youngest child of the family, Ann.*
2   *James is the Reverend James Pascoe who married Ann Bennet.*

last several pages relate to me only and tho' in the beginning even our accounts are itemised ? with each other, yet you can without much difficulty discover the part that belongs to yourself and the part that belongs to me, not forgetting however, in the midst of it to reckon the Redeemed Land Tax of Trethill and Penhale as your own for whatever hereafter may be the decision as to the Land Tax yet I should tell you that I have not reckoned it as mine in those accounts as I understand Mr Paynter intended it for you. The Redeemed Land Tax for Trethill is £4:17:0 a year and £2:2:0 for Penhale a year. I have also drawn out a sketch of the Gwinear Tythes for the same two years but not a copy as it would take too much time and if you wish it I will send it with the copy of the accounts passed before the Court of Chancery in the manner and at any time you will name.

If it would be more satisfactory to you to have a copy I can procure someone here to do it but I would not take upon myself to have it done as it will be attended with some expense and the acknowledgement I have made will I think answer every purpose. It appears by the sketch I have made that for the first year a balance of £410:9:11 was due to you from the Receiver after the payments were deducted which sum it seems was afterwards paid into Court. On the second year after the payment to our Solicitors there seems to be a balance of £414:3:8 due to you from the Receiver. You of course can tell whether you have ever received the £410:9:11 paid into Court and whether you have ever had it.

I observe what you said in the latter part of your letter of our separation and I cannot help repeating how very sorry I am that there should be any truth in those reports with which the County so much abounds and is astonished. I could say much but I will desist. Whenever you wish the papers sent and will tell me by whatever conveyance I will forward them to you. Wishing you a happy and merry Christmas.

Believe me to be,

Your faithful Brother

M. Wallis Bennet.

PART TWO

CHAPTER 5

The merry, merry lark was up and singing,
And the hare was out and feeding on the lea;
And the merry, merry bells below were ringing,
When my child's laugh rang through me.
Now the hare is snared and dead beside the snow-yard,
And the lark beside the dreary winter sea;
And the baby in his cradle in the churchyard
Sleeps sound till the bell brings me.

                    Charles Kingsley. *A Lament.*

On the 3rd January 1820 Richard Gully Bennet and Loveday Basset were married in the Parish Church of Saint Enoder. The Basset family had its seat at Tehidy Park in the Parish of Penwith near Redruth. The Bassets, a noble Cornish family, came from Normandy with William the Conqueror. The first Cornish born son of the French emigres was Ralph Basset who was created a Justice of England and invested with the unique privilege of sitting in any Court he pleased for the administration of the law. He was said to have been an able judge and died in 1120 having founded an illustrious pedigree which dominated many parts of Cornwall and produced magnificent families for generations to come. Lord de Dunstanville who was a natural son of King Henry I was, in 1140, raised to the dignity of Earl of Cornwall. His son Walter de Dunstanville's sole heiress, Cecilia, married William Basset and from that union descended Sir Francis Basset, Vice-Admiral of Cornwall. A later descendant, Francis Basset, married an heiress of the Cornish family of Pendarves and it was from a son of that marriage was descended Edward William Wynne Pendarves who became a close friend of the Bennet family as appears from his appointment as Guardian of Richard Gully's only surviving son and Trustee of Richard Gully's estate.

Loveday Bennet was welcomed at Tresillian as Lady of the Manor and there the young couple, Richard Gully aged twenty-six and his young bride aged twenty-two, established their matrimonial home at the beginning of 1820. George III died on the 29th January and was succeeded by his elder son George IV who had been Prince Regent for nine years. Following the English victory at Waterloo in 1815 the Corn Laws had been passed in an endeavour to keep up prices. The national debt had risen from £231 million to £861 million. Taxation was high. Life throughout the country was anything but easy. Mydhope Bennet, a poor curate, received a small stipend and relied upon income from his Estates to preserve his standard of living. The accounts arising from the case against Joseph Norway and Major Bennet continued to exercise his mind and cause him great concern as appears from letters written by him to his brother Richard Gully throughout 1820.

East Looe
Friday morning
5th January 1820

My dear brother
I met Billy* last evening as I was going out to dinner and as I

Chancel: Parish Church of Saint Enoder

could not return the same evening I have rode home this morning and hasten to scribble a few lines. In the parcel I sent you a copy of the accounts passed before the Court of Chancery, and as our accounts are there intermixed you will be able to subtract both the receipts and payments relating to yourself. The last page of this copy relates to me only and you will observe that I have turned it down that you might not waste any time in looking over those accounts which belong to me.

The accounts in this copy, as you will see, begin at Ladyday 1812 and end at Ladyday 1814 – being two years – and if you can make out that your accounts commence only at November 1814 you will be entitled surely for the receipt of rents for that half year. This copy which I send will also give you an insight into the allowance of £500 which was made by the Court of Chancery for your maintenance etc. I also send the Tythe Account being the original sent to me from London by Mr Vanheythysen and on examination you will find it, I believe, to accord with what I said in my last letter to you. You must take great care of this and I will thank you to return this as well as the other papers as soon as you have done with them, by Post if you have no opportunity of forwarding them otherwise.

Another paper which I have enclosed will show you how the £33:13:1½ (which I before mentioned to you) is your due. I also send you a statement made by Mr Paynter shewing how the costs of the suit were paid, and on glancing my eye over it I observe that £142:12:5 was paid out of the Gwinear Tythes money – therefore I imagine that this sum must be deducted from the larger sum due to you according to the Tythe Account.

I also send you an account between us made by Messrs Paynter & Son and corrected by them when I was last at St Columb. By this you will see that I have credits for the sums received from Ladyday 1812 to Ladyday 1814 according to the accounts passed before the Court of Chancery and that I also allow the payments according to the same accounts, so that this paper in most respects is only a repetition of what is in the accounts passed before the Court of Chancery.

You must take care of this as it is the only copy I have to shew in defence of myself and allow me to hint to you not to let any of them out of your hands but when you have made a proper use of them to return them to me by Post. I cannot help observing that in my opinion it would be much to your benefit if we could jointly have gone over these accounts having all the papers relating thereto before us – for it is almost impossible for either of us to make them out to our satisfaction as we are much concerned together and as our accounts are so much intermixed. If this is agreeable to you I shall only say that if you like to come over here at any time, and will give me notice, I will willingly look over the accounts with you and I am sure it would tend to our mutual benefit.

If you write Wightwick of Oxford you might I think discover which money has been paid to Exeter College as I understand Jones is now the head of that College and he is an intimate friend of Charles Wightwick. Tho' Wightwick is now in the country yet I suppose he will be at Oxford about the 20th of this month and if you write him I dare say he would make enquiries for you tho' you must recollect to pay the postage of the letter. If Robert Paul is at Exeter College, by writing to him, if you dislike the former plan, you might I dare say accomplish your purpose.

The £331:19:8½ you speak of in your letter to me agrees exactly with the sum due to the Receiver on the two years according to the accounts passed before the Court of Chancery. I hope you will be able to read this, if not, and should you have any further enquiries to make, I will with pleasure answer them if I am able. In the meantime, believe me to be, my Dear Brother,
                    Yours very faithfully and sincerely
                    M. W. Bennet.

                                        East Looe
                                        Wednesday morning
                                        January 13th 1820

My dear brother
    Tho' I have so lately written you I have no scruples of conscience in taking up my pen again as I am sure you will gladly be at the expense of and for the postage of a letter by means of which you will be able to gain £6:5:0 which I have no doubt you can do if

---

Billy was a groom employed by Mydhope

you please by what I am about to tell you. In examining the accounts passed before the Court of Chancery you will no doubt find much difficulty so much as they may appear to be somewhat obscure. I will allude to the attitude pursued by Messrs Paynter & Son with regard to them which if you have their account it will make all things easy and clear and you will observe that when the two years accounts were closed with the Court of Chancery by Mr Paynter there was a balance of £33:19:8½ due to the Receiver which sum of money tho' it was to come from me chiefly yet has been charged to you in your general accounts with Messrs Paynter & Son according to your last letter.

Now as you were shewn a debtor in the whole of their sum of £331:19:8½ when I ought to have paid the greatest part of it, it became necessary that an account between you and myself should be made and this account which exists between us I sent you last week by which as you will see that you gave me credit for the rents received on my behalf for those two years and I allow you for the payments and allowances made thereon according to the copy of the account passed before the Court of Chancery which I also sent you last week – so that the plan pursued may make it obscure to us, it comes to the same thing in the end whether I pay Mr Paynter £300 or thereabouts or to the Receiver on this account passed before the Court or whether you pay Mr Paynter for the whole sum due to him and I pay you my proportion of it excepting that there is something due to you for Interest which we must settle when some determination is made respecting the Legacy of £500 and the Interest accruing thereon. Tho' these things are involved in great obscurity yet this explanation will I think make everything clear and I should not have been so officious in entering so fully on this subject if I did not imagine that you would not wish to bestow so much time on your accounts as to discover the method in which the accounts between the Receiver, yourself and your humble servant are made to explain one another. By returning to the copy of the accounts passed before the Court of Chancery which you have, you will find that from the first year the sum of £343:15:0 is allowed for my maintenance (among the payments are £45 and £450 for the second year making altogether £838:15:0) whereas in the account between us I pay you only £270 and £562:10:0. (See that account in the very beginning) making altogether £832:10:0. So that the difference which is £6:5:0 is, I imagine, due to you from the Receiver because as I say and justly pay you only £332:10:0 so it cannot be right that you should pay the Receiver six pounds five shillings more on my account which you will do if you are charged with the whole balance of £331:19:8½. In short there appears to be no doubt but that £6:5:0 is due to you and if you should not be able to make it out I will readily explain it whenever we meet. When you have quite done with the papers you can send them to me as I purpose sending the Tythes Account to Vanheythysen as soon as we are both satisfied in our accounts.

Believe me, my Dear Brother

Yours very faithfully and sincerely,

Mydhope W. Bennet.

Wednesday evening

I had written this much when your letter arrived (and allow me to congratulate you on the progress you have already made and I hope will still continue to make in the examination of your accounts). The arrears in your favour at Ladyday 1814, if we include those of Mr Hawke appear to exceed £700!!! But whether these arrears were all paid by Michaelmas 1814 or some of them extended to the following half year I know not – at any rate these things ought to be looked into and tho' some of your Tenants may not have had receipts for what they paid, yet, you may I think justly expect and demand of Messrs Paynter & Son what the respective Tenants paid each half year and when you have done that you will easily find from the Tenants whether the sums agree with the rents they actually paid. This will be a good way for you to proceed I think if you find any difficulty in the obtaining of proper receipts. The expenses attending the Chancery suit according to the papers I sent you were, I believe, entirely paid by you excepting £111:11:0 paid by me to William Prater towards some part of them and by referring to the account between you and myself you will see that I pay you £525 for my moiety and two or three pounds I have since paid you when the final settlement took place.

You do not appear by your letter to reckon those bills which Mr Norway consented to accept for William Prater and this I should imagine is reckoned in the paper I sent you tho' without seeing the paper itself I cannot exactly tell respecting the £33:13:1. I certainly should ask Mr Paynter why he has not given you credit for the full sum tho' I must own that I doubt some idea that some deduction was to be made tho' I cannot tell to what amount or for what. If you were here I could satisfactorily explain to you what I have said tho' I fear you will not understand it by letter.

East Looe
Thursday evening
January 27th 1820

My dear Brother

Your letter this moment received has surprised me indeed. When your letter before this reached me I had prepared one for you and on receipt of yours immediately added a good deal to what I had written on the accounts and having previous to the receipt of your letter directed it to you by way of St Columb I was unable to alter it and therefore despatched it to you on the following morning. Judge then my surprise at finding that it had never reached you. It must now be pretty manifest into whose hands this said letter has fallen, and tho' I had quite filled it with explanations on the accounts I do not in the least fear what has become of it tho' I regret it very much. I will now take care to direct it to you by way of Michael and this delay will cause no inconvenience to you I hope.

In answer to your letter received this evening, I have to observe that the sums of £37:18:0 and £75:0:0 as interest paid me on the £1500 are correct. The sums paid you by me for board at Tresillian are as extracted from my account with Mr Paynter as follows – totalling £161:1:4 covering the period April 4th 1814 to January 16th 1817. Thus it appears by my account with Mr Paynter that I have allowed him £161:1:4 instead of £43:6:8 for you and you certainly are entitled to such a sum being credited to you instead of the paltry sum of £43:6:8. If you wish to see my account with Mr Paynter you may at any time have it but you may depend that the above is a correct copy.

I shall make no comments on this extraordinary affair but proceed to other things.

I should think Elizabeth and Nanny must have paid for board at

Tresillian as soon as I did but I will make particular enquiries of Nanny and let you know. Respecting the £33:13:1 due to you on the account, I have to observe that the £20:3:5½ paid you by Francis Paynter is correct as far as it relates to him but then there is £3 due to you from Nanny which I will procure for you if you like and in that case I must have a line from you saying so much by Saturday week as I purpose going to St Keverne* on the following day and should not like to claim the £3 for you unless you desired it. The remainder of the money which would make the £33:13:1 namely £10:9:7½ but said to be according to the letters in my possession only £10:8:7 (which is only 1s:0½ too little) is set off against the £440 awarded to Mr Norway for setting forth his Answer to the Court of Chancery and as I have paid my half – that is to say £220 – you ought to be charged by Mr Paynter only £209:11:5 as there was due from Mr Norway £10:8:7 which ought to be deducted from your moiety £220 and which would reduce it as I have said before to £209:11:5. By referring to your account with Mr Paynter you will be able to see whether you are charged with £220 or as it ought to be with £209:11:5 and can act accordingly as £440 was awarded to Mr Norway so was £85 awarded to Major Bennet and for reasons which I have not room to give you here you should be charged with £32:1:6 on this account and not with the half £42:10:0. Look at your accounts and see with which of these sums you are charged by Mr Paynter. As I have much more to say by reason of my last letter being intercepted I shall not scruple to write to you again this week as I intend to give you a clue to the recovery of a few pounds more you would do well therefore to send to Michael a day or two after the receipt of this as you may then expect another from me. I will say no more here as I am fearful you will not be able to read it.

    I am,
        your faithful brother
        M. W. Bennet.

---

*Ann Bennet had by this time married the Reverend James Pascoe who had the living at St. Keverne.

East Looe
Saturday night
January 29th 1820.

My dear Brother

I again sit down to make a few more observations on the accounts tho' I fear from the lateness of the hour I shall not be able to make so good a hand of it as I did in the letter which never reached you*. I had taken great pains with it and therefore regret much your never having received it. Your being saddled with the whole sum of £331:19:8½ on the accounts passed before the Court of Chancery is thus explained and you will recollect you adverted to it in a former letter.

The balance due to the Receiver on those two years accounts is exactly £331:19:8½ and tho' I ought to have paid the greatest part of this sum (my rents not being sufficient to meet the payments) yet you are made debtor to Mr Vanheythysen in the whole sum and then it became necessary that an account between you and myself should be made out (which account I sent you for your perusal) and you will observe by it you give me credit for my rents for those two years and I allow you all the payments made on my behalf during the same period – so that it comes to the same thing in the end whether I pay Mr Paynter my proportion or whether you pay Mr Paynter for the whole and I afterwards pay you my part. If you view it in this light all difficulty (and great difficulty I confess does attend it) vanishes. But I should tell you that I give you credit only in my account with you for £832:10:0 for my maintenance and education tho' you by allowing Mr Paynter the £331:19:8½ pay him for the same £838:15:0 and therefore by that means you are a loser of £6:5:0 which by stating to Mr Paynter you will or ought to obtain and if you find any difficulty in so doing I would not refuse to make it out and prove it to Mr Paynter on your behalf without you would rather give up the £6:5:0 than claim it which I see no reason for doing. In examining the copy I sent you of the Accounts passed before the Court of Chancery you will soon discover that you are charged

---

The 'missing' letter did in fact reach Richard Gully, it was dated 13th January 1820 and has been set out above.

for the two years for my maintenance and education the different sums of £343:15:0. £450 and £45 making altogether £838:15:0 whereas by referring to the account between you and myself you will I believe in the very first articles see that I pay you only £832:10:0 by which you are a loser of £6:5:0. I hope therefore I have made this out sufficiently clear.

I observe what you said about the large sum paid by George Hawke and the other Tenants for one half year and the small credit given you thereon. I am truly astonished!!! but at the same time congratulate heartily in having made such rapid advances in your accounts and hope you will continue to do so until you are perfectly satisfied.

I cannot exactly tell how the expenses of the Chancery suit were paid by you as I have not the papers here but in addition to those payments mentioned by you in one of your letters I think you should reckon the acceptance of two bills by Mr Norway, the benefit of which either William Prater or Vanheythysen had, and you surely do not forget William Prater coming to Tresillian about it. The reckoning of these bills may probably make up the deficiency – and you should observe that you paid the whole of the expenses of this suit and I have since given you credit for my part in my account with you – see the £525 there mentioned for the costs of suit.

I will recollect what you say about Mr Whitfield and I shall be glad to employ him when I have anything for him to do. I return you many thanks for the wish you have expressed of seeing me at Tresillian. As both the letters I wrote on Thursday, and this are particular, I should be glad to know whether you have received them and you may then say whether I was clear in my explanations, by this method you are pursuing will no doubt be able to collect some sums of money and I heartily wish you success in it. At any time I shall be glad to hear how you have succeeded and if I can do anything I shall be happy to render my services.

If you can procure some of the receipts from the Tenants and would like to bring over the papers I sent you here we might I think make some discoveries only I should like in that case to have a little notice thereof. You will see by what I said in my last letter that you ought to pay Mr Norway £109:11:5 only (instead of £220) as I did for Mr Norway setting forth his Accounts to the

Court of Chancery and £32:11:0 (instead of £42:10:0 as I did) to the Major.

I am your faithful Brother

Mydhope W. Bennet.

St Keverne Vicarage
February 9th 1820

My dear Brother

According to your request I prepared a line for you tho' I am uncertain whether I shall be able to send it tomorrow and in case I should not shall take it with me to Truro on my return from this place on Friday.

I have made enquiries of Nanny respecting the board and after some difficulty she supposes (for she is not certain having no written accounts) that she must have paid altogether for two years and a half when she considers that she was absent at Flushing and at Exeter and thinks that for those times she could not have been charged for board by Mr Francis Paynter.

As it appears by your letters that you have had credits of Mr Paynter for three years and a half I have not paid him the different times for which Nanny paid board as she cannot speak with any certainty or exactly. And for my own part, if Mr F. Paynter has given you credit for three years and a half as you seem to say in two of your letters to me I should be inclined to think that you had received full credit for board on Nanny's behalf.

Nanny thinks Elizabeth should have paid for two years board – and it seems also by your letters that you have had credit for those two years (at the rate of £40 per annum) and upon the whole as far as I can see, no mistake appears to have been made, now you have received from Mr F Paynter another account giving you credit for some money received for board from me and from each of my sisters. I mean as far as regards my sisters, for of course you are entitled to a pretty large sum from Mr Paynter for a deficiency of board on my account.

The expenses of the Chancery Suit were paid, I believe, entirely by you at first, amounting to more than one thousand pounds but then in my account with you I pay you for my half of William Prater's bill of costs viz, £525:0:0 and afterwards I paid you £3:2:3 more on that account, so that I should imagine you ought to be charged with a similar sum and then again I have paid for my half of the sum awarded to Mr Norway viz, £520:0:0 and you ought as I said before to pay only for the same £209:11:5. I also have paid my half of the sum awarded to Major Bennet viz, £42:10:0 but you think for the same should only be charged £32:1:0 but it is impossible for me to explain how these things are so, by letter and if you refer to the account between us, you will see something of what I have said which I conclude has 'ere this been paid you for me by my Tenant William Gilbert. You should recollect at the same time that I borrowed of you when I was last at Tresillian. I consider this a better plan than taking the risk of sending the three pounds by letter tho' you cannot understand it fully without my explaining it to you in person. Suffice it to say that in my opinion you ought to be charged with about £1056 for costs and £209:11:5 and £32:1:0 for sums awarded to Mr Norway and Major Bennet. Nanny desires her love and is quite well as well as the babe.

    I am,

        your faithful Brother
        M. W. Bennet.

                  East Looe
          February 22nd 1820

My dear Brother

    On the other side I send you a copy of an account sent me from the office of Messrs Paynter & Son where you will see me charged for £42:10:0 for my moiety of the costs awarded to Major Bennet. The balance in your favour on this account is £10:9:0 which balance I paid you at Tresillian on the 27th July 1819 and you a day or two after sent in a line by me to Mr F Paynter signifying that I had discharged the above balance. You may perhaps recollect my paying you £1:16:0 for half a dozen of Madeira wine, and 2:6 for Gooseberry bottles at the same time making altogether the sum of £12:8:3. The £25 can be very easily settled between ourselves but first I must expect to have the particulars of William Henwood's bill shewn to me and as before the receipt of your letter I had written Messrs Paynter & Son requesting them to send me the particulars of several bills which they had paid for me while my accounts were in their hands, I should suppose they will send this among the others which I expect from their offices in a short time. I should however feel obliged if you will give them a hint of this when you see them as it may slip their memory at this moment. When satisfied of its being a proper claim on me there will be no difficulty of our settling the matter. If you have done with the papers which I sent you I should like for you to return them to me immediately as I am rather anxious to send them to London and the others I want for my own purpose. Do not forget to send the account between you and myself.

I am,

your faithful Brother

Mydhope. W. Bennet.

East Looe
February 26th 1820

My dear Brother

I have just received a letter from you and tho' it is Saturday evening when I am generally pretty busy I will reply to it. I confess I am not able to explain the costs of the Chancery Suit in any satisfactory manner, indeed who can when such different accounts are given by William Prater and Mr. Paynter. I know that £440 was awarded to Mr Norway and £85 to the Late Major Bennet by the Court of Chancery and also that according to William Prater the expenses of carrying on the suit amounted to £1056:4:6. Now as I have paid you my moiety of each of these sums, that is to say in the account between ourselves I have given you credit for £220 a moiety of £440 awarded to Mr Norway and £42:10:0 being the moiety of the £85 awarded to the late Major and £528:2:3 the moiety of the charge of £1056:4:6 made on us by William Prater it is my opinion that you must pay the different persons the full amount of these sums awarded to them by the Court of Chancery. So that as I have paid you £220, £42:10:0 and £528:2:3 you I think ought to be charged by Mr Paynter for double those sums and then you will only have paid equal to myself as those sums which I have paid you will be deducted therefrom. To attempt to explain how these sums have been paid by you it will be impossible in this letter tho' I think we might be able to manage it were I to see you here and I shall be glad if you will come over any time next week or whenever it may suit you. As it can only be my wish to get the really friendly part I should observe to you that you seem to have lost sight of your accepting two Bills to the amount of £145 which were afterwards paid by Mr Norway out of cash received by him to your account. This £145 went towards paying part of expenses of the suit tho' I am ignorant how the £145 came into the hands of Mr Norway but I dare say William Prater can explain this matter.

William Prater has given me an account how the expenses were paid, but if I were to copy it, it would, I fear, be only confusing you the more. If you come here do not forget to bring most of your papers with you as it will be impossible to do it satisfactorily without them.

I do not know that there is any truth in the report you have heard of my approaching marriage and I hope I shall be consulted on the subject before it takes place. Hoping to see you soon, believe me to be,

your faithful Brother

M. Wallis Bennet.

There is no possibility of our coming to any clear understanding of the costs without our meeting and I cannot possibly come over at this moment being much engaged. You had better come here immediately I think therefore and at all events you will do well to make full enquiries of the £145.

M. W. B.

East Looe
March 10th 1820

My dear Brother

On the other side is a letter to Messrs Paynter & Son which you can cut off from that part of the sheet and send to them and I should be obliged if you will pay them £1:13:7 for me as I owe it to them and cannot send so small a sum by letter. I will settle this with you when we make up our accounts. You can pay them soon as I should not wish much delay to take place.

Respecting the £50 I am almost positive it was paid at that time and I believe went to pay off some of your bills in Oxford. I know at many different times sums which I owed you were transferred to the payment of your debts in Oxford and what makes me convinced of this is that I never expected in my own mind to be charged by Messrs Paynter & Son for £50 and I am now clearly of opinion that that debt was discharged at the time but what bills of yours I paid with it in Oxford or whether it went to Oxford I am not quite certain. I have examined all my old bills and can find nothing relating thereto, not even your receipt.

Since writing the above I clearly recollect my telling one of the men at Oxford that I had paid £50 for the rooms for I well recollect the thought that I had paid nothing for them. If after this you are not satisfied you had better ask Elizabeth or Nanny as they are most likely to know something about it tho' I doubt not but that it is of too long a distance to be in the perfect recollection of anyone.

I think I had better settle with Messrs Paynter & Son about the £25 to William Henwood as I do not mean to allow it till they produce the particulars of the bill and you will see by my letter to them that they have as yet produced the particulars of none of the bills. I cannot think of being charged so much for bills and not to know what it is for – I wish you to notice this in your next letter to me and you can say how you discovered that it belonged to me and for an estate of mine that the bill is charged for. If you wish it I suppose I shall be able to hand you £100 or from that to £150 about the end of each month and as I was intending to put it into the funds if you take it I shall not think of charging you more interest than I should get for these which can be ascertained by seeing how the funds are when I lent it to you. Of course I cannot speak positively that I shall be able to lend you so much as it must of course depend upon the Tenants paying me their rent.

If under these circumstances the money will be of any service to you, you are perfectly welcome to it under those conditions. As soon as the papers I sent you are done with, you will of course forward them to me, but I do not wish to hurry you.

I was about to give you a hint that the postage of letters was expensive, therefore if we write each other now and then and continue to say as much as we have on the accounts in one letter it will be, I think, a good plan.

I am, My Dear Brother,
Yours faithfully
M. W. Bennet.

East Looe
March 20th 1820

My dear Brother

I am sorry to trouble you again with a letter so soon especially as our correspondence of late has been unusually extensive as well as expensive but you will, however, I hope, excuse it as I am greatly in need of your assistance at this moment. I am in want of the registry of my mother's burial at Newlyn, and if you will apply to Mr Pooley for it and on receiving it pay him his usual fee for the same, I shall be obliged. I fear, however, it will be necessary for you to see Mr Pooley yourself (except you can procure some gentleman to stand in your place) as the person who receives the certificate must make his affidavit in the manner and in the words hereunder written and as Mr Pooley is a Magistrate the affidavit may be made before him. As this is necessary to be done in law matters you will not I hope feel awkward in meeting Mr Pooley on this occasion especially as it is on business, but in case you do, you can, I dare say, get someone to get the entry and to make the affidavit required and see that it is properly filled up in his name, and as soon as this is done you can forward it to me. Indeed the best plan would be for you to carry a sheet of paper to Newlyn, on the first page of it make the entry and the affidavit and on the third side (but not on this side of the sheet) you can say whatever you like as in that case I shall be able to tear it off and send it to Exeter or London as may be required. The way in which it is to be done is this -

'(Here make an exact copy of the Entry in the Register at Newlyn)

Underneath you must word it in this manner -

'Richard Gully Bennet of Tresillian House in the Parish of Newlyn in the County of Cornwall, Esquire maketh oath and saith that he did on the   day of March in the Year of Our Lord Eighteen Twenty search the Register Book of Burials kept in and for the Parish of Newlyn and that the above copied extract is a True Copy or Extract of an entry made in the said Register Book of Burials.'

I have no doubt that you will understand by this that the copy from the Register must be made first and the affidavit in the words above written must be made underneath it. Aunt Roberts

78

came here this morning and intends to stay some time. She is very well and desires to be very kindly remembered to you. This as well as other causes will prevent me from coming to Tresillian till the latter end of April. You can say in your answer whether you think you shall be in want of the money and anything else that may have occurred. If you meet with anything else in the accounts and should like to ride over here before I come to Tresillian I shall be glad to see you. I am in haste, and believe me to be,

Your faithful Brother

M. W. Bennet.

Besides having to pay Mr Pooley for the Certificate from the Register you will also have to pay him, I believe, for swearing you.

M. W. B.

East Looe
Sunday evening Eight o'clock
28th March 1820

My dear Brother

I received the parcel with a letter for my Aunt as well as one for myself on my return this morning from serving my *fifth* Church and now that the duties for the day are over I sit down quietly to thank you for sending them.

My Aunt is from home, being staying at St Martins a mile from this place where her old friend Dr Michele lives, and as she does not return this evening it will be impossible for any answer to be given (should one be required) by the bearer, but when she arrives at St Columb, or perhaps before, you may I dare say expect to hear from her in answer to your letter. I immediately on receiving it sent it to St Martins for her and she has no doubt 'ere this received it.

Your last as well as your previous letter has quite astonished me respecting a certain gentleman of our acquaintance. I sincerely hope that my dear Sister will never hear anything which may be going on and if it is possible I hope there may be no quarrel between you and our friend for my Sister's sake, for such a thing would I know give her great uneasiness and I cannot bear to think on her untoward situation. We, however, can both of us profit by the past and this will not be seen nor felt by my Sister, and I don't doubt but that by taking care of ourselves we shall yet do well. I long to come over to talk it over with you, and do if you can go to the house, if you cannot take your meals there.

The £8:5:0 I have no doubt of throwing back on the proper person, *our friend* and as I see that such a thing will not be quietly settled without an interview I will ride into St Columb with you (when I come over to Tresillian) and then we cannot, I think, fail to bring the matter to a conclusion, and to such a conclusion as will not be prejudicial to ourselves.

The £25 must be left between Mr F. Paynter and myself, I believe, as he has not yet thought fit to give me the particulars of the bills required, and you cannot have any objection to such a plan, as in that case the £25 will go towards paying off the debt between you and Mr F. Paynter. You, of course, sent this letter to Messrs Paynter & Son which was written on part of yours and I conclude paid him what I desired you to do.

The burial certificate was very correct and I thank you for the trouble you must have taken in getting it. I cannot tell exactly when I shall be able to come over to Tresillian, as I do not know when Aunt Roberts leaves me, but certainly not to the very latter end of April or the beginning of the following month. We shall then, I hope, be able to arrange and settle all matters not yet determined.

Can the report circulated here be true that Mr Vyvyan of Truro is engaged to Miss Mattocks of St Columb?

About the wine, we will talk when I see you. I have no objection to taking a part. Could you intend to be absent from Tresillian any other days than those you mentioned you should, I think, let me know. You may be sure I shall come in the beginning of the week whenever I set out and if I do not hear from you again I shall conclude there will be no necessity of any writing you to tell you the exact day, as in all probability I shall not myself know very long before I take the journey. If you wish to hear beforehand you must write and say so. I have nothing more at present to say, I believe, and therefore shall subscribe myself,

Your faithful Brother
M. Wallis Bennet.

On the 31st October 1820 Loveday Bennet was delivered of her first child, a son, named after his father Richard Gully, who was baptized in Newlyn Parish Church on the 12th January 1821.

Between April and June of 1821 the renewal of the Lease of the Gwinear Tythes became the subject of negotiation between the Rector of Exeter College, Oxford, and Richard Gully Bennet. Gully took advice from his brother-in-law, Francis Paynter, and succeeded in bargaining for a lesser fine on renewing the Lease.

Exeter College
April 3rd 1821

R G Bennet Esquire
Tresillian House
St Columb
Cornwall

Sir,

The present extra-ordinary depreciation of the article of corn partly in consequence of the late abundant harvest does not appear to us to be a fair basis of the terms for a new Lease of any description of landed property. The calculation which I now send you is founded on the amount of your last Fine compared with the average price of wheat for the three years last passed, the usual lapse in the case of the Gwinear Tythes; by which Fine on the proposed renewal amounts to Four Hundred and Eight Pounds 16:0.

I have the honour to be,
Sir,
Your obedient servant,
J. C. Jones. Rector.

St Columb
9th April 1821

R G Bennet Esquire
Tresillian House

My dear Gully

From Mr Jones' letter I am inclined to think that you may by standing out a little be able to obtain the renewal for £350. The general opinion is that unless there is a very heavy duty on all

81

imported grain (which is by no means likely to be the case) the average value of wheat will never again exceed 8s:0 per Winchester bushel or 24:0 per Cornish bushel which will, as before stated to you, have the effect of reducing the value of Tythes. The poor rates too which are everywhere rapidly increasing particularly affect Gwinear. A large proportion of the population is out of employment and thrown on the Parish for relief.

From this you will perceive that the basis of Mr Jones' calculation is not a solid one. The poor rates he leaves entirely out of his account. The correct way of calculating is such to find the gross value of the Tythes. Then to deduct from it the received Rents payable to the College, the Vicar's pension, the poor rates and the way rates. It will then be found that the net value is much less than he imagines. I would take these facts to Mr Jones and make him an offer of £300.

I am obliged to you for your letter of Saturday and am only prevented from immediate attention to it by my intended absence from home in the latter part of this week.

Elizabeth unites in kindest remembrances, in haste,
Yours very truly
    F. C. Paynter.
P.S. Elizabeth desires me to enclose a recipe of your late mother's which when copied you will be so good as to return.

Exeter College
May 5 1821

R G Bennet Esquire
Tresillian House
St Columb
Cornwall

Sir,

We could not consent to admit the articles of poor rates and way rates into the calculation of our present Fine as extraordinaries; because the increase of the former may be owing to mismanagement and the chief cause of the latter is an accident which we understand is at this moment removed. In consideration however of the embarrassments which at this season are generally acknowledged to oppress the agricultural interests, the College has agreed to remit the sum of £50:16:0 from what it still considers a just valuation of the Tythes when compared with the former Fine. I am accordingly instructed to demand Three Hundred and Fifty Pounds as the price of the present renewal from which the College has determined not to recede.

I am, Sir, with due respect
Your obedient servant
J. C. Jones. Rector.

St Columb
11th May 1821

R G Bennet Esquire
Tresillian House

My dear Gully

On Monday next I go into the week pursuant to appointment in order to secure a pretty considerable sum and it will then be perfectly convenient to accommodate you with the £250 required. Since the College will not go below £350 you have no choice but to close with them. In writing, I think, however, say 'that in accepting their offer I was conscious of having paid more than the value of the Tythes.' What Mr Jones means by the poor rate increasing through mismanagement I am at a loss to grasp. If he can strike out any mode of rendering perpetual the valuable mine now worked out and of preventing the material increase of population the Parish of Gwinear will feel infinitely obliged to him.

Your accounts we shall be glad to close. The only difficulty seems to be with respect to the two remittances to Prater for which we must get his note of hand. It appears to me that the account should be two remittances with interest thereon from the time of the final settlement of the costs of the suit in London.

Elizabeth has a very feverish cold. The two younger children are fine as usual − poor little Edward growing weaker daily.* Elizabeth unites with me in kindest remembrance to Mrs Bennet and yourself.

Yours very truly
F. C. Paynter.

Edward died the following month.

83

Oxford

29th May 1821

R G Bennet Esquire
Tresillian House
St Columb
Cornwall

Sir,

By the direction of the Rector and Scholars of Exeter College I send you the Counterpart of your new Lease which you will be pleased to execute in the presence of one witness. I send you also the Fine and Fees and am to request you will remit the amount to the Reverend the Rector together with the Counterpart and old Lease when the new Lease will be sent to you.

    I am, Sir,

        Your obedient servant,

          Robinson Barker

Fine   £350:0:0

Stamp Fees £ 12:9:6

Exeter College

June 21 1821

R G Bennet Esquire
Tresillian House
St Columb
Cornwall

Sir,

I have to acknowledge the favour of your letter dated the 16th of this month enclosing a draft for the sum of Four Hundred and Eighty Two Pounds and 9s:6 the amount of the Fine and Fees for the Lease of Gwinear Tythes and two years Rent due at Ladyday last.

The Counterpart of the Lease is also arrived and the Lease itself with the College Seal affixed will be forwarded to you without delay.

    I have the honour to be, Sir,

        Your very obedient servant

          J. C. Jones. Rector.

The letters exchanged by the two brothers in December 1819 speak volumes of the pain and distress which arose from their dispute with the Receiver's Accounts and their sister's marriage to the Receiver's son. But time healed and the family of two brothers and two sisters remained close and loyal to each other. The year 1820 had been blessed with the union of Gully and his young bride Loveday followed that autumn by the arrival of their first child. And so into 1821 which was marked by the death of Napoleon at St Helena. Mydhope maintained a flow of letters to Gully.

East Looe
April 10th 1821

My dear Brother

I received your letter on Saturday only tho' it bears the date of the first of April. The same post that brought one from you brought one also, as you may suppose to my great astonishment, from Cock of St Enoder, Mason. His object in writing me is to get permission to work at Trewinion. Now, after everything you say of him, namely of his having lately carried off some stone from Bennallack, and after his having told you that falsehood of my having given leave to Zwintell that he should work there when in fact I do not know the man and never gave any such permission, I am determined that Cock shall do no part of the work on Trewinion for I will never support any man in such iniquity as he appears to be carrying on. I shall therefore be obliged to you if you will say so much to Cock on my behalf, and if you will also endeavour to prevent him from writing me any more letters by saying that they will not be taken up in future, or any other plan that you may think advisable to prevent him from writing to me again.

It appears Cock applied to Mr Cardell to do the work at Trewinion but that Mr Cardell referred him to me. How he could think of doing so after what I had said I cannot imagine. Will you therefore tell Mr Cardell that I am unwilling that he should do the work. Mr Cock, also by your letter, appears to be willing to pay the dues if I will give the account of them. But it should be recollected that William Cock has worked for these several years past on Bennallack in cutting stone and therefore it is impossible that during that time I can bring forward my account again to him. It is true I have an account of a few shillings which he owes me for dues which I accidentally found out, but it can never be supposed that during all that time I have kept an account against him when I have only known that Cock worked there for these two or three years past, as therefore Cock is so wicked as not to produce the account on anything approaching towards a reasonable account it will, I think, be a good plan not to allow him to work on Bennallack again till he will do so. It is not that I care whether he pays me or not, but this will be a good excuse for you not allowing him to work there again if he does not pay me. Should Cock therefore be determined to cut stones at Bennallack again, in opposition to us, I will thank you to have the notice given, a copy of which you sent me and you may also adopt any other method that may be likely to prevent him from going there again.

I will take care not to give anyone liberty to draw stones without acquainting you of it.

I am much obliged for the notices you copied out and sent me. William Gilbert owes me only £8:15:0 to last Michaelmas therefore I will endeavour to wait patiently for this small sum till June or thereabouts when I hope to visit you. The parcel I received very safe. Take care of my neck handkerchief. Is it my riding one? For I have lost it. Be sure to let Cock know that I will not employ him because he has acted so badly. Remember me kindly to Mrs Bennet and the Boy and I hope to hear when anything is determined about Cock.

I am,
Your faithful Brother,
Mydhope. W. Bennet.

East Looe
May 29th 1821

My dear Brother

I return you many thanks for the very fine ham which came safe to hand and for which I had intended to write before acknowledging and thanking you for the same and should have done so had I not some other things to mention which I could not do well sooner.

I was about to ask you, provided it was not giving you too much trouble, if you would be kind enough to collect a little money for me in your neighbourhood. Mrs Richards of Bennallack owes me £21:10:0 to Michaelmas 1820 which she promised to pay me in May or June. There are some deductions to be made from it, I believe, for timber to prop up the one side of the house, and also for repairing the Cart or Wagon House, provided those things are done. I am also willing to allow her a deduction of 5 or 10 per cent and at that rate provided the times appear to press hard upon her. She is a very industrious woman and therefore if she cannot pay me the whole I believe I must be content.

William Gilbert owes me £8:15:0 to Michaelmas 1820 and he I should think would be ready to pay part if not the whole of this sum. There are no deductions to be made except if you think he is entitled to the deduction at the rate of 10 per cent and then you will make it.

After saying this much you will I dare say be kind enough to make the best collection you can for me, at the same time recollecting that I would rather go without it than distress them for the money for I fear I shall not be able to come to Tresillian before I start for France, at all events it will be very inconvenient for me to come till the end of June or the beginning of July, and therefore I am anxious to ascertain what money I can raise before that period. I shall feel greatly obliged if you can collect these two sums for me.

I conclude the new house at Trewinion is going on as I have left almost everything to Mr Cardell's judgement relating to this house, there will be no difficulty I trust to meet with. But if so as I am not on the spot now and likely to be absent soon I will cheerfully rely on your and Mr Cardell's opinions should any difficult question arise as to the difficulty of building any part.

When you write I dare say you will tell me what Cock is about. I always suspect he is doing no good but I trust he is not having his revenge on me for refusing to let him work at Trewinion by drawing stones on Bennallack and carrying them away. You will not of course forget to speak about the grass for my mare and when the time approaches you can get someone to come to Liskeard for her as we talked of when last at Tresillian.

Mrs Bennet and the child, I trust, are well, to whom I beg to be kindly remembered.

I am almost sure that the Law Book I spoke of is 'Williams

Law Dictionary 1 Vol Octavo'. I enquired of Dr Michele and he said this was the name of it, at all events it is worth while to get it even if a certain risk does attend it as the price cannot be very great.

If I should not be able to come to Tresillian soon you will perhaps be able to send me a check on the Truro Bank for the amount some time hence for I am in no imminent want of it. How does Mr Hocken bear up under the sad affliction of his son's misfortunes. It must fall, surely, very hard upon such an old man.

I am, my Dear Gully,
    Your faithful Brother
        Mydhope. W. Bennet.

East Looe
July 12th 1821

My dear Brother

I received your letter safe, and am much obliged to you for receiving the money you mentioned on my behalf. It never, I can assure you, gave me any pleasure to think of quitting this Country without coming to Tresillian, but if we had abided by our original agreement I am afraid it would have been impossible for me to have accomplished it. However we have now altered the time of our departure to the 27th August and that will allow me to come. If agreeable therefore I think of leaving this place for Tresillian on Monday the 6th August. I then intend to come by way of St Columb on purpose to get Mr Norway to pay me the balance he has received on my behalf from the Treasurer of the Liskeard Turnpike Trust. I have written him repeatedly and cannot obtain any answer. If you think it is at all likely for me to succeed now that the Bank has stopped payment it is my wish to come to St Columb on the 6th and to wait on Mr Norway. If I find I cannot obtain the money I then thought of telling him that I should stay at St Columb till he paid me. This I imagine (and I still imagine if it is not impossible for him to pay me) would be the most likely mode of procuring the money as perhaps he would be likely to advance the money on purpose to get rid of me. In that case I should not in all probability be at Tresillian on the Monday nor must you expect me till you see me. In that case also I would not wish you on any account to tell anyone of my coming as if it came to Mr Norway's ears he would contrive not to see me. I am anxious to take him by surprise. If however after saying this much you are almost sure that I should not be able to get the money, and will write me so, of course my labour would be lost and then I should not come by way of St Columb. I sincerely hope you did not receive any of Mr Norway's bills on my behalf, and I greatly fear some of my Tenants have suffered by the stoppage of the Pydar Bank, if so do tell me. While I am on this subject I will ask you a great favour and I trust it will be convenient for you to grant it. I am greatly in want of the sum of Twenty Pounds and do you imagine that you could lend it to me? I am willing to pay interest for the same. The fact is owing to the badness of the times I am disappointed of receiving some of my rents, and as I am to make a journey which will be expensive I need to make up the sum necessary for the journey. Perhaps you could raise such a small sum easily enough but if I cannot get it I shall be obliged to sell out from the funds and that will be a great loss – a loss of some pounds at least. At all events if you will be kind enough to tell me as soon as possible, do try what you can do.

In coming to St Columb or even Tresillian I should like to appear decently and therefore I shall be obliged by your telling me at the same time whether it is necessary to put crape round my hat for the little boy. I should not wish to distress Elizabeth's feelings and therefore should be glad to know whether it is usual to wear mourning on these occasions. I have never yet done it for the little boy as I imagined we ought rather to rejoice than to mourn.*

I am much obliged for the observations you have made on the allowing of a percentage and agree with you in the matter all things respecting the mare and it can be left till I see you. I hope you will make no engagement for me as I wish to be pretty active about my estates while I am at Tresillian. If I can obtain the £20 by the 20th August that will do should earlier be inconvenient to you.

With kind remembrances to Mrs Bennet.

I am, your faithful Brother,

M. W. Bennet.

This refers to Edward Paynter, Elizabteh's infant, who had died the previous month.

I suppose we shall get the Turnpike money some time but when I know not. Many difficulties attend it. I shall enquire when next I go to Liskeard.

M.W.B.

East Looe
July 19th 1821

My dear Brother

I received your letter but was unable to return an answer to it by return of post. I wish I could raise the sum of Twenty Pounds by application to my Tenants but you must not look on my Tenants in the same light as you look on your own. Of those I have in the Parish of St Enoder, Richard Richards must not be called upon in consideration of his promise to lay out money on the house at Trewinion. Mrs Richards no doubt has paid the utmost she can scrape together. Mr Glanville we all know is always poor enough and finds it difficult enough to pay his rent when the year is up. And as for William Gilbert, he is not, I believe, too rich. As thus stands the case I fancy with my Tenants you will very much oblige me by procuring the £20 for me at 5 per cent Interest. I do not know whether you are still in the habit of borrowing money from Mr Francis Paynter, but if so, and intended to get me £20 there I dare say you would be kind enough to borrow it for yourself and then I will undertake to pay you. Perhaps you would have no great objection to do so even if you obtain money from some other quarter but of course I cannot press this if you have the slightest objection thereto. I understood you to say in your letter that you would be able to get it and therefore I make no doubt but that I may rely on you to do everything needful on my behalf.

I am glad to hear so soon an account of Gilbert's intentions. I am very thankful to you for your attention in this matter.

As Norway's affairs will not be settled till the 9th August I hope to come to Tresillian on the 6th and then I can ride into St Columb an early day in the week. You must not expect me till you see me and therefore on no account to wait dinner on the Monday.

I must sincerely apologise to Mrs Bennet for having done anything which has incurred her anger – but how can I regain her favour? for I am always desirous of standing well with the female sex.

I must, my Dear Brother, leave it in your hands, and through you implore forgiveness this time. I will candidly own that at the time of my last writing you I did think of my Godson* but how could I make enquiries for the *first* without dropping some hint about the *second* and especially my wishes that it may be equal to the first?**

I am very sorry to hear such bad accounts of Nanny. I could wish she would change the air for I think the air of St Keverne is very prejudicial to her health. I long to see her and could therefore wish that I was on a little better footing with James that I might be enabled to do so. Curgenven, Lord Falmouth's Steward has lately sent me in an account of £2:10:0 due to Lord Falmouth at Ladyday 1821 for quitrent for Trevorrick. In case James Tremayne should see Mr Curgenven in Truro before I come to Tresillian will you desire him to pay the amount for me and obtain a receipt and you can give James Tremayne the money out of that which you have received on my behalf. If this were done I should be able to get the receipt when I come to Tresillian which would be very desirable.

With kind remembrances to Mrs Bennet and to Richard Gully believe me to be my Dear Brother
    Yours faithfully
        Mydhope. W. Bennet.

                East Looe
          August 17th 1821
My dear Brother

I received the check on the Miners Bank Truro for the sum of Twenty Pounds on Tuesday last and am very much obliged to you for sending it in such good time. I conclude Mr Tanner waited on you early on the Sunday morning and I beg to say that I paid him for his trouble so that I sincerely hope he did not claim it of you also. He said he usually received 1s:6d from yourself and Francis Paynter for going to Tresillian and as we were old friends who

---

*Mydhope's Godson is Richard Gully Bennet, then aged nine months.
**Reference to the 'second' is to Mrs Bennet's pregnancy then in its fourth month.

had not met for some time I believe I gave him 2s:0d. I mention this because I fear he may have been paid twice.

Mr Puddlecombe* and myself have now fixed to go to Torpoint on Monday the 27th day of August so that Billy** may now set out per coach on the same day and then he will arrive at Torpoint about four o'clock in the afternoon. I will leave my mare at the Inn kept by Mr Oliver and where the mail coach puts up. I dare say he will be very careful on his return with my mare for since my return from Tresillian my mare appears to be crippled in her forefeet, and therefore should Billy find it too long a journey from Torpoint to Tresillian I have no doubt in that case you will not be angry if he does not reach Tresillian until the Wednesday morning. Nothing I believe but a run will cure her.

I believe I mentioned when at Tresillian my wish to have £50 from you in November besides the Interest that is then due. I have lately been making some calculations and I find that I should not be able to do without it except by going to Bodmin Gaol, and as you are about to attend the Agricultural Meeting next year I suppose you would not wish this to take place.

Remember me kindly to Mrs Bennet and don't on any account forget Godson as I am not willing to incur Mrs Bennet's displeasure being always ambitious to keep on good terms with the Ladies. Remember me also to Nanny if you see her and the whole house. I expect to hear from that quarter soon.

I am, my dear Brother,
Yours sincerely and faithfully
M. W. Bennet.
P.S. In a week or ten days after starting I hope to be in Paris.
M. W. B.

East Looe
August 24th 1821

My dear Brother
I enclose a check on the East Cornwall Bank for the sum of Fifteen Pounds as due to yourself, Francis Paynter and James Pascoe. The truth is on Wednesday last I received Twenty Pounds

---

*Mr Puddlecombe was a close friend of Mydhope and lived near him.
**Billy was a groom employed by Mydhope.

of Mr Anstis of Liskeard and for us four being £5 each and the interest due on the money which my Grandfather laid on the Turnpikes there and I understood at the same time from Mr Anstis that the Interest now paid was for two years, that is to say, from Michaelmas 1818 to Michaelmas 1820. Of course I have retained £5 belonging to myself and I will thank you after retaining the same sum for yourself to pay Francis Paynter and Nanny (or James Pascoe) five pounds each. Now with respect to the Principal (which is of more consequence) I beg distinctly to state what Mr Anstis said to me on Wednesday last. Mr Anstis is of the opinion that the funds belonging to the Turnpike Trust are in a very bad state and that if we do not take some steps to get the Principal it will be years before we can obtain it. On the other hand he thinks that by proceeding against them now we may be likely to obtain the money in nine months or less. To tell you the process by which it may be obtained, I cannot. Suffice it to say that Mr Anstis has the different Acts of Parliament relating thereto and that his mode of conducting it is different from that of Francis Paynter.

Now I have no doubt but that you and Nanny as well as myself will be anxious to have recourse to the latter expedient, that of obtaining the money by instituting some immediate proceeding against the Commissioners of the Turnpike Trust or the Gatekeepers. But whether Francis Paynter will be of the same way of thinking I know not. I wish therefore for you to make enquiries for as there is a meeting of the Commissioners fixed for September if we all wish for Mr Anstis to obtain the money for us without much delay it will be necessary before that period for some statement to be drawn up and signed by Francis, yourself and Nanny (or James) empowering Mr Anstis to act for us in this business and stating that it is with our consent that such proceedings are undertaken. If such is not done and sent to Mr Anstis before the 5th September he cannot then enter upon the business nor can he give notice to the Commissioners which, if we are willing to go on with it, he then intends to do, and as it is uncertain when another meeting of the Commissioners will be appointed.

I hope nothing will prevent you from forwarding by that time a letter to Mr Anstis stating that you are all anxious to obtain the money and that you wish him to procure it. It will be no use for you to write letter upon letter to know how it is to be done for nothing but an interview can explain it, much better in my opinion is it for us at once to agree to it and then no delay will be occasioned. If this is not done we shall never, in my opinion, have the money. If however Francis should refuse I hope you and Nanny will agree to it and then I trust it can be done – do therefore your utmost and see yourself that everything is done and then you may conclude that we shall have the money in a short time. If however this is not done other claimants on the Liskeard Turnpike Trust will appear and then it will be difficult if not impossible to procure the Principal. I am writing Mr Anstis the receipt of the Fifteen pounds may be acknowledged. I am going on Monday and hope Billy will be at Torpoint on that day.

Remember me to Mrs Bennet and Godson and believe me to be, my dear Brother
Yours faithfully
M. W. Bennet.

P.S. I have already given Mr Anstis authority to proceed on my behalf but that will not be sufficient except the rest agree to it.

London
October 15th 1821

My dear Brother

I have postponed writing you till I reached the Metropolis being well assured that you have heard of me through Elizabeth and Nanny and therefore concluding that to write to you under such circumstances would only be incurring an unnecessary expense. Mr Puddlecombe and myself arrived at this place on Wednesday evening last from Dover where we spent a few days after ending our voyage of six hours from Calais. Tho' we had spent a pleasant time in France we were both very glad at once more seeing the English coast. Nothing indeed after all is so good as old England and I think that every radical should take a tour to some foreign land for it is impossible not to admire the English Government after seeing the imperfections attached to that of other nations. France seems entirely governed by the military and compared with that nation I cannot but think that we enjoy a great deal of liberty. I will not however now enter into the detailed account of France as we are likely so soon to meet, but will proceed to tell you of our proposed plans.

Mr Puddlecombe and myself hope to reach Looe on Monday the 29th of this month or on the following day. It is our intention to come by way of Exeter and from there proceed to Plymouth and it will be impossible for me to come to Tresillian till I have procured a lodging or some kind of residence at Looe for it must be manifest to you that engaging a lodging and preparing for the following Sunday will be a sufficient employment from the 29th October to the 4th November. Besides the 13th November will not have arrived and as we should not be able to settle our accounts I will postpone coming to Tresillian till some time after the collection of your rents. Under these circumstances I shall be obliged by your managing something about my mare. I should wish if possible to have her sent to Looe on Thursday the first of November for by that time I shall be sure to have arrived. How this can be done I know not and will leave entirely to you. You no doubt can procure someone on my behalf to bring over the mare but I cannot tell how that person can return for the Coach does not come nearer than Liskeard which is 8 miles from Looe. It will also I think be a good plan to have her taken in from grass about the week before she is sent over to Looe as otherwise she will be in a miserable state and I dare say you will procure someone to ride her.

In all these things I will gladly allow any reasonable expense and of course you will keep an account against me and regulate the whole about it. I do not care if she is looking very thin so long as she is tolerably well so I therefore should think a week will do for getting her into some order but this I will also leave to you. Will you also pay for the people.

So I understand Mr Pooley is dead and I long to hear who is to succeed him and whether he is about to reside or keep a Curate in his stead. I was much surprised to hear that Mr Pooley was so soon gone.

Give my kind regards to Mrs Bennet and Godson and also to Elisha and tell her how much obliged I am to her for her letter, it arrived just in time, the very morning after I arrived here.

I have seen Tom Paynter and have walked with him about London – he is not yet in a situation but expects to be so shortly. He is very well and in pretty good spirits. He appeared much astonished to see me. Excuse this letter as it is written in the Coffee Room which is not the best place for such things.

If you wish to write before you send my mare a letter directed to East Looe will find me most probably on the 29th October.

I am, my dear Brother,
            Yours faithfully
                    M. W. Bennet.

                                            East Looe
                                    November 5th 1821

My dear Brother

I arrived here safe and sound this day week and received your letter on the Tuesday for which I return you many thanks. I am very sorry to find by it that my mare is lame but I trust under your management a short time will restore her to perfect soundness. I have been obliged in consequence of this to hire a horse twice but I must endeavour till my mare comes to do as well as I can without her. The first moment however you think it is safe to send her to St Austele, I will by you giving me notice of your intention send a man there to receive her from the hands of your servant. As this is the case I will if agreeable postpone my visit to Tresillian to any time that may be agreeable to yourself and Mrs Bennet. The beginning of December or January will suit me better than the week after the Court and therefore I shall leave it to you or rather to Mrs Bennet to decide. At all events I had now better leave it till all is over and comfortable of which I trust you will let me know as I shall be extremely anxious to hear that all is well. Give my kind regards therefore and good wishes to Mrs Bennet not forgetting the hunter who 'ere this I suppose has been in to the death of a hare.

I shall be very glad if you will pay Mrs Symons of Trerice for the keep of my mare and Mr Hawke the Principal as well as Interest – as for the rest of our accounts they will of course remain status quo till I arrive at Tresillian.

I am glad to hear of the good sport you have had in hunting; last week being a wet one I should imagine must have put a little stop to it again.

I am at present at my old lodgings and continue to serve the Parish of Morval where there is duty now twice again and therefore it is probable I shall entirely confine myself to that place. I hope you will be pleased with your new Vicar, Mr Polwhale. I hear that the Bishop has acted a most honourable part in giving it to him for I understand that Mr Polwhale was by no means known to the Bishop who gave the living to him entirely from hearing of his numerous family and also in consideration of his having been an author.

Mr Anstis whom I saw last week said how much obliged he was to you for the kind invitation you had given him, he was unable to accept it when he was last in that neighbourhood but when he goes there again he says he will not fail of giving you a call. Your letter authorised him to proceed on our behalf for the Turnpike Trust money did not reach him in time to lay before the Commissioners of the Trust but he hopes shortly to be enabled to do so. If you see Elizabeth, or write her, will you say with my love that I am here and that she shall hear from me next. Hoping to hear soon of my mare. Believe me to be,
my dear Brother,
    Yours faithfully and sincerely,
        M. W. Bennet.
If you should see any of my Tenants you might say that I am likely to be at Tresillian between this and Christmas and then they will be more likely to be prepared should I not be there so soon.
                    M. W. B.

                    East Looe
                    December 4th 1821
My dear Brother
    In compliance with your request I hope to send off by tomorrow's post Alison's sermons and will therefore prepare a letter to send therewith as well as thank you to forward the enclosed to Elizabeth the first opportunity you may have. You can pay for the carriage of the parcel which I shall be ready to allow when I come to Tresillian as of course you ought to be put to no expense in this matter.

    I am sorry my mare is not as yet much recovered tho' I cannot say I feel much the loss of her except that I should wish to have her for my journey to Tresillian. However I must make the best of a bad matter and I was about to purpose to start from hence for

Tresillian on Monday the 31st day of December. This must however entirely depend on its being agreeable to Mrs Bennet and yourself, I trust it will not be too soon. If I hear nothing to the contrary by the 20th of this month I shall conclude that it is agreeable and shall come. Therefore you will have no need to write on purpose.

Respecting my mare I cannot expect that she will be well enough to enable me to ride her from hence to Tresillian and therefore if I do not hear from you by the 20th inst saying that she is sufficiently recovered I shall proceed then to hire one for the week. So that your silence will imply that I may come on the 31st inst and that I must borrow a horse for that week as I am likely to be at Tresillian so soon I think at all events the firing of the mare had better be deferred to that period. For my part I would much rather allow a little time for her recovery than to proceed to such a remedy.

I have been thinking whether the 31st will be too soon, if so the seventh of January will do equally as well for me so long as I know in time and whichever of the two you fix on I will thank you to give notice to my Tenants accordingly of my intention of coming into that neighbourhood to receive my rents. A man would very well go round and I would readily pay him for so doing.

I think three feeds a day quite sufficient for my mare now she is idle. I do not wish to starve her but you must remember not to run the poor Curate up too long a bill. I do not wish you to send any money. I feel obliged by your offer of your young horse but of this we can talk when we meet.

I sincerely hope that by this time all is well and over with regard to Mrs Bennet as she caught me last time and then was sooner than she expected. So I hope it will be now. I look forward every day I can assure you to a letter from you. If however it should not take place till after the receipt of this you will then be able to mention all about my coming, mare etc.

With kind regards to Mrs Bennet and Godson, believe me to be,
Your faithful Brother
  M. Wallis Bennet.
I will defer saying anything about poor Charles till I see you. If

I come on the 31st on a hired horse of course you will not expect me till the evening.

On the 15th December 1821 a little boy named John was born to Gully and Loveday. He was baptised privately by his uncle, Mydhope. Seven days later Gully suffered a devastating blow. His young wife, Loveday, died at Tresillian aged 23 years. It was as if he had been struck by lightning. Elizabeth who lived a few miles away at St Columb immediately took the two infants, Richard aged fourteen months and John a week old. Gully faced his torment alone, save for servants, at Tresillian. His sister Ann wrote on the eve of Christmas:

> St Keverne Vicarage
> Wednesday night
> 24th December 1821
>
> I little thought my dearest Gully I should have had to address you on an occurrence so melancholy and so disturbing as the present nor can I express the grief I feel on contemplating your situation. To be deprived so soon and so suddenly of your wedded partner and mother of your children is a calamity with which few can fully sympathise but those who have experienced the same loss. You will believe however that I have felt most fully and bitterly this stroke now befallen to a beloved brother and that these feelings have alone prevented my writing earlier. To put consolation into the afflicted person is in the power only of Him who afflicts and my most earnest prayer is that the Almighty who has seen fit to lay this stroke on you will enable you to bear it.
>
> If I can be of any service do not hesitate to command me. I would not wish to make any intrusive offers on real grief but if you would like to confine either of your children to my care during their earlier years I would try in some measure to repair a mother's loss by discharging a mother's duty.
>
> Tomorrow I send to Helston on purpose for letters to give any intelligence of you for I trust Elizabeth has remembered my anxiety. I do not ask you to write, do it therefore at your convenience, a line will always comfort me if it does not distress you. To enter on any other subject would be painful both to you and to me, I therefore conclude with offering every kind wish

with that affection ever present and believe me, My Dear Brother,
to remain,

    Your most sincerely afflicted sister
      A. Pascoe.
    James begs his kind regards.

It was a grief stricken Gully who made arrangements for his young wife's funeral at Newlyn. Christmas that year was a bitter and lonely trial for the sorrowing husband. On Boxing Day the Masons, Carpenters and Labourers prepared Mrs Bennet's vault and the accounts tell all.

Paid the Carpenter's bill	£2:15:6
Paid the Mason's bill	£2:15:6
Paid carriage of bricks	£0:18:0
Paid the bill at the Public House for workmen's beer	£1: 1:6
Paid the bill for bar and spirits at Ship Inn Newlyn for Masons Carpenters and Labourers engaged about Mrs Bennet's vault	£1:1:6
To paid John Symonts -	
for a Hearse and Four	£6:6:0
for Mourning Coach and Four	£6:6:0
for Post Chaise	£2:0:0
Paid drivers of Hearse and Coach	£1:1:0
Paid Driver of Post Chaise	£0:7:0
Paid Clerk and Sexton	£1:1:0
Paid bill at the Public House for bearers and drivers etc.	£1:0:0
Paid spirits for the gentlemen attending Mrs Bennet's funeral	£1:0:0

Loveday Bennet, aged 23, was laid to rest on the 28th December 1821 in the Churchyard at Newlyn Parish Church. According to the Burials Register she was the fourth Bennet to be buried at Newlyn.

Gully's aunt, Ann Roberts, living at Landrake Vicarage, wrote to him on the last day of the year:

                    Landrake near St Germains
                    December the 31st 1821

My dearest dear Gully
    Would it were in my power to offer you any consolation or to

soothe those sufferings which I know must be most intensely acute. Your dear sister is I hope with you as her affectionate solicitude will aid her in doing all that can be done in a case where time alone can really effect any material relief. John desires me to say how sincerely he consoles with you and that when you can bear to see him he will go down to Tresillian for a day or two. I will only add at this suffering period that to see you at Landrake is my first and earnest wish and you will see no company, not a creature – and your poor Aunt feels as distressed for you as she would do for either of her own children. Ann is by no means in a good state of health but fully alive to the deep affliction of her dear Cousin.

Be assured my beloved nephew that I am always your affectionate and now most sympathising Aunt.

Ann Roberts.

Two months later Aunt Roberts wrote again, at the foot of a letter from her son John.

Parish Church of Saint Newlyn

Landrake Vicarage
St Germains, Plymouth Dock.
February 18th 1822

My dear Gully

It was fully my intention of being with you some part of the last week but I was obliged to be in attendance on my sister who is gone off to Sidmouth. I am now called on a good deal in a professional way and therefore cannot say when I shall be so disengaged as to be at liberty to leave this place for a few days. My mother and myself are at present the only inmates of Landrake Vicarage and if you My Dear Friend will favour us with your company we shall be delighted to see you and will do everything in our power to soothe your severe affliction.

I remain my dear Gully
    Yours sincerely
      J. Roberts.

I often think of you with the tenderest sympathy my dearest Gully and most earnestly entreat you to come to us without delay. The ride is not a very long one and I hope it may be in our power to benefit your health and spirits. You will never be intruded upon and you may almost think yourself in the Deserted Village. The dear sweet babes* are I trust well and with kindest remembrances to dear Elizabeth.

I am my beloved nephew very affectionately and faithfully yours
      Ann Roberts.

In 1822 Gully was appointed a Magistrate for the County of Cornwall and his new found duties coupled with his own activities as Squire of Tresillian relieved his loneliness. Both infant children had been taken by his sister Elizabeth and lived with Elizabeth and Francis Paynter, growing up with their cousins. Mydhope remained unmarried.

East Looe
March 16th 1822

My dear Brother

I fear you will think me a miserable correspondent but you

Richard Gully was then aged only sixteen months and John was aged three months.

must recollect I am not an idle person but have a profession to occupy my time the duties of which must be performed. I am very glad to hear of the determination you have come to respecting your dogs and horses. You will I think enjoy equal pleasure attended with less expense and will no doubt soon find the determination to be most wise and prudent. The huntsman's wages also will be saved and altogether I think you will now be able to pay off by degrees some of the mortgages with which your estate is encumbered. I am also glad to hear of your intended visit to Looe and trust the Solicitor's wife will accompany you. I have said so much to her and whenever it is agreeable to both shall be ready and happy to receive you.

I told John Roberts that I conclude you intended to pay them a visit at that time. He was here last week and spent two days with me and you can hardly imagine it to be possible that John could make so steady a clergyman as he does. Indeed at this moment he is doing wonders in his Parish and perhaps excels most of those of his profession as far as regards the duties which are imposed on him, few, if any, in my opinion, can be found who are so altered in so short a time.

Ann is at present at Sidmouth having been absent from Landrake more than a month. Had I been most sanguine I could never have supposed that I could have had any chance, especially if any account is to be taken of her conversation, therefore I must suppose she is looking farther than to a Curate.

I have been thinking much of late of Gilbert, he promised to pay you £8:10:0 on my behalf at all events by the middle of last month. If he has not done so by this time, the best plan, I think will be to threaten to distrain him immediately if he did not give up the Estate and be allowed for the corn which he has now in the ground as well as for that which is not thrashed. I thought if an adequate person, perhaps it must be a professional man (and if so I should like to have Thomas Hawkey or Whitfield) were prepared to distrain before the 25th of March, and would go to his house and threaten to do so, provided he would not give up the Estate, he would be inclined to accede to the terms. After considering the matter however more fully I wish to give Mr Gilbert notice to quit the Estate at Michaelmas next. The year goes in and out at Michaelmas and therefore a notice given before or on Ladyday will remove him at that time.

I do not know whether the notice must be signed by myself but if there is no need I authorise you to do so on my behalf.

This, I think, is the best plan, for I cannot distrain him, and if do lose money by it, I shall be glad that I have got rid of him. There is now corn in the ground respecting which it will be an after consideration whether I am inclined to pay myself part of the arrears out of it.

If you have any essential objection to this plan of mine, I do not wish to get the notice served for I understand but little of these matters. I will give you notice for Gilbert at the end of this letter and if it will do and you think it advisable for me to give him notice as *I cannot* distrain, I wish you would have it served it on him. If you do this perhaps also you would be kind enough to get someone to be on the alert and to see that he does no injury to the Estate as he is so soon to leave it. I am thinking of letting Richard Richards have it from year to year only as the times are now so precarious and when I come over your way can see about it. In the meantime I should wish for everything necessary to be done to the Estate and I am ready to allow anyone for the same.

I, Mydhope Wallis Bennet hereby give William Gilbert notice to quit the Estate of Trefullock in the Parish of St Enoder in the County of Cornwall on Michaelmas Day next.

Dated the sixteenth day of March one thousand eight hundred and twenty two.

Mydhope Wallis Bennet.

East Looe

Excuse this letter as I have not time to write it over to you. So Mr Paynter is dead, I heard from Elizabeth but have not written her as I expect to hear from Nan again shortly. I hope to hear from you shortly and am much obliged for your receipts for the mare which is now in very good order. I hope Richard Gully is well, of the babe I hear very good accounts.

I am my dear Brother
Yours truly
Mydhope W. Bennet.

St Columb
13th April 1822

My dear Gully

One of my clerks shall serve Hawke with an ejectment the beginning of next week as arranged.

I have been repeatedly with Norway on the subject of the balance due to you on the account of the sales of stock by Mr Rashleigh. This morning he has assured me that nothing shall prevent my having the account immediately after his return from the Sessions and with your approval I will therefore wait till the end of next week in the hope of saving you the expense of an application for the account in London. Should I be once again disappointed I will without further reference to Mr Norway apply to Mr Rashleigh through my agent for the required papers and when the amount of the balance due to you is ascertained it will be for you to determine on the expediency of adopting measures for the recovery of it.

I am, my dear Gully
Yours very truly
F. C. Paynter

My dearest Brother

Are you sure there is a coach which goes this road to Liskeard if so I have determined to accompany you and take Margaret. Perhaps a week after the time you first thought of would be better for me but do as you like. I think we shall be a great many for Mydhope's one servant, I would therefore have you mention that I could bring my apprentice who is able to do a great deal and if we could continue to go on a Wednesday I could send her off by Cazier's cart the Tuesday for Liskeard, but think this over. – In haste E.P.

I don't think I could stay above a fortnight and you may not bargain for no visiting.

St Columb
25th April 1822

My dear Gully

I have received on your account Forty Seven Pounds Seven Shillings and send you enclosed as detailed my draft on Lubbock

& Co for the amount. You may if you please endorse it specially.

In consequence of my late father's death it has become necessary that I should with as little delay as may be call in all sums due to the late firm of F. Paynter & Son, and shall therefore feel obliged by your favouring me at your first convenience with a remittance in part payment of the balance due from you.

Elizabeth and the children are well as is also your little boy. She unites in kindest remembrances to you.

My dear Gully,

     Yours very truly,

     F. C. Paynter.

                          St Columb
                    June 20th 1822

My dear Gully

Mydhope proposes being here on the 8th of July and wishes you to fix your plans and then let me write. He proposes being here at dinner that day and of proceeding to Tresillian Tuesday evening or Wednesday morning. Now I think you had better let us see you here to meet him on the Monday and suffer us to have John christened the Tuesday, I can then ask Mr Aldrich to take his dinner here with Mydhope in a family way without anyone else. Perhaps you had better invite the Polwhales on the Thursday that Myd may have his last day at command. I will come out in the morning. He wishes to fix Mr Cardell to a particular time when he can be sure of finding him at home, any part of the Friday he says would be excellent.

Of course you know that Mrs James has lost her infant.

As to letting little John home you will of course soon find the measles are now all about, perhaps on that account it might be a bad time and there is no obstacle to his remaining only I must know long enough for to give Mrs James some notice and you should be on the lookout for a good steady servant. I did hear Mrs Polwhales had parted with one on whom she had perfect reliance as a child's maid. You are pleased with Philly in the kitchen, why not continue her tho' in my opinion there are many objections to her as a child's maid and I cannot in justice to you or the lovely legacy so awfully bequeathed suffer him to return to his paternal mansion without intimating that to my certain knowledge your darling Richard was at one time kept many days without washing properly. I speak not from the tittle tattle of servants but after my sister's eyesight, she on this occasion would not grudge my having informed that I have not wished to be a meddler, the months that are past must speak. In fact I should not now but in so young a child the result might be pernicious.

Francis we expect home tonight, he has at length gained information of Mr Norway's debt to you thirty-eight Pounds but seems to think it will be difficult to recover. I sincerely hope you will get it.

Adieu and believe me to be your affectionate sister,

E. Paynter.

Francis will be off again on Monday – let me hear as soon as possible.

St Columb
21st June 1822

My dear Gully

Yourself and Norway

I have been recently in London and whilst there called on Mr Rashleigh for the purpose of investigating the state of the accounts as to date sold out on the death of the last tenants. I make this communication to you and await your further instructions.

Yourself & Hawke

I hope the settlement of this rent is to your entire satisfaction and that the rents will follow with interest at Michaelmas without giving you further trouble.

In haste, my dear Gully
F.C. Paynter

St Columb
12th July 1822

My dear Gully

Mr Norway has promised to let you have your account this day a month and says that by that time all his affairs will be arranged and his accounts ready for delivery and settlement.

In haste,
very truly yours,
F. C. Paynter

St Columb
Friday night

My dear Gully

I have this moment had a letter from James with the comfortable tidings of my beloved sister's safety. She was delivered of a fine boy yesterday morning but had contended with a very severe labour the whole of the day and night before. I am sorry to say your little John is very unwell indeed suffering a vast deal from teeth and perhaps some other impossible cause. Everything we can think of is doing for him and Mr Mountsteven duly attentive so that I hope very few days will relieve our anxiety on his account.

Our kind regards attend yours,
Ever your affectionate
E. Paynter.
Let Mr Cardell know this.

On the 26th September 1822 the infant John Bennet died at St Columb aged nine months twenty-two days. Gully took this further blow with the calm and resolution with which he had faced the death of his wife nine months earlier. His sister Ann wrote on the 30th September 1822.

St Keverne
Monday evening : 30th September 1822

It was with the greatest sorrow my dearest Gully that I heard on Saturday of this severe and recent affliction you have sustained in the loss of your dear child. That his being removed thus early from this life of trouble is really an act of mercy to the infant no one can doubt, but it is hard for the parents to part and a severe stroke to you my dear Brother. I trust that time will soften it and enable you to regain your accustomed composure.

I had many times intended writing since my confinement but put it off from time to time indefinitely now however I am able to inform you that my health is much improved and that my children are well, the little one thriving exceedingly and thought to resemble me more than the other. He is called James and I hope will do well.

Dorothy is now with us and has not been quite so well of late, Humphrey I think very ill and the winter will try him greatly.

Mary spent a day with us lately, she expects to be confined before Christmas.

I heard from Myd Saturday giving an account of Sir Francis Burdett's visit to Looe. Next week we are to lose our surgeon who moves to reside at Helston being nearer the centre of his business. His departure will be a great loss to us for tho' not out of the district we cannot send that distance on every occasion. James unites in kind regards and accept dear Gully the affectionate love of your sincerely attached sister;

A. Pascoe.

A kiss for dear Richard.

Mydhope's letters continued with regularity.

East Looe
November 11th 1822

My dear Brother

I have a little more time now on my hands then when I wrote you such a hasty line on Saturday last. You must know I went on the Monday according to agreement to Fowey where I stayed till the Saturday morning and was surprised that Mr Basset should dispatch a messenger to me here without first apprising me of it. He must have been aware that he could not calculate with any degree of certainty on my being at home. Accordingly his messenger was detained here from Thursday evening to Saturday noon owing to my absence. He also presses me to return him an answer immediately. It was morally impossible for me to come to terms on such an important matter at a moment's notice and therefore I wrote him to say I could have no objection to being granted a set provided the terms offered were fair, at the same time referring him to Mr Cardell whom I have authorised to come to terms if they are in any way fair and reasonable.

Lord Falmouth has granted a deed and in case we can agree it will be necessary I conclude for me to grant one also. In that case I have requested Mr Cardell to procure Mr Whitfield to draft the same. The only point of which I am ignorant is this, and which you can speak to Mr Cardell if you should see him, namely whether it is usual for the takers to indemnify the Lord for any land they may injure. By Lord Falmouth's deed a clause appears to be made to this effect and if it can be done in my case I should like it.

I should not on any account like to grant the barn at Trefullock for the purpose mentioned in your letter and you are perfectly at liberty to say as much if you should hear anything more of the subject. By the 20th instant or thereabouts I conclude I shall receive the money from you. At the same time you will mention in your letter the particulars of the account between us that I may compare them with the account which I have. It appears by your letter that £4:19:6 was awarded to Mr Gilbert for preparation for tillage but I do not exactly understand what the deduction of 19s:9d is except it be for want of Gates and a coat of dressing for the clover field. Mention this when you write.

I am glad you have received from William Gilbert all the money that is due to me. Is the allowance for the barn exactly 4s:3d? State all particulars when you send your account. I wish also to have a copy (verbatim) of the paper which I signed for the allowance of Twenty Pounds per annum to Betty at Newlyn, and this I should be anxious to have when you next write.

Have you ever made an agreement with Richard Richards for the preparation tillage at Trefullock? After viewing the Estate Mr Richards acknowledged to me at St Columb (when he took the Estate) that it was worth £6:10:0 therefore I see no reason why I should take a less sum for the £4:19:6 was awarded to Gilbert yet I conclude somethings were set against it such as the circumstance of his cutting the field twice to hay in one year which I now find to have been contrary to the Deed granted to Mrs Richards of Benallack. If you have not made an agreement with him will you do so shortly as it cannot be so easily done when the preparation for tillage is not to be seen. It will of course not be advisable to take a less sum than the £6:10:0.

The quarry at Trewinnion is already or immediately to be filled in. I shall therefore feel particularly obliged if you will plant some pinisters round the little orchard which I am about to make. Mr Rendle of St Austle has called here this morning and offered me some apple trees for 2s:0d: each. I believe this is a fair price, and if you also think so, will you desire Richard Richards to select as many as he wants (I believe 30) from the nursery of Mr Rendle and plant them. They will be better if planted before Christmas I

110

think provided it is not frost. Mr Rendle has given you the prices of the trees which he sells, I find I wish to know before I give him an order whether you consider them to be fair. Perhaps you may receive this on your birthday. If so, or otherwise, I beg to wish you many returns of the day and with a kiss to Godson, believe me to be, my Dear Brother yours faithfully,

M. W. Bennet.

Mr Rendle informed me some sycamore trees would be very good to plant round the orchard in as much as their leaves come out very early and would shelter the blossom of the apple trees. I shall be very glad to allow you anything for what you may plant round the orchard. I have always understood that anyone living within ten miles of the Bank he draws on, can draw legally a check on the top of a letter. If you like you can draw the check on the top of your letter I believe instead of enclosing a check on the Miner's Bank and this will save double postage. Francis Paynter, if you see him, will tell you how this can be done.

M.W.B.

East Looe
November 28th 1822

My dear Brother

I hope you are not alarmed at not hearing from me sooner relative to the check for £100:6:6 which came safe to hand in due time. To that part of your letter which regards the reduction of interest I cannot at present return a decisive answer. I should be most willing to give you an answer in the affirmative were I persuaded that it was the general practice for a reduction of interest to take place on mortgages, I will not say between strangers, but between relations, but I think if that is not the case, it will be too much to expect me to make such a reduction especially when it is considered that more than a quarter of a year elapses before I receive the interest even after a year's interest is due and when it is also recollected that I charge you no more than 4 per cent for the sum of £140 when it was in my power to have obtained from you 5 per cent interest. At all events I must at once object to my conduct being regulated by that of Mr F. Paynter as in all probability his mode of acting will generally differ most essentially from mine. I do not mean to insinuate that it is your wish that I should do anything of the kind and I am willing to make enquiries forthwith as to the custom of a reduction of interest taking place at this time between relations and to abide by that custom at the same time if it is your intention to ground anything of it I shall consider myself bound in honour to return you an earlier answer on this subject than I should otherwise do. You will perceive I do not complain of the interval which takes place between the interest becoming due and the time of you paying me the same. I only state it as a ground for a non-reduction of interest. The account you sent me was I believe perfectly correct and therefore the balance accounted as by your check to £100:6:6.

You forgot in your last letter to send me an exact copy of the paper which I signed for Betty at Newlyn and I should be particularly obliged to you if you will procure it for me immediately and forward it. You said Jack who goes to Newlyn every evening could get it and therefore I hope you will lose no time in sending it to me. When you speak of obtaining trees from London for half of Mr Rendle's charges, do you include the expenses of carriage which I should imagine would be considerable.

I shall rely on your planting the Pinasters and seeing the orchard at Trewinion is put to rights. You do not say whether the apple trees at 2s:0d are a fair price. I am much astonished at your intention of ceasing to keep hounds. As far as it regards myself I should never allow the permission to shoot over Nuncall which has been granted by Lord Falmouth to Mr Betallick's son to weigh with me to such an extent tho' if there be any other ground for relinquishing them the case is very different and the determination you have formed may be very prudent and judicious. I cannot however for a moment imagine that the step which Mr Betallick has taken can materially affect your keeping of hounds especially when you must have such good hunting ground even at this moment.

Mr Whitfield informed me when last at St Columb that two deeds with the proper stamp for Trefullock would cost £3:13:6 but one deed and stamp and another without it would be only £2:7:0. If Mr Richards agreed to take the one without stamp (which I am sure he would be glad to do save the expense) do you think it would be advisable to let Mr Richards do this? or it is in your opinion a bad plan?

Have you any idea whether the £8:10:0 for the preparation for tillage at Trefullock is a fair price and will you tell me for what reason the 19s:9d is deducted from the £4:19:6 as appears by your former letter? You of course recollect the £4:19:6 was awarded to William Gilbert for preparation for tillage, but for what is the 19s:9d deducted from it? Do tell me in your next.

I hope you will answer this letter shortly as I wish to have some correspondence with you on another subject for which I have not room in this letter. Remember me kindly to Godson and believe me to be, my dear Brother
    Yours faithfully
        M. W. Bennet.

East Looe
January 7th 1823

My dear Brother

Yesterday's post brought me a check on the Miner's Bank for the sum of Thirty Five Pounds which Richard Richards had paid you on my account. Having occasion to write to Richards about a week since I mentioned to him that I was not aware whether he had paid you any money for me and that if he had not I should expect a pretty large sum from him at Ladyday. If Richards therefore should speak to you on the subject you can satisfy him that I have received it. Indeed, between ourselves, I did not wish that you should enclose it to me and in future you had no need to take that trouble except I should particularly wish it to be sent or except you should not like to keep so much money in the house.

I cannot imagine how you could think I was coming in your neighbourhood in February. I never recollect having such an intention or having said so much to anyone. I certainly did intend to volunteer a visit to yourself and Elizabeth some time after Ladyday, in the month of April, and had some thoughts if it was agreeable and convenient to both of you and I could get my Church served, to spend the fortnight, staying over one Sunday, when I might also be able to go over the whole of my Estates in St Enoder Parish. I should not wish for this plan to be known generally in as much as I would not on any account that any engagement should be made for me to dine out, and I am also very anxious to escape the Sunday duty. Recollect therefore you do not whisper anything of the sort into the ear of Miss Marianne – above all things let not the Pencorse Family hear it. When I could not succeed in procuring the paper from Betty through you I wrote to Mrs Cardell thinking it likely Mrs Cardell might know some of Betty's acquaintances through whom she might easily obtain the contents of the paper. I however left it open as to what plan had better be adopted in procuring it. Consequently Mr Cardell called at Newlyn on Betty and was unsuccessful – after this and considering my anxiety to obtain a copy I should think you could have no objection on their application again for any money to refuse it till they bring you an exact copy of the Paper. This must have the desired effect – I at the time I put my name to the Paper accommodated you and I am sure you will not in return refuse me a similar accommodation. To convince you I took no offence I shall give you an exact copy of a letter as far as regards the business I alluded to which I wrote you about a fortnight since, but which has by this time perhaps reached you. For fear however that it has not, I will give it to you. With love to Godson, I am my dear Brother, yours faithfully

M. W. Bennet.

East Looe
December 26th 1822

You no doubt recollect that a year or two since our attention was directed to the consideration of the Redeemed Land Tax. In endeavouring to ascertain at that time to whom the Redeemed Land Tax of Penhale and Trethill of right belonged, an opinion was taken by me of a professional man by which it appeared that if the Redeemed Land Tax of Penhale and Trethill was meddled with, a question might arise whether such a step would not involve the whole of the Redeemed Land Tax both that which belonged to you as well as to me and that eventually a very different distribution of it might be made than at present exists. In consequence of this the subject was dropped and as a doubt may hereafter arise whether you legally possess the Redeemed Land Tax of those Estates you now hold, and whether I also am entitled to the Redeemed Land Tax of Penhale and Trethill which would in all probability involve our posterity, if not ourselves, in a Law Suit, the object of this letter is to know whether you will agree to a plan which might at once put an end to any law suit which this subject might occasion. The plan I propose is for each of us to make an assignment of the Redeemed Land Tax to each other, that is to say for you to agree to have a deed drawn bearing your signature assigning over to me the Redeemed Land Tax of Penhale and Trethill as well as of those Estates which I now have in St Enoder Parish, and for me to agree to have a deed drawn bearing my signature assigning over to you the Redeemed Land Tax of those Estates which you now hold. If you will agree to this I will immediately obtain Mr Bond's opinion on the practicability of it, and in case it can be done, we can employ, if you please, Mr Whitfield to draw the deeds, you bearing the expense of the deed which secures to you your Land Tax which I think would be fair, and I will bear the expense of the deed which may secure my Land Tax to me.

I wish however for us to understand each other and in case you should think there may be more doubt of my right to the Land Tax of Penhale and Trethill than there is to your right of possessing Land Tax you now have, and consequently you should be unwilling to adopt this plan, I am sure you will have no objection to another, which is to have the opinion of an Eminent Counsel, and to abide by the opinion of that Counsel, even if it should occasion the Land Tax to be distributed into other hands than now hold it for this must necessarily follow the opinion of the Counsel, should that be his opinion.

My object as you will see by this letter is to have the subject at once decided and I will agree to either of the plans you may chose.

My reason for being anxious for an early decision is to prevent ultimate ruin to either party for should either of us be wrong in receiving the Land Tax we at present do, a delay of many years if the case were then brought forward might be almost ruinous in its consequences. Will you therefore consider this subject and then let me have your opinion. I can assure you truly and honourably that I have no other wish in introducing this subject than that of averting any ruin which by delay might be impending over our heads for many years.

115

January 7th 1823

I am sorry if Mr Cardell has said anything which has irritated Betty's husband.

Say in your next if you will adopt the plan I suggest relative to the obtaining the contents of the paper of Betty.

East Looe
February 25th 1823

My dear Brother

I have lately received from Mr Anstis two years' Interest on the Deed Poll from Michaelmas 1820 to 1822 both for you and Elizabeth or should I rather say Francis. The sum for both of you amounts to £10:0:0 – £5 each – but then I have paid Mr Anstis' charge of £1:1:0 out of it, so that there is due to you the sum of £4:9:8 as well to Elizabeth. The same deduction has been made out of Nanny's and my portion of £10:0:0. The charge made by Mr Anstis is not only for receiving the money now as well as in 1821, but also for the trouble he has taken in endeavouring to get the Principal etcetera. I have not enclosed a check for the amount, both because I know not whether you may not have received some money of my Tenants out of which you can take it, and also because I am likely to be so shortly with you. If however you wish it, write, and I will give you a check. Indeed if it should be particularly convenient to you to do so I shall be obliged by your paying Francis the sum I have above mentioned and he can acknowledge the receipt of it as well as that of Five Pounds which he received in August 1821 for two years interest from Michaelmas 1818 to 1820, in the same letter in which Elizabeth writes me. Do not forget to mention this to him as I never received a receipt for that paid in 1821.

You do not understand me about Betty. I not only ask you to threaten to deprive her of the money but also to carry the threat into execution – to keep back the money in reality provided she will not give a copy – and this must have the desired effect. It can neither entail any hardship on Betty, nor can she reasonably complain of it, and as I obliged you in signing the Paper I am sure you will not but oblige me in endeavouring to procure it for me. Will you, therefore, when the next application is made, adopt this plan? I shall be exceedingly thankful if you will. I do not expect you to give any answer respecting the Redeemed Land Tax till I see you. You had better, however, keep the letter which I wrote respecting it as we may one day have occasion to refer to it.

I think I recollect you once lost a great many bottles of cyder by placing them on the wrong side or end. As I am about to bottle off a good quantity will you tell me how they should be placed. I believe on their ends and not on their sides – am I right? I confess I do not wish to purchase my experience at so dear a rate as you did.

I am perfectly astonished at Miss Basset's conduct. I should like to have asked her when she spoke of Elizabeth's conduct and want of feeling, what she could have felt, who could, on the very day of the funeral of her sister, melancholy indeed as it was, give orders to a younger sister to copy the pattern of Elizabeth's cap or frill, during our absence in attending her sister's remains to their last home.

I fear it will not be in my power to come in your neighbourhood till the beginning of April as I wish to get someone to serve my Church for one Sunday. I cannot mention the time at present but will let you or Elizabeth hear that I shall be in time to attend the wedding.

I do not hear that Elizabeth's boy is christened, if I am mentioned or thought likely to be asked to be one of the sponsors, throw as much cold water on the subject as you possibly can, and I shall be particularly obliged to you (this between ourselves).

Take the earliest opportunity of stating my objections to that of standing to children, tho' of course you will not say I have spoken of the subject.

I am, my dear Brother,
Yours faithfully
  M. W. Bennet.

P.S. Please give a kiss to little Richard from Uncle Mydhope. Do not forget planting at Trewinion and I hope to hear shortly in answer to the former part of the letter.

During the early summer of 1823 Mydhope was taken ill with abdominal pains which caused anxiety to his brother Gully and the two sisters, Elizabeth and Ann. Elizabeth and Gully visited him at the end of June.

23rd June 1823.

My dearest Brother

A letter last night from Myd in which he asked me to tell you how glad he will be to see us. Should you like to take the third of a chaise it will be more comfortable to me to go that way and if we go the Lostwithiel road. Francis and I both think it will be more reasonable for all parties I shall then take Jane with us and for the child it will be far less tedious. If I do not see you this week I wish you would let me know whether you accede to this plan that I may write Myd for the old Bachelor is in a thousand fidgets as to the hour for ordering dinner – much obliged for your procuring the tea.

Francis joins in kind regards.

Ever Yours

Elizabeth Paynter.

Doctor McGrath of Plymouth was Mydhope's doctor and he felt obliged to take a second opinion from Dr Fox an eminent physician also of Plymouth. Gully was deeply concerned by his brother's condition when he visited him at East Looe and wrote immediately to both doctors who replied in rather vague terms.

Woodside
Plymouth
July 12th 1823

R G Bennet Esquire.

My dear Sir

It will give me pleasure to reply candidly to your enquiry respecting your afflicted brother. You know my opinion of his state prior to my consultation with my friend Dr McGrath, I copied my letter to you and it contained my honest and deliberate assessment of his case.

Still however, one should not be warranted in omitting those means which Providence has entrusted us with. Many patients have recovered whose situation I have thought desperate. You are doing everything for your brother which duty and affection demand. You ought not to relax.

I am, yours truly

Joseph Fox.

Doctor McGrath wrote to Gully a few days later:

Plymouth
24th July 1823
Tuesday evening 7 o'clock

Dear Sir

Until my return this morning from a distant professional journey I did not receive your letter and it would have been more promptly attended to although I truly confess that I feel no little difficulty in replying to some parts of it and especially that in which you say 'if there is no ultimate chance of recovery it is to be hoped that he should be sustained with medicine and thereby prevented from sinking by weakness.'

In justice to myself and to my colleague Dr Fox I am bound to state that the measures which we recommended when we saw your brother were not experimental or speculative but the result of mature and deliberate reasoning deducted from previous similar cases and the symptoms which presented themselves to us; and under the presumption that they were best calculated to relieve him without hazard or unnecessarily distressing him.

With respect to my 'candid opinion' I have little to add to that which I truly and unreservedly submitted when at Looe. His case is unquestionably one of an aggravated nature involving much danger and the prospect of protracted suffering; but still under present circumstances I should not consider it by any means a hopeless one. I have seen some analogous maladies where the symptoms were not so exaggerated but were terminal unfortunately; and I have met with many others where the appearances were less encouraging, the symptoms more violent, and the growth of the abdomen to a much greater extent than in your brother's instance, end satisfactorily. I therefore feel the necessity of caution in giving a prognosis as to the probable events and in doing so I would appeal to all those best acquainted with the difficulties of medical investigation and pathological indication as to the propriety of circumspection from the uncertainty in which maladies of that nature are revealed; but I would add that the resources of the medical art furnishes us with many alternatives should the plan now in adoption not succeed.

119

Before concluding I think it only honest to state to you that no medical man can prescribe for a patient so circumstanced as your brother upon the report or representation of another as there can be many such points and shades of consequential difference constantly arising which are only cognizable by professional experience in analogous cases that I should feel great delicacy in venturing to recommend any change in the treatment or his removal without seeing him, or to give any opinion as to the deficiency or inefficiency of such a step, as an opinion so given would be very liable to error.

I am, Sir, your obedient servant,
S. McGrath.

During this time, on the 18th July 1823, Gully was appointed Deputy Lieutenant of the County of Cornwall. Mydhope, who was, as the doctors made plain, in a serious state of ill health, made his will on the 20th July 1823.

This is the Last Will and Testament of me Mydhope Wallis Bennet of The Borough of East Looe in the County of Cornwall, Clerk, being of sound and disposing mind memory and understanding, praised be God for the same, I give devise and bequeath unto my sister Elizabeth Paynter and the heirs of her body lawfully begotten or to be begotten all those my Estates called or commonly known by the names of Trewinion and Trevorick situate lying and being in the Parish of St Enoder in the aforesaid County of Cornwall together with their rights members and appurtenances and also Redeemed Land Tax of the same premises and for default of heirs of her body lawfully begotten or to be begotten then I give and devise the said premises unto my own right heirs forever. I give devise and bequeath unto my sister Ann Pascoe and the heirs of her body lawfully begotten or to be begotten my undivided moiety or half part of in and throughout the Tenement of Trethill in the Parish of Sheviock in the said County of Cornwall with the rights members and appurtenances to the said moiety belonging or appertaining and also the Redeemed Land Tax of the said moiety and for default of such heirs of her body then I give and devise the said premises residue and remainder of my real and personal Estate of every description I do hereby

120

give devise and bequeath the same unto my brother Richard Gully Bennet and his heirs executors administrators and assigns forever and I hereby make nominate constitute and appoint my said brother Richard Gully Bennet sole Executor of this my said Will.

This Will was witnessed by Peter Rogers and Thomas Pengelly. On the 22nd October 1823, his physical condition having made no improvement, Mydhope wrote a codicil.

1.   I do request (which request as well as those expressed underneath) I do earnestly hope will be strictly attended to by my friends that in case my present illness should terminate in death I may be buried in a retired spot in the Churchyard at Morval, that, as I dislike all pomp and show on such occasions I may be carried to the grave by a sufficient number of well disposed persons who are to be paid handsomely in money for so doing and who on no account are to be allowed malt liquor or spirits as it is too often the case and renders the funeral a drunken scene, but who, instead of it, if my friends think fit, are to have a good breakfast or dinner.

2.   I also request that my body be not opened after my decease.

3.   I also request that within six weeks after my death Ten Pounds be given in money to the poor of the Parish of Morval, the distribution to be entirely at the discretion of Mr Puddlecombe.

4.   I request that Thomas Pengelly who has so faithfully attended me in my sickness be handsomely paid for his trouble.

5.   I request that my servant Peggy Little have a handsome present made her in addition to the wages which may be due to her at my decease in consequence of the additional trouble and fatigue which she has undergone during my long illness.

6.   I request that my coffin may be a plain one as in my opinion better becomes an occasion.

7. I request that the allowance of 1s:6d per week which I make to William and Sarah Clapp late of Bagmills near Trethill be continued to them after my decease as long as they shall live.

8. I request that the allowance of 1s:0d per week which through Mr Messer I promised to make to Patience Lance of Truro be continued to her during her life and that in case Mr Messer and Mrs Orchard should withdraw their allowance during the natural life of the said Patience Lance that then the sum of Six Guineas be paid her annually.

9. I also request that my mare which has carried me so many years well and so safely may after my decease be taken the greatest care of and never suffered to be used harshly or cruelly.

Mydhope Wallis Bennet.

Shortly after this Mydhope seemed to have overcome the severity of his illness and by Christmas of 1823 he was conducting his Parish work as normal albeit tiring easily. On September 26th 1824 Mydhope added to his Codicil:

I gave a Five Pound note to Thomas Pengelly on the 30th December 1823 as a recompense to him for his attendance on me from Midsummer to Christmas 1823 with which he seemed perfectly satisfied.

I gave Five Pounds to Thomas Pengelly this day for his attendance on me to Midsummer 1824 with which he seemed quite satisfied – June 24th 1824.

I made a trifling present to Peggy Little for the additional trouble which she had undergone on account of my illness on the 24th day of June 1824.

I wish that the Coppice Wood go with Trethill Estate, but not Bag or Bagmills – Mydhope Wallis Bennet.

It is my request and particular desire that my new silver teapot, the two dozen of silver forks and the two plated nut crackers be given to my dear eldest sister. It is also my desire and request that the silver tureen ladle the silver fish slice and the dozen of desert spoons be given to my dear youngest sister and I am sure I may rely on my dear brother's carrying these requests into execution notwithstanding the provisions of my Will which I made some time since and deposited in the hands of Mr Bond.

East Looe
September 26th, 1824
Mydhope Wallis Bennet.

Shortly after this Elizabeth visited Mydhope and then wrote to Gully:

My dearest Brother

Mydhope was not well enough to do duty on Sunday but exhausted very much towards the end of it, he meant to go to Landrake on Monday Henry tells me besides this account which I had from Myd himself that Mr Messer was so much alarmed as to go immediately to Looe. I have unconsciously felt today for the old pair at St Enoder the last tie to existence seems rent asunder by this conduct in their favourite son. From one of the family we learn the debts amount to Seventeen Thousands – awful sums the manner in which most people now-a-day seem to be going on, show and expense being the rule of their conduct. You and I God grant my Dear Gully may learn to stem the tide and confine our wishes to our circumstances that we may leave to our children strict behaviour and the means of subsistence. Nanny winters under certain depression of spirits and from her account of her health she must be very bad. I wish we could continue anyway to obtain the truth for accounts so vary that I am bewildered.

Kindest love,

Ever your affectionate sister,
E. Paynter.

On the 7th November 1824 Mydhope died at East Looe. Gully settled his brother's accounts and took charge of the funeral arrangements.

In deference to the wish expressed in his Codicil made twelve months earlier Mydhope's body was taken to the tiny Parish Church of St Wenna nestling in the sheltered wooded valley of Morval, one of the most beautiful corners of Cornwall. The church, originally founded in the tenth century, was damaged during Cornish opposition to William the Conqueror, and was presumably rebuilt of its present granite and slate stone after the Conquest. In 1244 the Priory of St Germans exercised the privilege of nominating its

123

vicars and receiving its tithes. Mydhope Wallis Bennet was laid to rest in a large rectangular tomb standing some three feet above the ground and beside the main door of the church. Today the lichen covered tombstone is as a sentinel on duty, still serving the church Mydhope loved so much.

A memoir was published in the *Gentleman's Magazine* of December 1824:

Memoir of the Rev M. W. Bennet

November 7. At East Looe after a long and severe illness the Reverend Mydhope Wallis Bennet, B.A., second son of the late Reverend John Bennet of Tresillian House in Cornwall, by Elizabeth daughter and co-heir of Mydhope Wallis Esquire, the representative of the ancient family of Mydhope of that County. The death of this amiable young man has been the source of unfeigned grief to his family and friends, in whose recollection his memory will ever be cherished with the sincerest affection and esteem. His deep sense of piety and gentleness of disposition united to a suavity peculiarly his own, rendered him a bright example of all that is esteemable in a clergyman and a man. The most unpretending manners

Parish Church of Saint Wenna: Morval

were in him found joined to no common solidity of judgement; and whilst scrupulously careful to avoid wounding the feelings of others, he possessed a firmness and independence of mind which those only who knew him intimately were able to appreciate. Whether contemplated as a Christian, a clergyman, or a gentleman, his character claims unqualified admiration and affords to those who loved him a mournful but heartfelt consolation. The poor of the neighbourhood in which he resided have lost a benefactor whose kindness of heart and unostentatious conduct 'did outsell the gift and yet enriched it too' and whilst by his purse he contributed to their comforts, his enquiries and advice manifested that he was truly interested in their welfare. Of the many who esteemed him none felt more respect and affection towards him than the writer of this inadequate but sincere tribute to his virtues; and although he deeply deplores the loss of a friend to whom many years of intimacy and a perfect knowledge of his character had strongly attached him, he joins fervently in the expectation of all to whom he was known, that he has attained that final reward which it was the object of his most anxious thoughts to secure. Mr Bennet died unmarried and was buried in a spot selected by himself in the Churchyard of Morval, which Church, previous to his illness, he had for some time served.

The last of the surviving family letters of this period was written to Gully by his sister Ann in the spring of 1825:

Monday evening
April 6th 1825.

My dear Gully

We were much surprised to hear from the newspaper on Saturday last Mr Messer's sudden death. We have now lost two out of the three Trustees appointed in our marriage settlement. As James thinks it prudent to have at least one if not two in their place I lost no time in applying to you as the nearest relative to each of us to ask if you will be kind enough to take the office. I suppose that the settlement which Mydhope always kept in his possession came into your hands at his death, and as we never understood that it had been subsequently forwarded to either of the other Trustees, you can of course look into it and let me hear at your earliest convenience.

Mr Hosher who returns to Ellinghaze for a few days has kindly promised to convey this to you. His wife's health is far from good. I hope you have comfortable accounts of Richard's health and improvements, mention him when you write and also how our sister is, and if you consider her complaint dangerous. Hearing only from herself I have no opportunity of ascertaining the real state of her health. I think it is a pity that she should undertake the journey she now contemplates.

What an insufferable fog! It has lasted three days and there seems no prospect of a change. Poor Mr Prater too! It makes one melancholy to see these old friends dying around us.

James unites in kindest regards and I am my dear Gully,

  Your very affectionate sister,
    Ann Pascoe.

CHAPTER 6

And he began it by observing
How reason dictated that men
Should rectify the natural swerving,
By a reversion, now and then,
To the well-heads of knowledge, few
And far away, whence rolling grew
The life-stream wide whereat we drink,
Commingled, as we needs must think,
With waters alien to the source;
To do which, aimed this eve's discourse;
Since, where could be a fitter time
For tracing backward to its prime
This Christianity, this lake,
This reservoir, whereat we slake,
From one or other bank, our thirst?
    Robert Browning. *Christmas Eve.*

The three years from 1825 to 1827 were largely uneventful for the Bennet family. Further north in England the first railway from Stockton to Darlington had been opened in 1825. The arrival of the railway in Cornwall was still thirty-eight years away. Richard Gully Bennet consolidated his estate with those lands inherited from his brother Mydhope. His duties as a Magistrate and Deputy Lieutenant of Cornwall added to a very full life as a conscientious squire to which he had the burden of being a single parent to his infant son who was five in 1825. Gully's able foreman was William May who was still managing the estate at Gully's death. A woman, referred to simply as Betty and sometimes Betsy, was the housekeeper of Tresillian. A number of grooms and maids made up the household.

Young Richard spent those three years at home with his father and quickly showed his love of the country and all its rural pursuits. Coursing, hunting, riding his pony about the estate and accompanying his father on horseback to nearby Newlyn Church Town and St Columb became regular events.

At Michaelmas 1828, shortly before Richard's eighth birthday, Gully took him to Plymouth where he attended a preparatory school conducted by Mrs Vavaseur at 10 Devonshire Place. The early weeks at school must have been a bewildering experience for the young country boy who had not known his mother. But Master Bennet took quickly to his lessons as appears from his first school report contained in a letter written by Mrs Vavaseur to Gully at the end of the term:

Plymouth
December 7th 1828

Sir

We have taken this liberty of sending our quarters' account for your son's education to you and when I tell you that it is our invariable custom to do so I am sure you will not be offended. I hope in every respect you will find your dear little boy improved. I can assure you a more docile good natured little fellow we have not in our school, the only thing we want in him is a little more activity which by his mixing with boys of his own age we hope he will soon obtain. Next quarter we intend trying him in French as he gets on so very well with his history and Latin etc. I must say that his improvement has been most rapid as when he first came he could not settle his mind steadily so as to retain anything or commit it to memory but his abilities to bring forth are certainly above the common standard. His health has been invariably good.

My mother and sister beg to write with compliments.

Louisa Vavaseur.

In his diary Gully was to note: Good account from Mrs Vavaseur of Richard's disposition and activities.

Christmas 1828 passed amid heavy rain and showers of hail. Gully's diary of 28th December 1828 reads: Hoary morning and the ground very wet. Went to Tregonning coursing – Richard turned out a hare which showed us good sport – fine weather.

And on January 1st 1829 Gully wrote: The New Year commenced with dry wind. Took Richard on his pony to see a hare coursed but she was gone. The rest of the day at home.

At the end of January Richard was taken back to school by Gully. Gully's cousins, the Roberts family, lived at Landrake Vicarage a few miles from Plymouth and their home provided a convenient staging post on the long ride from Tresillian to Plymouth. The 18th December 1829 saw Gully and his son making the return ride to Tresillian after Richard's first full year at school. Mrs Vavaseur's report dated 14th December 1829 made pleasing reading:

Plymouth
December 14th 1829

My dear Sir

I am happy to return you your dear little boy in high health and spirits and I am sure what will gratify you more a most exceedingly good little fellow not only as regards his improvement in his studies since he has been with us but his general good conduct and the improvement of his mind within the short space of a year and quarter is truly astonishing. You must be pleased with his proficiency in his grammatical knowledge when you question him – indeed you may be proud of your son.

Richard continued at Mrs Vavaseur's preparatory school until Lady Day 1831 when he was enrolled as a pupil at Taunton College School where he remained until Lady Day 1837.

Gully's diaries together with letters written to him by Richard give testimony to the strong bond between father and son. In particular Gully's diaries provide a lively chronicle of the daily life of a Cornish squire divided as it was between running his own estate and performing his duties as a Justice and Deputy Lieutenant of the County. He faithfully records the minutiae of every agricultural activity with a daily reference to wind, rain, hail, snow, weather good and weather bad. Of his lands, details of preparing, improving, manuring, planting, hoeing, reaping, gleaning and cleaning and the names of all employees are duly noted. We read of his cropping; buying, breeding, fattening and selling cattle; lambing and pig-rearing. His farming was undoubtedly successful. Nearly every Monday was taken up with a Justices' meeting at Newlyn Church Town with his colleagues Hosken and Andrew. On Tuesdays he rode over to St Columb for his Justices' meeting with Molesworth, Willyams and Lyn after which he invariably dined with his sister Elizabeth Paynter before riding home to Tresillian. The Quarterly

Sessions at Truro and Bodmin, each usually of four days duration, made up his legal year. And so a peep into those diaries between 1831 and 1836 and a reference to letters from Richard and his Headmaster's reports make up a picture of the two Richard Gully Bennets during that period.

8th March 1831

Walked to Goenhoskyn this morning. Sent a heifer to Blackwater for Phillips. Left home about five this evening for Newquay in consequence of the miners having assembled to prevent the shipping of barley.

9th March 1831

Left home at seven this morning to meet Willyams at Newquay and on our commencement to read the Riot Act the miners dispersed – a heavy shower before but very fine afterwards – returned about half past one.

18th March 1831

Met Willyams and Molesworth at a Deputy Lieutenants' meeting St Columb – breakfasted and dined at my sisters – found Aunt Roberts there – very fine weather.

30th April 1831

At home all day. Sent Samuel to the Blue Anchor with some papers to be circulated respecting the ensuing contest for the County. Sir Charles Lemon and Mr Pendarves against Lord Valetort and Sir Richard Vyvyan.

10th May 1831

Left home a little after six in the morning to attend the County Election at Lostwithiel. Took up Hawkey on the Moors. Fine weather. Pendarves at the head of the poll.

11th May 1831

At Lostwithiel – fine weather – Pendarves, Lemon, Vyvyan, Valetort.

12th May 1831

At Lostwithiel – fine weather – the candidates same as yesterday.

13th May 1831

At Lostwithiel – fine weather – candidates same as yesterday.

14th May 1831

The two latter candidates gave up the contest about four this afternoon. Pendarves – 1815, Lemon – 1804, Vyvyan – 901, Valetort – 811. Reached home about twelve in a postchaise.

16th May 1831

Went this morning to the Blue Anchor to see a colt three years old. Purchased two cows for £30 this afternoon – very fine weather.

17th May 1831

At home all day – very fine weather – sold a heifer to Parkes and two cows and eight sheep.

2nd June 1831

Went to Lower St Columb Church Town at nine this morning to decide whether a person building a house there had encroached on the highway. My decision was that he had not. Very hot weather.

16th June 1831

Went to Bodmin in the phaeton this morning – some very heavy showers – returned with Richard about half past seven and dined at eight.

21st June 1831

Met Willyams and Molesworth at a Justices Meeting St Columb. Richard accompanied me and we dined with my sister. Very fine weather – commenced cutting hay with four men this morning.

25th June 1831

Walked to the Blue Anchor this morning and committed Benny for an assault with intent on his own daughter, a child under eleven years of age. Rain the whole way home and for some time afterwards.

27th June 1831
Richard accompanied me to the Justices meeting at Newlyn.

4th July 1831
Left home with Richard about six this morning in the phaeton.
Breakfasted at Truro and reached St Keverne about two – some
misty rain.

5th July 1831
At St Keverne and stood godfather to my sister's child –
named John Bennet.

25th July 1831
Took a ride with Richard to the seacoast – very fine weather –
returned about one. Charles Parks here on our return. Cardell and
Farmer Whitford called in the evening.

29th July 1831
Purchased fifteen wethers of Hawke and sold three bullocks to
Bray – very fine weather.

30th July 1831
Purchased 40 wethers of Rowe of Cargoal – very fine weather.

1st August 1831
Richard and self and Rowe of Cargoal went into the
neighbourhood to see some horses – very fine weather – Charles
Parkes on my return.

7th August 1831
Went to Newlyn Church and attended a large meeting in the
Churchyard after service for the purpose of addressing the Bishop
on the removal of William Poleshill – Prater arrived about eight
this evening.

17th August 1831
Went on horseback to Bodmin with my son, the Regulator
Coach being full at the Blue Anchor. Reached Exeter this evening
– fine weather but very cold in the evening.

18th August 1831
Left Exeter at eleven in the forenoon for Taunton through Tiverton – very fine weather.

19th August 1831
Left Richard at the College School at two o'clock this afternoon – got upon the coach immediately for Exeter – very fine weather.

29th August 1831
Met the hounds at Mitchel this morning by eight o'clock – fine weather – found one hare, a short run but did not kill – very bad scent.

30th August 1831
Wallis Roberts and Prater arrived this evening.

31st August 1831
Prater left this morning and Whitwick Roberts arrived by the mail coach. Attended an appeal of the taxes – returned to a four o'clock dinner – some rain.

1st September 1831
Went as far as Nancolleth to meet with hounds – returned in consequence of the rain – Roberts and his brother went out shooting.

2nd September 1831
Took a ride to Nancolleth to meet the hounds but did not fall in with them – fine weather – Roberts and his brother shooting.

3rd September 1831
Met the hounds at the Indian Queens – did not find until half past one had a good run for half an hour two killed – fine weather – Roberts and his brother shooting.

4th September 1831
At home all day – Whitwick Roberts gone to St Columb to dine with my sister – rain.

5th September 1831

Met the hounds on Newlyn Downs found only one hare – very little sport. Returned between two and three. Prater arrived about half past four. Roberts and his brother shot 8½ brace – rain at night.

11th September 1831

Went to Newquay on horseback this forenoon with W Prater – fine weather. Roberts dined with my sister and Prater rode into St Columb in the afternoon.

18th September 1831

Prater left at a quarter past seven this morning. At home all day – very fine weather. A parcel containing two books and five shillings to be sent tomorrow for Richard.

24th September 1831

Drew Laddock Wood for a fox at an early hour this morning. Found and earthed him at Trenwith Wood with only a couple and half of hounds the remainder having pursued a hare. Prater called in the morning and in the evening with F.C. Paynter.

27th September 1831

Met hounds at Summercourt – very excellent sport and large field and killed two brace – very warm weather.

3rd October 1831

Found a fox on the Downs ran him to Nancolleth and in consequence of its coming on to rain lost him – met Hosken at a Justices Meeting Newlyn Church Town for the appointment of Way-Wardens.

7th November 1831

Found a brace of foxes in Laddock Wood – no sport – very cold wind with heavy showers of hail – returned a little after one – commenced ploughing in the higher field for wheat.

24th November 1831

At home all day. Sent 30 bushels of barley by William May to

Newquay for shipping – very fine weather – John Bassett and Mr Cardell in the forenoon.

29th November 1831

Found a fox in Laddock Wood and ran him in cover for some time and killed – very fine weather.

30th November 1831

At home all day – frost – but very fine weather. Sent 20 bushels of barley to Newquay for shipping. Robert Peter arrived this evening.

1st December 1831

Peter and self met the hounds at Nancolleth, a fine run to a hare and killed the other side of the Downs. Drew Laddock for a fox but did not find.

3rd December 1831

Two fine runs to hares on Newlyn Common – killed one. Peter accompanied me and returned about twenty minutes past three – some misty rain.

5th December 1831

Met the hounds at Laddock Wood at nine – no fox – found a hare near the Kennel and ran her nearly one hour and killed – a little rain in the forenoon but more in the afternoon accompanied by wind.

9th December 1831

Two good runs with the hounds about the Indian Queens – returned about four – rain in the evening – Robert Peter arrived about six.

14th December 1831

Met the Regulator Coach this morning and charged the guard to bring Richard with him tomorrow. Found a fox afterwards in Nancolleth and after a short run went to earth there.

15th December 1831

Met Richard at the Indian Queens. Captain Paynter returned with us in a postchaise.

Taunton College School
Christmas 1831

	£ s. d.
Gully Bennet Esquire to the Reverend W.R. Crotch.	
Half a year's board and tuition for Master Bennet	18. 7. 6.
Washing	1. 1. 0.
Mending and sundries	10. 6.
Writing and arithmetic	1. 1. 0.
	21. 0. 0.
Weekly allowance and tickets for concerts	10. 0.
Six books, parcel, letters, taper	12. 3.
Soap birthday presents and miscellaneous	15. 3.
Mr Stone : French Master	3. 3. 0.
Mr Denhall Shoemaker	13. 9.
Mr Thrusher Tailor	3. 6.
Mr Poole Stationer	1. 6. 11.
Mr Bridge Tailor	5. 12. 6.
Cash for journey	2. 10. 0.
	36. 7. 2.

The Scholars will reassemble on Friday January 27th after which time no indulgence of absence can be permitted except in cases of illness as the classes will be formed and absentees will thus forfeit any claim to Prizes.

12th January 1832

Ran a hare about one hour and a half and killed on Higher Tresillian. Richard accompanied me. Several showers – Prater dined here and gave Richard a watch.

14th January 1832

Met the hounds at Trewarthen – good sport and killed a brace of hare – Richard accompanied me – returned about three o'clock. Frosty morning and a fine day.

20th January 1832

At home all day – cold weather. Richard spent the day ferreting rabbits with his Uncle and Cousin. John Cardell drank tea here and purchased 20 bushels of barley for shipping.

23rd January 1832

Met the hounds at the Kennels, killed three hares and Richard and myself returned to a three o'clock dinner – cold wind. Paid Mr Stephens towards the expenses of endeavouring to dig out a fox.

25th January 1832

Left home this morning about half past nine with dear Richard and put him on the Regulator Coach at the Blue Anchor – returned immediately – some rain.

14th February 1832

Met Molesworth at a Justices Meeting St Columb – dined with my sister and returned in the evening – very cold weather. Received a letter from Richard.

28th February 1832

Took the drag of a fox in Laddock Wood and found him in Vincent's Eastern Downs and killed near Plummers Paper Mills after a run of two hours and forty minutes. Fine weather – found the fox nine minutes before twelve and ran him into eight parishes.

4th March 1832

Drew Laddock Wood and land adjoining for a fox – a blank day – returned about two. Wrote Richard this evening – a misty morning but fine afterwards.

2nd April 1832

Met Hosken and Andrew at a Justices Meeting at Newlyn – walked there and returned about half past two – very fine weather – found Butcher Phillips on my return and sold him two steers.

3rd April 1832

Went on horseback to the Easter Session Truro – returned about nine – very fine weather.

5th May 1832

Held my Ladyday's Court this day – at home – plenty of rain in the afternoon.

16th May 1832

Left home this morning at six to obtain signatures to a requisition to the High Sheriff for a County Meeting. Met with Johns and Lieutenant James in St Columb – they came here to dinner. Robert Peter in the evening.

18th May 1832

Mr Trenman, Charles Parkes, Richard Cardell and Mark Symons shot rooks and dined here – 143 bagged – very fine weather – at home all day.

24th June 1832

Richard accompanied me to Newlyn Church – fine weather but wind very hard.

25th June 1832

Met James Hosken at a Justices Meeting at Newlyn Church Town – Richard accompanied me – we returned to Tresillian to dinner – fine weather.

29th June 1832

Commenced cutting hay with four men this morning – at home all day – fine weather.

1st July 1832

Richard accompanied me to Newlyn Church – very fine weather. Committed two vagrants this afternoon.

12th July 1832

At home all day – took a ride round the farm with Richard – fine forenoon but plenty of rain afterwards. Farmer Whitford called in the morning respecting a cargo of coals.

30th July 1832

Met Peter, James Hosken and Andrew at a Justices Meeting –

Richard accompanied me – returned a little after five – very fine weather.

31st July 1832

Met Willyams and Molesworth at a Justices Meeting St Columb – Richard accompanied me – all dined – very little business – fine weather – returned about eight.

15th September 1832

Drew Nancolleth at seven this morning found two or three foxes and ran one principally in cover and killed him. Full one hour and a half. Killed a hare afterwards and ran another.

25th October 1832

Met Willyams at St Columb to swear in two extra constables in Newquay – fine weather. Returned to dinner. Merry Andrew put to death this morning at the Kennel aged 18 years and 5 months – fifteen years of which he carried me.

21st January 1833

At home all day – very cold wind. Sold five bullocks and three pigs to Butcher May for £72.10.0. Sold sheep, bullocks, calves from the 3rd January last to the present day amounting to £471.18.10 – profit £178.18.10.

29th January 1833

Met Willyams and Molesworth at a Justices Meeting and appeal of the tax, St Columb. A vast deal of business – arrived home ten minutes before six to dinner.

21st March 1833

At home all day – two women brushing out wheat, 860 sheaves altogether, which produced 11 bushels and 10 gallons of best and 17 gallons of bread corn.

24th March 1833

Walked to Newlyn Church. Mr Johnson gave us an excellent sermon – 90 Psalm – v 12. About two o'clock a heavy shower of snow.

27th April 1833

At home all day, laid up with the gout for the first time. Nanny Richard and daughter weeding in the lower part of the lawn half a day. Mr Cardell drank tea here. 1280 sheaves.

28th April 1833

At home all day – gout somewhat better but cannot yet put on my shoe.

1st June 1833

At home all day, very fine weather. Held my Ladyday's Court. Two women cutting up potatoes half a day.

5th June 1833

Nanny, Susannah and one girl in the Kennel Moor. At home all day. Commenced putting out manure for turnips in meadow.

23rd July 1833

Mary, Nanny and Mary Rowe in the Barn winnowing – 1269 sheaves. Plenty of rain but a remarkably fine afternoon. 17 bushels of best wheat and about 3 peck of bread corn. Nanny Tinney had child today.

28th July 1833

Mary and Nanny hoeing turnips. Susannah and Mary Rowe in the garden. Very fine weather. Mrs Salmon in the evening.

29th July 1833

Richard accompanied me to Newlyn Church on horseback – very fine weather.

9th August 1833

Nanny and Mary Rowe hoeing turnips. Went on horseback to the Blue Anchor to see Richard off for Taunton – very fine harvest weather.

16th August 1833

Sent Philp to Newlyn Church Town for newspapers – received a letter from Richard dated Monday last.

7th September 1833

Met the hounds accompanied by Roberts at Goenhoskyn to begin the season. Very dry – ran three hares and killed only the first – returned about one – very fine weather.

6th October 1833

Sent a parcel consisting of three books a letter and one sovereign to the Indian Queens to be forwarded per coach tomorrow morning for Richard. At home all day.

11th October 1833

Children in Tresillian Moor taking up potatoes and then picked stones. Took out eleven fat sheep for sale and put them into the lower long meadow.

19th October 1833

Men sowing wheat and ploughing in Tresillian Moor.

22nd October 1833

Met Willyams, Molesworth and Lyn at a Justices Meeting St Columb. Returned to dinner. Not much business. William May thrashing oats.

13th November 1833

Commenced thrashing barley. Rode the fox pony to Newlyn Church Town. Two men thrashing.

5th December 1833

Two men in Tresillian Moor making hedge – some heavy showers. William May sent for some brandy – bowel complaint. Several persons on justice business.

22nd December 1833

Plenty of rain – no going to Church – Richard arrived last evening.

23rd December 1833

Two men thrashing wheat – some heavy showers and high wind. Met Andrew at Newlyn Church Town at a Justices Meeting

– little business.

24th December 1833
Met Willyams and Lyn at a Justices Meeting St Columb – little business and returned to dinner – Richard accompanied me. Two men thrashing wheat.

21st January 1834
Some rain – met Willyams, Molesworth and Lyn at a Justices meeting St Columb – Richard accompanied me and we dined with my sister.

27th January 1834
Two men thrashing – Mary Rowe in the barn – some rain. Met Hosken and Andrew at a Justices Meeting Newlyn Church Town. Richard accompanied me – returned to a fine six o'clock dinner.

28th January 1834
My dear son left this morning for Taunton – accompanied him to the Blue Anchor. Penhallow Peters dined here. Two men thrashing.

8th May 1834
Sent William May with 20 fat wethers to Summercourt Fair. Not sold.

17th June 1834
Richard arrived a little before five this morning – Mary Solly and daughter and Susannah May weeding.

19th June 1834
Commenced cutting hay in the Chapple Cloths. Susannah May and Betsy Rowe hacking potatoes. Richard gone to St Columb.

22nd June 1834
Richard accompanied me to Newlyn Church.

Taunton College School
Midsummer 1834

My dear Sir

Your son has acquitted himself with that propriety of conduct and diligence to his studies which I have always had the pleasure of witnessing in him. He has enjoyed excellent health – and will I trust reach you in safety. I am my dear Sir
  faithfully yours
    William Robert Crotch.

17th September 1834
Men preparing the ground for the foundation of a new wainhouse.

18th September 1834
James Veal commenced building the new wainhouse this morning.

College School Taunton
October 30th 1834

My dear Papa

I resume my pen to thank you for your kind present half of which is gone to the party cooks for a cake for my birthday. Mr Crotch has not told us whether we are to have a half holiday tomorrow afternoon but I trust he will not refuse your first and only time of asking.

I hope the Taunton newspaper gave you a good account of that terrible conflagration in London of the Houses of Lords and Commons which though I dare say was a beautiful and magnificent sight at the time must rise the taxes a little more than usual in order to rebuild new ones and I see that the King has offered the old Palace at St James to make up the deficiency for the time. There is a groundless report that Windsor Castle was burnt to the ground but the coachdrivers nowaday make up such tales about different things that there are only a few that we may at all credit.

My best trowsers are sadly wearing and I think it would be a good thing if I was to get some cheap sort of trowsers now, such as pepper and salt, and they would serve for hunting when I come home, else I shall not have but my fustian trowsers for hunting and those must be washed some time and while they are washing and drying I shall not be able to go out hunting.

I have made up my mind to come down by the Defiance next holidays if it is not full and if I arrive in Exeter the day before it starts and I shall stop at St Columb. I shall then see Camelford and Wadebridge and all the country on that road which I have never seen before.

For these last few days I have been ill but had it the slightest of them all, as seven or eight of the boys have been ill as well, but I am now alright, tight and jolly.

I hope the Gun will be quickly sent down, or again I shall be disappointed. If I was you, I would not have a Gun from him at all if he did not quickly send it down, but I have one from someone else, if I have not one next holidays I shall be terribly disappointed as I have been thinking of nothing else all the time I have been here this halfyear.

I hope you will write soon to let me know how Aunt Paynter is, as I am very anxious to know about her. I suppose Mrs Moorman attends her but she ought to have Mrs Jewel of Tregoning. Only one whole month more to the holidays.

Give my best love to Aunt, Uncle, Anne, Betsey – and accept the same for yourself and believe me your dutiful son.

Richard

P.S. On Tuesday morning last at a quarter before seven the lady of the Reverend W K Crotch of a son – who is as well as can be expected.

(The Houses of Parliament at Westminster were destroyed by fire in 1834.)

20th December 1834
    Richard arrived from Taunton this evening.

25th January 1835
    Dined at Newquay with Mr Cardell. The first lamb this season born in the afternoon.

College School Taunton
June 18th 1835

Mr Crotch presents his compliments to Mr Bennet and is happy to return his son in good health and with the appearance of his having continued to merit Mr Crotch's regard. He is senior of his class and would have brought home a Prize had he not, perhaps from some mistake, contented himself with the mere routine of school exercises without any extra work. If he is not to return Mr Crotch will take this opportunity of expressing his admiration of his very good qualities of mind and heart. Of course, Mr Bennet will see that his education is far from completed, Mr Crotch's object having been to lay a firm foundation.

19th July 1835

Went to Newlyn Church – an excellent sermon from our Curate Mr Snowe – Mary and Millicent Bassett there being no morning service at St Enoder.

20th July 1835

Sent William May to purchase some sheep – did not deal.

22nd July 1835

Sent William May again to purchase sheep, did not succeed, the farmers saying they would not sell until after harvest.

College School Taunton
August 5th 1835

My dear Sir

I beg to acknowledge with many thanks the receipt of your cheque for thirty three pounds nineteen shillings – I shall be most happy to see your son whenever you think it right he should resume his studies as I consider him a promising and most praiseworthy pupil.
I remain my dear Sir
William Robert Crotch.

25th November 1835

Farmer Whitford died this afternoon about four o'clock.

28th November 1835

Attended Farmer Whitford's funeral – buried at Newlyn.

6th February 1836

One of the ewes had a ram lamb this afternoon the first for the season.

9th February 1836

Susannah shaking straw. Met Willyams at an appeal of the taxes and dined with my sister.

25th February 1836

A fall of snow this morning. Two lambs this evening – a ram and ewe lamb.

College School Taunton
April 25th 1836

My dear Papa

As it is now a long time since I have sent you a letter I must now try to scrape up something to tell you. Perhaps you will be surprised to hear that we had ten days holidays at Easter, and that I spent the first part of them at Mrs Goffey's and the remainder at Mrs Woodland's; they both live in the town and have sons at our school. I spent a very pleasant holidays and rode out twice on Mrs Woodland's pony but I found a difference between him and Fox. I went to the theatre the Sheriff's Night (who is a namesake of ours) and was very much amused, and I dont think I ever laughed so much before as at the last piece, which was called 'My Neighbour's Wife'. I also went to the theatre last Friday night with four other of our boys who spent the evening with Mrs Moore. I am the luckiest fellow imaginable as I have been to two new places, besides the old ones, this half. I go out more than any of the other boarders, and although I have no relations here nor did I know a single person when I came here first. I expect to dine at Mrs Goffey's the first Thursday in May when I expect to meet Cousin Anne. I have been at Mrs Goffey's twice this half, besides the Easter holidays, which I consider very kind. On Thursday last all our boarders dined at Mrs Woodland's and had famous fun in the evening. We had dancing from eight to eleven, and I danced every dance. I have been to three dances this half already, but as summer is coming it will be left off. We have another new day boarder and have lost none. How surprised I was to hear of Mrs Pattison's death which happened a night that I was spending out. Mrs Liddon has desired me to come and tell her when I can come to her house, so one day I shall run over and give her a hint. Cousin Anne desires her love to Aunt etc who, I hope, is well. So Aunt Pascoe is going to call her youngest after you. I suppose you will be Godfather. We had a very heavy calendar of prisoners here, more than half of whom are to be transported – one is hung and another condemned but it is expected he will have a reprieve. I did not try to get in Court all the holidays as I do not like it well enough. Give my love to Aunt and believe me

Your affectionate son

Richard

P.S. I have not been unwell this half as yet, I hope I shall continue so – I hope you are as well as I am. Please to send me a newspaper soon. How changeable the weather is now; I suppose it is the same with you. I am invited out for the two next Thursdays, first at Mr Liddon's whom I saw yesterday after Church and he made me come in to see Mr Anstis, who is just come from Oxford. Goodbye
Richard.

20th May 1836

Went to St Columb – saw Wallis Roberts, Aunt Roberts very ill in bed – Dr Yeo sent for – she died at six this afternoon aged next month 78.

22nd May 1836

Went to St Columb this morning to ascertain when and where Mrs Roberts was to be buried. Her remains are to be conveyed on Thursday next to the vault at Sheviock – the burial place of her father and mother.

24th May 1836

Met Molesworth and Captain Rogers at a Justices Meeting in St Columb – dined with my sister, Ann Roberts, Wallis, John and Whitwick.

1st June 1836
Held my Ladyday Court.

15th June 1836
Commenced sowing turnips in the Chapple Close this afternoon. John Laver shorn 10 ewes and 17 young wethers.

17th June 1836
Richard arrived from Taunton this evening.

9th July 1836
Richard and Betsy gone to Truro in the Pony Carriage.

11th July 1836
Richard to the Miners Bank Truro with 4 cheques amounting to one hundred and fourteen pounds.

1st August 1836
Two men on a charge of felony from the Parish of Mawgan – cutting down 69 apple trees. George Collins attended and dined here.

18th August 1836
Richard left for Taunton.

College School
September 19th 1836

My dear Papa

Having been back a long time, I think that I must try to scrape up a few lines for you.

On Thursday the 18th of last month Mr Cross came to see me for about ten minutes on his road towards Exeter from Bristol and he contrived to lay out half a sovereign for me. And on the next Sunday, who should come up here to see me in the morning but Cousin Whitwick Roberts whom I did not know at first. I dined with him on that day and breakfasted with him the Thursday after which day he left here for London. He was here on some King's Bench business about the Grand Western Canal, but I do not know whether he won or not. All I know is that he also contrived to lay out a sovereign for me. This is the best half that I ever had.

I went to a party the other night with another of our boys and had very good fun. I saw our Taunton races the only ones I ever saw; there were a few good horses but it seemed as if it was determined by the jockeys who should win. I went to the theatre in the evening of the second day. As there is nothing going on here I can hardly tell what to say. Cousin Ann is very well as well as myself. I suppose that you have finished your barley harvest as it is not finished here – weather unsettled.

We have had some wild beasts here which I went to see but they were nothing very grand. I hope you will send me some newspapers oftener. I hope you are very well considering the weather. I hope Uncle will come here to see us and I hope Aunt has prevailed upon him so to do. To whom as well as Uncle, Margaret, Billy etc I hope you will kindly remember me. And in the meantime

believe me
your dutiful son
Richard.

20th September 1836
Met Willyams at St Columb on two excise cases – dined with my sister.

27th September 1836
Met Molesworth at a Justices Meeting St Columb – returned to dinner – William May commenced ploughing Tresillian Moor.

28th September 1836
William May ploughing Tresillian Moor.

29th September 1836
William May ploughing Tresillian Moor.

30th September 1836
William May ploughing Tresillian Moor.

2nd October 1836
   Hard wind during the night and some rain – wintry weather – very cold.

3rd October 1836
   William May ploughing Tresillian Moor.

4th October 1836
   William May ploughing Tresillian Moor.

5th October 1836
   William May finished ploughing Tresillian Moor about 12.

12th October 1836
   Heavy rain all the afternoon and stormy wind during the night. Damage done to the buildings. Two men making up gaps in hedge close field in the forenoon.

15th October 1836
   Weighed the wool and sent it to Hawkes, St Columb.

18th October 1836
   Met Willyams at an appeal of the taxes at St Columb.

12th November 1836
   Solomon and Ellery – William May's daughter and the daughter of James Jenkins and men bringing in mangle whurzels with horse carts.

22nd November 1836
   Met Mr Lyn and Mr Molesworth at a Justices Meeting St Columb.

25th November 1836
   3 children – John Fithick – Phillips – Ellery and Solomon about potatoes.

That was his last diary entry. He died in December 1836 aged only forty-three years and was buried in Newlyn Churchyard.

Gully had made his will three years earlier and appointed two respected friends, Edward William Wynne Pendarves and Thurston Collins to be his executors, trustees of his estate and Richard's guardians. To his housekeeper Elizabeth Mountsteven Tinney (referred to in his diaries as Betty or Betsy and sometimes as Nanny Tinney) he bequeathed an annuity of £60 a year. To her four children he bequeathed £25 a year until each attained majority whereupon each child inherited £200. The rest of his estate passed to the trustees to hold on behalf of Richard with a direction reading: 'And I hereby direct and request that my Mansion House of Tresillian aforesaid with its several offices be duly taken care of and occupied by a servant during the minority of my son.'

Richard, now in the care of his guardians, returned to Taunton College School in 1837 where he remained until Lady Day when Mr Pendarves, then a Member of Parliament, placed him with a private tutor, the Reverend Robert Bateman Paul who resided near Bridport, Dorset.

During the summer of 1837 Richard accompanied by another pupil, the Honourable Arthur Schomberg Kerr, and a former pupil Edward Linzee, then keeping terms at Oxford, were taken by Mr Paul on a tour of Norway and Sweden lasting eight weeks during which they visited Hamburg, Kiel, Copenhagen, Elsineur, Helsingborg, Gottenburg, Wenersburg, Frederiestadt, Christiania, Drontheim, Ostersund, Sundsvall, the iron mines of Uppsala, the silver mines of Sala, Stockholm and Lubeck. Richard's diary records that he spent his Christmas vacation 'at the house of that kindest and best of guardians, Mr Pendarves.'

The summer of 1838 saw Richard accompany Mr Paul on another tour, that time to Scotland lasting six weeks. The journey from London to Edinburgh was made by steam vessel. Thereafter he visited Stirling, Loch Katrina and Loch Lomond, Inverary, Oban, Staffa, Iona, Fort William, Caledonian Canal, Inverness, Bonan Bridge, Thurso, John o' Groats, Wick, Culloden, Elgin, Gordon Castle, Aberdeen, Glen Tilt, Blair Athol, Killiekrankie, Dunkeld, Perth, Dunblane, Glasgow, Falls of Clyde, Gretna Green, Carlisle, Lancaster, Liverpool, Birmingham, and thence to Exeter and home.

At Lady Day 1839 Richard, then aged eighteen, left Mr Paul and went to read with the Reverend William Airy at Keysoe Vicarage near Kimbolton until October of that year when following his 19th birthday he began to keep terms at Trinity College Cambridge under the tutorship of Mr Whewell. As an undergraduate Richard lodged at a bookseller's house in Rose Crescent and in the same house lodged his friend from Cornwall, Edward Coode.

During the long vacation of 1840 Richard made a tour on his own to Switzerland. He left London on 14th June by steamer for Antwerp and visited Cologne, Mannheim, Baden, Stuttgard, Schaffhausen, Zurich, Grindelwald, Reichenbach, Interlaken, Berne, Fribourg, Lausanne, Geneva, Dijon, Paris, Le Havre and then to Southampton by steamer arriving on the 1st August.

Richard spent the long vacation of 1841 in Cornwall, principally at his guardian's home, Pendarve House, until the 20th August when accompanied by a friend, Arthur Hale, he travelled by steamer from Falmouth to Dublin and together the two young men embarked upon a tour of Ireland visiting Glendalough, Newry, Belfast, Fair Head, Giant's Causeway, Londonderry, Donegal, Enniskillen and back to Dublin where they took a steamer to Holyhead and returned to St Columb via Bangor, Shrewsbury, Hereford and Taunton arriving on 20th September. He returned to Trinity College in October and spent the winter vacation in Cornwall.

On the 20th January 1843, aged twenty-two years, Richard passed his final examinations at Cambridge and on the following day he was admitted Bachelor of Arts. The *West Briton* published on the 27th January 1843 recorded under the heading Cambridge University:

> Among the other gentlemen on whom the degree of B.A. has been conferred, we notice the names of Mr Coode, son of the Clerk of the Peace, of Mr P.W. Molesworth, son of the Reverend William Molesworth of St Breock and of Mr Bennet of Tresillian.

And under the heading From the *London Gazette* the same newspaper recorded that day:

> Friday, January 20th 1843
> Commissions signed by the Lord Lieutenant of the County of Cornwall.
> Royal Cornwall Militia, or Duke of Cornwall's Rangers –
> Richard Gully Bennet, Gentleman, to be Lieutenant.

On 20th February 1843 Richard was admitted to membership of the Inner Temple where he read law for a year with W. Carpenter Rowe and lodged at 3 Little Ryder Street, St James. That summer was spent in Cornwall and on the 17th October 1843 at the Quarter Sessions held in Bodwin Richard took the oaths and was sworn in as a Magistrate. His studies at the Inner Temple continued until 19th March 1844 when he gave up his London lodgings and returned to Cornwall. The Vicar of Newlyn, the Reverend E. Dix, invited Richard to take up quarters in the Vicarage while Tresillian House was being prepared and furnished for his return which took place on the 20th April 1844. Once more there was a Bennet of Tresillian residing in Tresillian House.

CHAPTER 7

When I some antique jar behold,
Or white, or blue, or speck'd with gold,
Vessels so pure, and so refin'd
Appear the types of woman-kind;
Are they not valu'd for their beauty,
Too fair, too fine for household duty?
With flowers and gold and azure dy'd,
Of ev'ry house the grace and pride?
How white, how polish'd is their skin,
And valu'd most when only seen!
She who before was highest priz'd
Is for a crack or flaw despis'd;
I grant they're frail, yet they're so rare,
The treasure cannot cost too dear!
But Man is made of coarser stuff,
And serves convenience well enough;
He's a strong earthen vessel made,
For drudging, labour, toil and trade;
And when wives loose their other self
With ease they bear the loss of delf.

John Jay. *To a Lady.*

On the 21st April 1846 Richard married Mary Jean Hosken, fourth daughter of Richard Hosken Esquire. The bride's uncle, the Reverend Cuthbert Edgecumbe Hosken performed the ceremony in the fourteenth century Parish Church of Cubert two miles from the sea and about two miles west of Tresillian. The Hosken family had provided Vicars of Cubert for over one hundred and fifty years and were descended from John of Goenhoskyn then part of Richard's estate inherited from Gully. Richard and his bride departed for London travelling by coach via Devonport and Bath.

154

On the 7th May Richard and Mary Bennet left for a grand tour of Europe which lasted until the 20th August and took them to Belgium, Germany, Switzerland and France, in many cases following the route taken by Richard in 1840.

As soon as he returned to Cornwall, Richard began planning to rebuild Tresillian House which had stood for some five hundred years and in which Sir John Tresillian, Lord Chief Justice of England under King Richard II had been born. A beautifully produced and illustrated book titled *The Mansions of England and Wales* edited by Edward Twycross and published in London by C.J. Greenwood in 1846 contains a magnificent line drawing of a double storied house of substantial proportions described as: Tresillian the seat of Richard Gully Bennet Esquire. It was accompanied by the following text:

> Tresillian, the seat of Richard Gully Bennet, Esq., is situated in the Parish of St Newlyn, in the Hundred and Deanery of Pydar, ten miles to the north of Truro. The old house will shortly give place to a new structure in the modern style, a view of which we have been enabled to give through the kind assistance of the architect. Mr Bennet possesses

Cubert Church

several family portraits by Bordwell and other artists, and one very fine picture from the pencil of Murray, the pupil and successor of Sir Peter Loly. Tresillian was originally held by a family who bore that name; and Sir John Tresillian, Lord Chief Justice of England, who was executed at Tyburn in 1388, was Lord of the Manor. With his daughter and heiress it passed to John Hawley, and subsequently, by purchase, became the property of the family of Davies, who sold it, in 1694, to Samuel Gully, Esq., of Leigh in the County of Devon, ancestor of the present inheritor.

Richard's architect produced a most detailed specification of the intended works. After thirteen pages of details and costings the final specification was summarised -

Removal of existing House	£14: 8s: 0d.
Diggers' Works	£32:12s: 6d.
Masons' Works	£944:12s: 5d.
Slaters' Works	£66:10s: 0d.
Plasterers' Works	£310:12s: 4d.
Carpenter and Joiners' Works	£924: 2s: 4d.
Smiths' Works	£108:16s: 0d.
Bell Flanging	£26: 6s: 6d.
Plumbers' Works	£235:11s: 2d.
Glaziers' Works	£47: 7s: 0d.
Painters' Works	£39: 1s: 8d.
	£2750: 0s:11d.

The item headed Bell Flanging for £26: 6s: 6d. is interesting and demonstrates the size of the new house designed to replace the old:

Bronze door pull	0:15: 0
Library two pulls	0:15: 0
Hall two pulls	0: 8: 0
Drawing Room two pulls ivory	1:10: 0
Dining Room two pulls ebony	1: 0: 0
Bed Rooms eleven pulls	1:18: 6
Sixteen bells, carriages, cranks, springs and wires	20: 0: 0
	26: 6s.6.

Richard's diary reveals that it took fifteen years before the new mansion was finally completed although he and his family moved into one wing of it as early as September 1849. His eldest child Kathleen Tryphena, was born in the farmhouse but both sons and his second daughter were born in Tresillian House.

March 28th 1848
Left the old house and took up residence in the farmhouse close by.

April 5th 1848
Commenced dismantling old house

May 3rd 1848
Foundation stone of new house laid – site the same as old house with one alteration.

May 7th 1848
Kathleen Tryphena Bennet born. She was christened at Newlyn on June 12th.

December 23rd 1848
New House covered in.

September 19th 1849
Left the farm house and occupied the wing of the new building.

October 24th 1849
Edward Gully Bennet born: christened at Newlyn on December 4th.

December 13th 1850
Ferdinando Wallis Bennet born: christened at Newlyn on January 17th 1851.

November 12th 1852
Held my Court in new Dining Room and began hence forward to occupy it.

February 1858

Sold my tenement at Retyn in St Enoder to Mr John Johns for £1550: that being an undesirable holding in consequence of the whole Farm being shared by five landlords. Rent £46.6.4. With the produce of this sale purchased, jointly with my cousin, the Miss Paynter, the farm of Trewinian in St Enoder from Mr Vivian of Pennalenick for the sum of twenty eight hundred pounds (my portion thereof being fourteen hundred pounds) – Rent (total) £105.

May 27th 1858

Edith Mary Bennet born about 7 o'clock in the evening – christened at Newlyn on June 22nd.

1st December 1862

Sold my reversionary interest in Bospolvans in St Columb Major – viz., the moiety of a meadow about three acres held by Elizabeth Brewer for her life to Mr Humphry Willyams for £193.

7th November 1863

Put up shutters in Drawing Room. House finished, with the exception of mantlepiece for said Room.

In the chapter headed Parish of Newlyn in *A Complete Parochial History of the County of Cornwall* published in 1870 appears this reference to Tresillian House:

The Manor of Tresillian descended through an heiress to Richard Gully Bennet Esq., the present proprietor. The heiress of Tresillian married, temp. Edward IV, Carne of Glamorganshire, who assumed the name of Tresillian, and was the ancestor of the Tresillians of Wendron, St Burian, and St Levan. Chief Justice Tresillian of this family was put to death temp. Richard II. The family arms are – Gules, a Pelican in her nest with wings displayed, feeding her young, or. Tresillian House has of late years been much improved, and is now a handsome seat, surrounded with a fine lawn, well sheltered with trees and ornamented with luxuriant shrubs.

The younger Richard Gully Bennet had restored the family seat to an extent which would have given immense pleasure to his loving father.

CHAPTER 8

Perhaps there lives some dreamy boy, untaught
In schools, some graduate of the field or street,
Who shall become a master of the art,
An admiral sailing the high seas of thought
Fearless and first, and steering with his fleet
For lands not yet laid down in any chart.
                                        Longfellow.

Richard Gully Bennet and his wife Mary presided over Tresillian for sixty years until their devoted partnership was dissolved by Mary's death shortly after her eighty-third birthday. Their story is one of a loving family, of concern for their children and of their devotion to Cornwall and its institutions. Richard, so ably supported by Mary, was outstanding in his public service.

Richard and Mary's marriage coincided with the long and glorious reign of Queen Victoria. After the defeat of the French in 1815 agriculture in England experienced troubled times. Richard was a typical country squire, his fortunes depended upon his success as an enlightened landowner. From 1815 to 1846 the Corn Laws determined the role of the English farmer. The repeal of the Corn Laws in 1846 was a victory for free trade but also marked the triumph of the manufacturer over the landowner. The countryman's dominant figure faltered and so began a new era in which the townsman became ascendant. In 1850 one in every six males throughout England over the age of ten years was a farm labourer.

Cornwall faced its own peculiar tragedy which began in 1860 and was to last for another forty years. By the middle of the nineteenth century fifty thousand Cornishmen were employed in the county's flourishing tin and copper mines. Cornwall was the largest copper producer in the world mining two-thirds of the entire global supply. But in the 1860s copper deposits were discovered in Canada and tin deposits were discovered in

Malaya. Production costs at the new mines were lower than those in Cornwall and so one by one the many mines throughout the county closed. Copper production was reduced from thousands of tons to a few hundred tons each year. Hundreds of Cornish miners were thrown out of work; many of them emigrated to work in the new mines in other lands. The once busy mines became silent ghosts. Tall chimney stacks, the pump houses and mine buildings decayed and fell into ruins. The tragedy was felt in every town and village throughout Cornwall.

For thirty years after the repeal of the Corn Laws farming remained important, especially was this so in the county which had lost its mining industry. New industries in the rest of England and with them the growth of towns and cities brought new markets for the countrymen. Farm prices were largely stable and profits from the land reasonably good. New market places brought about improvements in the roads and extensions to the infant railway system.

Rowland Hill had introduced his penny post throughout Britain in 1840. The Bennet family were natural correspondents and their letters and diaries provide us with an interesting picture of this Cornish family living in Victorian England.

In the second half of the nineteenth century schools provided almost exclusively for the upper and middle classes. It was customary to employ a governess to teach children at home until they were old enough to attend a suitable school as boarders. Richard's four children all received their early education at Tresillian. Four days before her seventh birthday Kathleen wrote to her father in immaculate copperplate:

> My dear Pappa
>   We are going to the farm today to see the little children picking stones. I hope you will have a pleasant drive today and bring back some fish for Mamma's dinner.
>   From your little maid,
>   Kathleen.

Two years later and on his eighth birthday Richard's second child, Edward, wrote in even more immaculate handwriting:

> My dear Pappa
>   I am very glad that I can write you a letter and I will take so much pains to do it well that I hope you will be pleased with it,

and that you will show us the Magic Lantern on Saturday as it will
be my Birthday.

    I am your affectionate son
        E. Gully Bennet.
Tresillian House
October 23rd 1857.

One can imagine that the Magic Lantern gave immense pleasure to
Kathleen, aged nine, Edward aged eight and Ferdinando then almost seven.

It is not known to which school Kathleen was sent, indeed she may have
remained at home with her governess. Edward and Ferdinando after early
days at home were educated at Kings College, Sherborne, from whence they
both took up careers in the British Army. Edith, born ten years after Kathleen,
remained at home until her sixteenth birthday after which she attended a
ladies school conducted at Strathallan House in Wetherby Road, South
Kensington, London.

In 1852 the three first children were infants. A Press cutting from the
Cornish Gazette of the 28th December that year carried the story of a Grand
Ball and Supper given in Truro by Miss Prideaux Brune. The reporter
enthused:

> We had known for some time past that the spacious Council Hall of
> the Borough had been most courteously placed at the service of Miss M.
> Prideaux Brune, of Newham, for the purpose of giving a Ball and Supper
> with more convenience to herself and in a manner more conducive to the
> enjoyment of those friends who were to be honoured with invitations.
> These it will be seen could neither have been few nor inconsiderable;
> comprising as our list of the company present does the names of persons
> of distinction from all parts of the county, as well as from this town and
> neighbourhood.
>
> Great as were the expectations from the taste and costliness displayed
> in the preparatory arrangements, the result we believe far exceeded them,
> and surpassed anything of the kind ever before witnessed in Truro.
>
> The hall was furnished with the utmost taste and elegance and
> splendidly lit with a profusion of wax candles, and two elegant branches,
> dependent from the ceiling, disposed in circles, which displayed
> innumerable small jets of gas like stars of dazzling brilliancy, and doing
> great credit to the clever superintendent of the Truro Gas Works.
>
> Dancing commenced between 9 and 10 o'clock, and was kept up with

unabated spirit till a late hour of the morning. The band consisted of a select number of the celebrated Plymouth performers, and, of course, the music was most excellent. In fact, everything appears to have been well managed, and to have gone off admirably.

There seems in short, to have been nothing wanting to give completeness to the entertainment; and we fear that, with our too imperfect information we can have tendered it but a scanty measure of justice. We will, however, close our brief account by adding, what it would be inexcusable not to do, that the gracious reception afforded by Miss Brune to her assembled guests enhanced exceedingly the pleasure of the evening; and rarely has so munificent a lady been honoured by visitors whose dresses were of such surpassing elegance, and whose appearance altogether when mingling in the joyous dance must have been enlivening beyond compare.

Among the list of one hundred and fifty guests was noted the presence of Mr and Mrs Gully Bennet.

A day later the same Miss Prideaux Brune gave a Grand Costume Ball for 'her distinguished friends in the county'. Again the *Cornish Gazette* gave detailed coverage of the event:

We very much regretted our inability to do full justice to the elegant Ball and Supper given by Miss M. Prideaux Brune to her distinguished friends; and so faultless was that splendid entertainment considered by all who partook of it, that we scarcely thought it possible that another fashionable reunion following with the interval of a day only, could sustain the same high character of unmingled commendation. That such, however, has been the case, we can now with pleasure and in confidence affirm. Upon each occasion the success was complete. But if the best description we have it in our power to give of the entertainment, which took place on the evening of Thursday last, at Trelissick, should be deemed by any of our readers less perfect than might be wished, they will please to remember that it was not an easy matter to describe with minute correctness, a scene of such dazzling brilliancy, where the dresses generally were so exceedingly handsome, and where a large proportion of the gay assemblage were arrayed in costumes which would have done honour to the Court of Her Most Gracious Majesty Queen Victoria. Difficult indeed it is, to say whether the hospitality and warm welcome of the highborn lady and gentleman of the mansion, or the desire manifested by their assembled guests to do them in return all the honour that costly dresses and courtly bearing could exhibit, should stand highest in our record.

Gully Bennet was listed in the Hon. Mrs Prideaux Brune's Waverley Quadrille in which he was joined by many sons and daughters of his father's friends – Miss Willyams, Miss Molesworth, Miss Vivian, Mr Collins, Mr Coode, the Bullers and the Rashleighs. It is recorded by the *Gazette* that Gully's costume was that of Evan Dhu MacCombich while the Quarter Sessions Chairman, and Gully's colleague on the Bench, Sir Colman Rashleigh, wore his Court Dress as High Sheriff. In a final comment on the costumes the *Gazette*'s reporter wrote:

> We need scarcely add that it was the opinion of those present, who had been accustomed to frequent fancy balls that the costumes generally were exceedingly handsome and correct.

But all was not social pleasure. In 1845, a year before his marriage, Gully had been appointed Chairman of the Guardians of St Columb Major Union, a duty which he discharged for many years with great seriousness. In 1832 the Poor Law of England, that is the legislation for the relief of paupers, had remained unchanged since the Statute of Elizabeth, almost three hundred years earlier. A commission appointed in 1832 led to the Poor Law Amendment Act of 1834. Poor Law Commissioners formed Poor Law Unions by fusing parish responsibilities and building workhouses the general administration of which was vested in Guardians, some elected by the ratepayers and others appointed *ex officio*, principally local magistrates. The Guardians of the poor were responsible for the regulation and administration of relief within the Union.

In April 1853 an election had taken place for the office of Auditor of the Guardians of St Columb Major Union. A Mr Lawrence was elected and at once wrote to Gully:

April 2, 1853

My dear Sir,

> It is no slight gratification to me to receive today Mr Anstis's report and to find myself the duly elected Auditor. As such I doubt not to be able to give satisfaction to the Poor Law Board and to the public.

I have to thank you for your support on the two last divisions – and yet I must confess to have felt no slight mortification that you were not among my earlier supporters, to whom, I must feel myself mostly indebted. That you preferred another and a much younger man to me was no slight disappointment especially as I believe you scarcely knew him when I last canvassed for the situation, and of course it has proved that you held lightly the tie of relationship between our wives – which, I am bound to say, she and her family have felt severely. Besides, I had a right to think that my services for your relations, the Norways, might have gained me your early support. Had I lost my election I should have blamed you for it undoubtedly. As it has proved my majority was a large one and I could have dispensed with the votes of all but my *sincere* friends.

The situation is of no common value to me and therefore to my family – nor have I any fear but that I shall perform the duties of it to the satisfaction of all parties.

Regretting that I should not have met from you that cordiality I had expected and with Maria's and my kind regards to Mrs Bennet.

> Believe me, dear Sir,
> Yours very faithfully
> N. H. P. Lawrence.

Gully replied on the 4th April 1853 but endorsed his copy of the letter with the words: withheld for three weeks:

Sir

I beg to acknowledge the receipt of a letter you have just thought it becoming to address to me in reference to the recent election of Auditor. In your hour of need three letters you then sent to me were supplicant and importunate; in your hour of success – a success I had helped you to achieve – the tone is changed, all is reproachful and audacious. Reproachful of what? That I forfeited my pledge? No! but for daring on one out of three occasions to vote against *my wife's cousin's husband*! And is this franchise given to me to advance the interests of those who happen to be connected with me by blood or marriage? You affirm the proposition for you say that my voting as I did 'has proved that I held lightly the tie of relationship between our wives' — I do hold it a trivial matter and one that ought never to weigh in the balance. I confess, however, and I avow it with shame, that in voting for you I did yield to this feeling! and I acknowledge further that had it not been for that connection you never would have had my vote.

You think it not beneath you to observe in your letter that you 'had a right I think that your services for my relations, the Norways, might have gained you my early support'. A petty reason truly. Do you always show a kindness on the quid pro quo principle? And what may these services be? You may have shown some, but what they are I have no knowledge. Pray do you know that at the last election for Auditor I voted for Hughes and against my *connection* Norway! You will find it true, and singular enough, no one of the family — not even the *rejected* candidate had sufficient acerbity of temper to write me a letter of reproach.

You say further; 'had you lost your election you would have blamed me for it undoubtedly.' Under such an imputation sleep would have been hopeless. And you wind up by saying that 'as your majority was a large one you could have dispensed with the votes of all but your *sincere* friends.' Your *sincere friends*! When did I lay claim to be considered one of your '*sincere friends*'? Why, if you could have dispensed with votes, did you write me an urgent letter even after Mr Vowles had resigned?

My reasons for voting for my old friend Archer — that 'much younger man' — I decline to canvass with you. They must be unsatisfactory to you, seeing that there is no bond of connection between him and either me or my wife.

Allow me in conclusion to express my hope that in discharge of your duties as a Poor Law Auditor your decisions will be arrived at solely from the consideration of what is right and just; and that no feelings of *consanguinity or affinity* may lead you astray from the path of righteousness.

I beg to subscribe myself, Sir,
>> neither your admirer,
>>> nor your 'sincere friend'
>>> R. Gully Bennet.

Such then was Gully Bennet, a man of great principle who took his public duties seriously and expected all others to do the same.

Between 1853 and 1867 there are no diary entries and no letters to reflect the activities of Gully and his family. A receipt dated 2nd March 1854 discloses that Mr Pentreath, an artist living in Penzance, was commissioned to paint the children then aged six, five and four respectively. Throughout these fourteen years Gully served on the Committee of the Cornwall Agricultural Association and was its President for seven of them. The Show Catalogue for 1856 reveals two competitions which would hardly survive the twentieth century:

> To the cottagers in Kenwyn, Kea, Feock, St Clement, Merther and Probus, who shall have brought up the largest family with the smallest means, in the best possible manner, without parochial relief, and being of a good moral character – two prizes £5 and £3. Given by the Right Hon. Lord Viscount Falmouth.
>
> To the servant or labourer in husbandry, who shall have lived the longest period in one continuous service, and being of good moral character – Two Prizes £2 and £1. Given by the Society.

CHAPTER 9

> In the name of the Empress of India, make way,
> Oh Lords of the Jungle, wherever you roam,
> The woods are astir at the close of the day
> We exiles are waiting for letters from home,
> Let the robber retreat – let the tiger turn tail
> In the name of the Empress, the Overland Mail!
> Rudyard Kipling. *Departmental Ditties.*

Edith Mary Bennet was born on the 27th May 1858 and christened at Newlyn Church on the 22nd June. Ten years later, on the 14th October 1868, her elder brother Edward was gazetted in the Army and appointed to the 48th Regiment on the 4th December 1868. In the same year Ferdinando Wallis Bennet, aged eighteen, entered the Royal Military Academy at Woolwich. On the 19th December 1868 Edward sailed to join his Regiment in Malta and the twenty-one year old Second Lieutenant began to keep a diary.

> On December 19th 1868 I started from Southampton for Malta. After a stormy passage arrived at Gibraltar December 25th. After a charming voyage down the Mediterranean arrived at Malta on December 28th at 1 a.m., and proceeded to the Imperial Hotel. Slept at Imperial and reported myself next day December 29th. Found the Regiment very nice and got comfortably settled the same day. Found the Maltese a nasty set of dirty villains swarming around you the minute you appear offering boats, go-cars, etc. Houses all built of sandstone, fearful glare. Steps to the sea innumerable. Opera very fine and nice. Library comfortable and books a great pleasure. Commenced my drill and at the end of January went to Pembroke Camp for musketry instruction which I completed first.

Edward was a very good shot and his diary records obvious pleasure from the next three years of army training and discipline in Malta. Swimming and sailing were undertaken with much enthusiasm despite frequent references to his being stung by jellyfish. The opera provided an enjoyable distraction when he was at Valetta.

February 7th 1869. Sunday. Saw breakfasts. Took detachment to Church. Went to Sliema Church in afternoon; Townsend preached (Miss Moore's friend, an awful duffer). First day of Carnival, only allowed to go to Valetta in undress uniform and sword.

February 8th, Monday. Went to Valetta to see Carnival. Comfits flying in all directions. Bands playing and people dancing. Men dressed as women and vice versa. Streets thronged. Dined at Headquarters and went to Opera. Heard the Barber of Seville, very poor. Returned home heartily sick of the whole affair and glad to get to bed.

February 22nd 1869. Monday. Left Pembroke Camp and was quartered at Marguerita, filthy hole. Lost £1:3s:0: stolen from my drawer. Went to Opera Crispino.

February 26th 1869. Friday. Had a row with servant having suspicions as to his honesty. Kept his situation on trial. Mess night but none there.

February 27th 1869. Saturday. Went to Valetta. Saw Rigoletto in the evening. Cortesi's benefit night, sang extremely well – did not get home till 12.30 a.m.

March 3rd 1869. Wednesday. An invite to Col and Mrs Crea accepted; went to Opera, Lucia di Lammermur very good.

March 10th 1869. Went to Opera 'The Huguenots' very pretty. Cortesi and Moro both appear.

March 16th 1869. Went to Opera 'Ophelia'. Dont care much for it.

March 17th 1869. General Tyson dined at Mess. Gave him three cheers on departing at which the Majors were very angry.

March 20th 1869. Played the Lord Warden took 5 wickets each innings and made 7 and 35 not out. Totals 48th 86 and 75 for 3 wickets Lord Warden 119 and 162. Heard Rigoletto.

March 21st 1869. Sunday. Read Queen's Regulations.

March 22nd 1869. No Opera for the week.

April 7th 1869. Went to Opera 'Don Carlos'. Fair put under arrest for signing his name to a false certificate.

April 10th 1869. Cricket match, made 21 67 were beaten on the first innings by 90 runs. Heard Opera 'Don Carlos'.

April 13th 1869. Awfully hot day, went out in skiff and was almost burnt up.

April 15th 1869. Went out sailing with Rogers and Scott, very pleasant but none of us knew anything about it. Saw Sicily very plainly.

April 17th 1869. Cricket match at Valetta. Subalterns v Brigade. Were beaten by 11 runs on first innings. Made 26 and 64 comprising two 6s one over the better to square leg the other a drive.

April 18th 1869 Sunday. Did not go to Church. A windy day, no boating, read all day, went to bed early.

April 28th 1869 Wednesday. Dismissed my drill. Best of all subalterns so the Major said.

April 30th 1869. Ellis, Howe, Bowen, Rylain went on leave via Messina went on board and found all very nice but rather crushed.

May 1st 1869. Very dismal nobody hardly left, went to Opera,

Moro's benefit night. Very full.

May 3rd 1869. Bathed early in the morning and went to Valetta in afternoon but saw nobody, went to Opera 'Trevatore'.

May 7th 1869. Garrison Sports but too hot to enjoy them.

May 16th 1869. Went to Civita Vecchia with Durrant – beautiful drive. Met Eden out there – went to the Cathedral which is very handsome with an inlaid marble altar piece and a very handsome roof. Went to the Catacombs, saw where the Saracens slept, washed, prayed and everything else, bought some coins said to be dug up there and the tongues of the Saracens as they said but really sharks' teeth. Saw St Paul's cave where he is supposed to have lived 3 months and his marble statue. Went to Musta into the Dome the third largest in the world. Very fine roomy place but very bare, all sandstone, built by volunteers for nothing. Went back and dined with Lynch and came home about one o'clock.

May 22nd 1869. Went to Opera heard Faust. Theatre crammed, chorus too weak, especially the old men. Last scene of Moro going to heaven very fine indeed.

June 2nd 1869. Queen's birthday, fired a fou de joie from St Angelo, went to Governor's Ball in the evening.

July 3rd 1869. Went to Valetta met Lynch who came bathing, had an early dinner and went to Opera to see Conjurer Ville.

August 10th 1869. St Lawrence's Day Patron Saint of Viltoriosa, were asked into the Casion a branch of the Malta Club in Valetta and were very friendly with the natives who were uncommonly civil and gave us filthy Port Wine to drink. Our band played in the square below the Palace.

September 21st 1869. 87th dined here prior to their departure to Pembroke Camp. Very pleasant evening, played whist until 4 a.m.

September 23rd 1869. 24th dined here on their arrival at Ricasoli from Floriana. Played vingt et un up to 7 a.m. and having won £3 went to have breakfast.

October 4th 1869. Went to the Opera in the evening. Heard Polinto which with the exception of a song in the third act is not worth listening to. Miss Miller very pretty and ladylike.

October 9th 1869. Went to Regimental theatre which opened on the 7th and was very good.

October 16th 1869. Went to Opera which was full owing to Crocodile and fleet.

October 17th 1869. Went to Dockyard Church. Went on board Crocodile, met Halifax 19th Regiment, very nice fellow. Went to bed early owing to Gun Drill which commences tomorrow.

December 10th to 13th 1869. On the sick list with Maltese Fever.

March 26th to April 11th 1870. Gradually growing hotter. On April 10th Bowen returned from leave and on April 11th Power, McLaughlin and Durrant went on summer leave.

Back at home on the 4th April 1870 Gully Bennet completed twenty-five years as Chairman of the Guardians Union. A most handsome silver candelabra was presented to him to mark the occasion. The engraving read:

> Presented on 4th day of April 1870 to
> Richard Gully Bennet Esq., by the
> Guardians of the St Columb Major Union
> in appreciation of the valuable services
> as their Chairman for 25 years.

In Malta Edward was enjoying the best weather. His diary continued:

April 18th and 19th 1870. Naval regatta, beautiful days. Went on board Lord Warden, fell in with Callaghan.

April 20th 1870. Our sports – beautiful day rather cold. Met G. Shaw and had a long talk with her. Fellows did not like it. Fair on sick list. Fawkes won mile.

April 27th 1870. Very cold. Played for Garrison against Navy made 33 won by one run – very exciting.

The rest of 1870 and the first nine months of 1871 passed with very little comment in the diary. The next major entry dated 24th October 1871 read:

Went on leave preparatory to going to India.
Was ill the whole time.

Edward's diary continued in January 1872 when he embarked for India but before resuming his story mention should be made of Kathleen and Ferdinando.

On the 4th January 1871, in the same batch to leave Woolwich as Lord Kitchener, Ferdinando was gazetted to the Royal Engineers and was posted to Chatham where he remained for the next two years.

Kathleen, then twenty-three years, had received a proposal of marriage from Major William Vigor Fox of Northwich, Cheshire. Gully and Mary Bennet approved and the marriage was to take place in August of that year. The months of June and July saw feverish activity by the Major and his lawyers to arrange a marriage settlement satisfactory to Gully. The letters speak volumes.

CHAPTER 10

The common law does not regulate the form of agreements between spouses. Their promises are not sealed with seals and sealing wax. The consideration that really obtains for them is that natural love and affection which counts for so little in these cold Courts.

Atkin L.J. in the case of Balfour v. Balfour, [1919].

Davenham Hall
Northwich
June 6th 1871

Dear Mr Bennet

I do not know which of us should have the settlement made out but if you will let me know if I am to do it I will put the matter in my lawyer's hands at once. I have taken the land in Lincolnshire which is 164 acres. I find it produced rather more than £300 a year. I have to pay a man to look after it so that with that and other charges I do not get much more than £300 a year.

Land in Lincolnshire	£300:0:0
Charge on my brother's estate	£162:0:0
North Eastern Railway guaranteed 4 per cent £2000	£ 80:0:0
£2000 in Union Railway guaranteed by Midland & North Eastern	£ 80:0:0
	£622:0:0

I think the farm at Lynn might be sold and I would rather not include it in the settlement. I can however put in that in addition if you like in case at any time my brother should wish to pay off the charge.

I am
Yours sincerely
W. V. Fox.

Davenham Hall
Northwich
June 15th 1871

Dear Mr Bennet

Harper has my Deeds locked up with his own in his strongroom so until I can get the key I cannot put them in my solicitor's hands to copy. I have seen him (the lawyer) and he has little doubt that I can settle the money (£3333) that is a charge on my brother's estate but cannot be quite certain till he has looked at the Will. He recommends me not to put the land in Lincolnshire into the settlement as it makes it so inconvenient to make any alteration in the terms with the tenants, give leases etc. I think the following securities ought to be as safe as the land:

	Interest
£3333 on my brother's property	£162:10:0
£2000 Consolidated Stock guaranteed by C.W.R. 5 P.C.	£ 97:10:0
N.E.R. guaranteed shares	£ 80: 0:0
£2500 in stock guaranteed by L & S W Rail 4 P.C.	£100: 0:0
£1500 which is to be paid in on July 20th at 4 P.C. say	£ 60: 0:0
1000 London Dock I took at 2½ P.C.	£250: 0:0
	£740: 0:0

That would allow for a considerable depreciation in value in any of the securities and the £600 a year might be paid out of that to my wife for her life by the Trustees in the same way that I suppose it would be if it was all in land. I do not however care much if you prefer the land and will have the copies made out as soon as I can get at the Deeds.

We have had some delightful rain here and I think have every prospect of a good crop of grass. I hear Lucy has got lodgings so hope to see Mrs Bennet & Kathleen on Monday.

I am

Yours sincerely
W. V. Fox.

98 Mount St.
Grosvenor Square
London
June 21st 1871

Dear Mr Bennet

I have shown the 'scheme' to W. Harper and we can neither of us find anything to object to in it. William thinks it had better be put into the lawyer's hands at once and I will send the scheme to Messrs Davies & Brooke my lawyers in Warrington at once and William will see them about it on Saturday morning. Will you send the address of your solicitor to them (Messrs Davies & Brooks) so that no time may be lost. If you approve of my proposition about the other securities they might be easily substituted for the land. The scheme can be sent back to you as soon as the lawyer has seen it.

I am
　　Yours sincerely
　　　W. V. Fox.

Trethill
10th June 1871

My dear Richard

It is quite sufficient to include Nos 1, 2, 4 & 6. The preparation of the settlement is in practice with the solicitor of the Lady – here he will require extracts or copies of the Deeds or Wills under which Mr Fox is entitled to the Estate in Lincolnshire and to the Mortgage or Charge of £3400 on his brother's Estate and these Mr Fox should instruct his solicitor to make forward to you – just enough he may say to his solicitor to enable your solicitor to prepare the settlement for you waive investigation of title which is often troublesome and expensive.

That you will have prepared an epitome of the proposed settlement and forward it to Mr Fox.

The above will enable you to write to Mr Fox and impress on him the necessity of his solicitor soon forwarding the copies or extracts you have referred to as the want of them will estop the way.

I retain the schedule to enable me to write out the analysis but return Mr Fox's letter.

We have been thrice tantalized with a quarter of an hour's rain and thus are terribly suffering from the drought.

Kind love to all
    Your affectionate cousin
       Wightwick Roberts.

                   Trethill
               16th June 1871

My dear Richard

Enclosed is a proposed scheme for settlement to be sent to Mr Fox and with any remarks you like and invite any remarks he may wish to make or his solicitor and you should agree as to who should be the Trustees and I should say Edward on his sister's behalf – at first it may be necessary he should sign a few papers to enable the income of the Railway Stock etc. to be received and afterwards most probably for many years the Trustees will have nothing to do and Mr Fox should name his and a younger person than W. Harper would be desirable.

When you agree on the scheme and Mr Fox's solicitor send the copies or extracts referred to in my last letter these will be full instructions for the Lady's solicitor to prepare the settlement – I don't believe he will undertake to prepare the settlement without Counsel and if Counsel be required I should be glad if the papers went to my friend Mr Murray Browne of Old Square Lincolns Inn who is very competent and very satisfactorily prepared Joyce's settlement – where is the rain?

Kind love to all
    Your affectionate cousin
       Wightwick Roberts.

                   Trethill
               June 21st 1871

My dear Richard

Evidently the £3333 or rather £3333:6:8 is no doubt as we imagined 1/3rd of a charge of £10000 on a family Estate and be assured any questions of Mr Fox's power to deal with it is moonshine. The land may be entailed and without any power to endow a wife out of it and if so the land must of course be omitted but otherwise Mr Fox may be assured his comfort and convenience will be best secured by including the land for again the lawyer's difficulty is moonshine for as you observe it is proposed by the analysis to give Mr Fox a full power to lease and without any dictation as to the mode of cultivation – Mr Fox now proposes including property producing an income with a margin over the £600 a year the wife taking the one and someone else the other but that would cause additional trouble to the Trustees who would thus have to keep an account with both parties and moreover would involve the necessity of including more of the convertible property than is otherwise necessary, the consequences of which both Mr Harper and ourselves pointed out. If, however, Mr Fox persists in his view I don't see it is for you to object. It is quite right to discuss all these points – I return Mr Fox's letter.

Anne has postponed her return until Saturday. The rain has been of immense benefit to us – there were many apparent vacancies both in Mangols and Turnips but now every row appears complete and our prospect of hay is we think increased by at least 10 tons but even these will be no better than half a crop. John is wonderfully well and was in the saddle yesterday having rode to Plymouth for nearly 4 hours without dismounting and apparently without the slightest fatigue – I am going to drive over to Trewin to congratulate Mrs Staples on her younger son having carried off the 2nd prize for Latin in a school of near 60 and then mean to call at Trevis to call on Reginald Pole who is there and to enquire for Mrs Pole who I fear is in a critical state. We all remarked Edward promised to be or rather already was a capital shot.

Yours affectionately
Wightwick Roberts.

Davenham Hall
Northwich
June 28th 1871

Dear Mr Bennet

I am very sorry for not having answered your letter sooner. I have written to my solicitor to send you the Settlement Scheme at once to which I quite agree. He will also make the copy your solicitor requires and send that as soon as possible. I forgot to

177

mention the name of my Trustee, Thomas Horatio Marshall, Hartford Beach, Cheshire. I am going to Aldershot on Friday next and shall leave any other business there may be as far as I can to my brother-in-law, W. Harper.

We have had plenty of rain here and the grass crops are looking well, we now want some settled weather for the hay which people are just beginning.

    I am

        Yours sincerely
        W. V. FOX.

Royal Hotel
High Street
Aldershot
Saturday 1st July 1871.

Dear Mr Bennet

I wrote to my Solicitor to make out the copy of the Deeds you require this week. I heard from him yesterday but he had a great dislike for some reason to my settling the property in Lincolnshire in the way we first proposed. He says it will involve us in great expense and trouble. He proposes a mortgage of the property to the Trustees as being the best plan if the property is to go into the Settlement. I hardly know what to do. I have a great fear of having the matter badly arranged so as to lead to a law suit or trouble in after times. I have sent the letter to W. Harper to look over and have written to the Lawyer to know his reason for objecting to the first proposal. I suppose I shall hear in a day or two and shall then be able to decide. I cannot see why the mortgage should be a better plan than the other. I am sure I have given you good reason to suppose I wished to put off the wedding but if I had wished it put off longer than the 16th you may be quite sure I should have let you know without going to the lawyers to help me.

The school does not open here until Monday morning so many men have not come up.

    I am

        Yours sincerely
        W. V. FOX

Trethill
7th July 1871

My dear Richard

It is I agree exceedingly provoking that Mr Fox who is evidently inexperienced in business did not take the proposed scheme for Settlement and your explanatory letters to his lawyers or Mr Harper and thus have made real progress whilst now we are very much where we began. I do not myself see the slightest indication of Mr Fox shrinking but what is very obvious is the lawyers are very inexpert to their business – for instance they now assign as a reason why the land should not be included is that it is old family property whilst I should say there could not be a stronger ground for including it for it is thus preserved – and as to the expense of investigating the title or being damaged by the links of the last deed you volunteered to waive the one and asked only enough copy of the last deed as would enable the Settlement to be prepared – in fact, all was anticipated and explained so far as their objections go and all difficulty removed – and you are right and so is Mr Fox in saying a mortgage is as bad as the Estate – if they are still of opinion they would be better off for you to accept the other securities and quit the land the safety is the same and therefore you need not object the sooner or later they would find their mistake.

Yours affectionately
Wightwick Roberts.

Warrington
11th July 1871

Dear Sir

On the other side we send copy letter written by us today to your Solicitors on the subject of Major Fox's Settlement. We will do anything that may be necessary to prevent disappointment on our part.

We are
Yours truly
Davies & Brook.

R. Gully Bennet Esquire
Tresillian House
Cornwall.

Warrington
11th July 1871

Dear Sirs

Major Fox's Settlement

We are referred to you in this matter by Mr R. Gully Bennet, who informs us that the marriage is fixed for the first week in August.

The proposal for the Marriage Settlement is sent herewith and (if you have not seen it before) we think that you will not find it difficult to carry out. You will receive an abstract of such parts of the Will of the Revd. Wm. Fox, Major Fox's father, as relates to the devise of his Lincolnshire property at Barton Upon Humber and Goxhill to Major Fox, and an abstract of the Conveyance of two closes bought since by Major Fox himself. The abstract of the Will also contains the directions to raise the £3333:6:8 one third of the sum of £6000 and £4000 therein mentioned, which is to form part of the settled property.

The scheme calls the Lincolnshire property a messuage and farm, but we have no list or schedule of it and on referring to the deeds we find that it was acquired in parcels, one of which comes under a Deed of Partition and Deed of Confirmation containing 28 skins between them.

There are other deeds besides, but no abstracts, and the expense of deducing a title would be very great. The two abstracts of the older title contain 172 sheets.

Under the circumstances, we think it useless to put Major Fox to the expense of deducing a title. The devised in his Father's Will is really the best commencement and we have written him for a schedule or list of the property to be inserted at the foot of the Settlement to which may be added such general words as 'all other his hereditaments at Barton Upon Humber and Goxhill' or like.

Of course we shall be happy to supply abstracts or whatever else may be required but a Settlement (as you are aware) differs from a purchase in the fact that the Settlor can settle only such property as he possess whether the title be good or bad.

Please telegraph if you can thereby save a day at any time.
We are,
>   Yours truly
>>   Davies & Brook.

Messrs Whitford & Sons
St Columb
CORNWALL.

>   Warrington
>   13th July 1871

Dear Sir

We hope you have got our letter of Tuesday. We are not aware that we have done anything to deserve so severe a letter as yours of yesterday's date. There was not an hour lost after receiving positive instructions, and as our staff is large we could get anything that may be required out of hand without delay. Our only object was to save expense.

We are,
>   Dear Sir,
>>   Yours truly
>>>   Davies & Brook.

R. Gully Bennet Esquire
Tresillian House
CORNWALL.

>   Royal Hotel
>   Aldershot
>   July 13th 1871

Dear Mr Bennet

I am really very sorry you have had all this annoyance but I cannot make the lawyers go faster. I had a letter a day or two ago for some information for which I was obliged to write to the man who looks after my Lincolnshire farms. I wrote by return of post and hope the information will be given by Saturday so that the documents your lawyers want ought to be ready by Monday or Tuesday. I know the time is getting very near but I have done all I can lately to hurry them.

181

We have had a great deal of rain here rather damaging to our drill. There is a good deal of hay out here and I understand that in Cheshire they have had more rain still. I hear most gloomy accounts of the hay harvest.

I shall write to Kathleen tomorrow. I hope you are all well at home.

I am
> Yours sincerely
> W. V. Fox.

In the event the terms of the Marriage Settlement were agreed, the Settlement was executed, and on the 16th August 1871 Kathleen Tryphena Bennet married Major William Vigor Fox. The settlement was not referred to afterwards until almost forty years later following Gully Bennet's death whereupon his co-Trustee, Thomas H. Marshall wrote to Edward Bennet seeking his consent to become the new Trustee in place of his deceased father:

> Parkstone
> Dorset
> 4th February 1910

Dear Colonel Bennet

Some correspondence has passed between Mrs Vigor Fox and myself as to the appointment of a new Trustee of her Marriage Settlement in the place of your late Father who was co-Trustee with myself. Mrs Fox tells me that you are willing to act as Trustee and in her opinion and also in mine, you are the proper person to do so. Will you kindly let me have a line to the address above, where I expect to be for the next two months, to say whether this arrangement will suit you, and whether you are willing that the Deeds relating to the Settlement should remain in the schoolroom at Tresillian House, where I believe they are at present and where Mrs Fox seems to wish them to be kept.

She tells me that she has always received the rents from some Lincolnshire property on which part of her Settlement is charged, herself, and that the dividends from some Railway stocks have been paid to her direct through Parrs Bank, Kensington High Street. I have never had anything to do with these payments and suppose they will go on as heretofore. Of course it will be necessary to have your name substituted for that of your father on the original Settlement Deed, but that I should say could be done by any local Solicitor subject probably to the consent of Mrs Fox and myself, which could be obtained in writing from each of us.

    I remain

        Yours sincerely

           Thos. H. Marshall.

PART THREE

CHAPTER 11

The music-room on the top floor of No. 5 was filled with the 'Aladdin' company at rehearsal. Dickson Quartus, commonly known as Dick Four, was Aladdin, stage-manager, ballet-master, half the orchestra, and largely librettist, for the 'book' had been rewritten and filled with local allusions. The pantomime was to be given next week, in the downstairs study occupied by Aladdin, Abanazar, and the Emperor of China. The Slave of the Lamp, with the Princess Badroulbadour and the Widow Twankey, owned No. 5 study across the same landing, so that the company could be easily assembled. The floor shook to the stamp-and-go of the ballet, while Aladdin, in pink cotton tights, a blue and tinsel jacket, and a plumed hat, banged alternately on the piano and his banjo. He was the moving spirit of the game, as befitted a senior who had passed his Army Preliminary and hoped to enter Sandhurst next spring.

Rudyard Kipling. *Stalky & Co.*

The *West Briton and Cornwall Advertiser* of 2nd January 1873 carried a detailed report of the Epiphany Sessions just opened:

> The Epiphany Sessions for this county were commenced on Tuesday morning at the Shire Hall, Bodmin. Gully Bennet Esq. presided, the Grand Jury was sworn.
>
> In addressing the Grand Jury, the Chairman said that although there was a slight increase in the number of prisoners, 22 against 18, as compared with the corresponding period of last year, yet the offences charged against the prisoners were of much less magnitude. There were then nine different cases of breaking and entering, but at the present time there was but one. The number of prisoners committed under the Criminal Justices' Act was the same as last year, but there was an increase of three – four against one, of those committed under the Juvenile Offences' Act; but taking the total number of criminal prisoners received into the Gaol during the quarter there was, as compared with the same period of last year, a diminution of ten, the number being at the present time 142,

whilst last year it was 152. He therefore thought they had reason to be satisfied that crime was not only not increasing, but that it was actually diminishing in the county, and, in fact throughout the whole of England. He was not prepared to enter into the causes of this beyond remarking that he thought it might be clear to all of them that the demand for labour was so great and wages had so much increased, that there was an absence of that poverty which prevailed some twelve months or two years ago. He was happy to be able to tell them that there would be no increase in the county rate at the Sessions, and as there was now no occasion for further borrowing on the part of the county, he hoped that their existing debt would speedily be reduced and that this would be followed by a diminution in the rates. He was also pleased to be able to report that there was a marked reduction in cattle disease and sheep scab in the county. The latter disease had been diminished in twelve months from about four thousand to only six hundred and twenty-eight cases, and of this number no less than five hundred and ten seemed to be in the police district of Liskeard. With regard to the foot and mouth disease, he would just remark that if farmers would only make their purchases in their own county instead of from places about which they knew nothing, there would not be anything like so much cattle disease amongst them. The county business was then proceeded with. After receiving reports dealing with the County Asylum, rating of mines, the Adulteration of Food Act, cattle disease, proposed new railways in the county, licensing matters and the Chief Constable's Report, there followed the Criminal trials.

TRIALS OF PRISONERS
(Before Mr. R. Gully Bennet)

Mary Oliver, 58, charwoman, pleaded guilty to stealing various articles from Frederick Truscott at Lansallos, and she was sentenced to three months' imprisonment with hard labour.

Robbery at Falmouth

Mary Jane Rogers, Elizabeth Troon, Amy Andrews and Anne Goodman were all found guilty of stealing four sovereigns, the property of Henry Dickson, at Falmouth, and they were each sentenced to three months' imprisonment with hard labour.

Theft from Wheal Basset Mine

Henry Tregenza, 35, miner, admitted that on the 5th December he stole some timber from Wheal Basset Mine, and there being a prior conviction he was sentenced to six months' imprisonment with hard labour.

False Pretences
William Thomas, 28, seaman, pleaded guilty to obtaining money by fraudulent means at Penryn, and he was sentenced to three months' hard labour.

The Alleged Wife Beating at Torpoint
The Grand Jury ignored the bill against John Uffen, charged with cruelly ill-treating his wife in the parish of Antony.

Robbery and False Pretences at Redruth
Bessie Kneebone, 14, servant, was indicted for stealing two watches, value about £5 and £10 respectively, the goods and chattels of Jacob Schwerer, of Redruth, in or about the months of July and November 1872. She was also indicted for obtaining by false pretences from John Webber of the same place, on the 17th December, divers pieces of flannel, velvet and terry ribbon. It appeared that the prisoner had been in the habit of going to various shops and getting goods to be charged to other people. She was found guilty and, considering her youth, sentenced to four months' imprisonment with a severe admonition.

Stealing a Shawl at Maker
Susan Ham, 36, was indicted for stealing a scarf shawl, of the value of £1, the property of George Avery, at the parish of Maker, on the 17th October. She was sentenced to four months' hard labour.

Stealing Oysters at Constantine
Mary Richards, 53, hawker, was indicted for stealing 500 oysters of the value of £2, the goods and chattels of John Tyacke, at the parish of Constantine, on the 1st December last. It appeared that this was not the first time the prisoner had been convicted of stealing oysters and other things, and she was sentenced to six months' imprisonment.

On 14th December 1872 Lieutenant Edward Gully Bennet left Madras to attend a course of Army signalling in Bangalore. His diary for March 1873 continues:

189

10th March 1873. Arrived back from Bangalore, passed good exam, and have to go again for night signalling. Hot weather commenced.

9th April 1873. Started on a shooting trip with Powlett. Bullock Bandy to Hospet. Rode to Hooligi and crossed the river, horses had to swim the river, boats for luggage. Shot doves made camp. Powlett's tent very nearly blown down. Rode on to Indri, no shooting although plenty of game; bears, cheetah and peacocks, quail, hares; stayed 10 days. Rode on to Copal, tent in the cutchery. (An Indian Magistrate's office or Courthouse.) Stayed some time, tahsildar (an Indian Revenue officer) called a doctor, we had great climbings, saw a bear within 100 yards. Shot a jungle cat, had shot at black buck, missed; could not judge the distance, standing in a hollow. Rode to the river, crossed at Wolaverator and stayed at Bellahaunez. On to Nainakainkey, paddy fields but nothing in them. Brahmin boys were civil, great bathing in a well, on to Nanglapoor, pretty ride, lots of quail, did not get breakfast till 3 p.m. as no chance of shooting went on to Ranandroof stayed ten days and had great sport picnics by Fraser and Dynely went out shooting but got nothing. Walked down to Yetton Gully, rode on to Kurtain arriving about 12.30 a.m. Had a chop and slept till 11 next day. Rode into Bellay same evening. Pennale very seedy sent to Droof, Blaine on sick list and Lewe all with fever. Very cool plenty of rain. Came back on the 9th June and found myself in excellent health and ordered to Bangalore for Garrison Course.

Edward spent the remainder of 1873 and the first few months of the new year on Army duties until on the 14th March 1874 he set off on six months leave and a grand hunting expedition part of which he described in a long letter to his parents dated 7th May 1874:

Mundagudda – Shemogah 18 miles
May 7th 1874
Here we are on our return south from the Falls and enjoying the luxury of rain. But my last letter was from Meligi, I think, so I will resume. From there we went 20 miles west to Hoolical where we met Barker, Beetham, Meiklejohn, Brookes and Howlett forming a party of 8. With 8 guns we sallied forth next morning,

190

drawing lots of course, for places. We had about 40 or 50 beaters, and they beat up to our line of guns through a jungle where bison had been marked down. They had been in about an hour (I was on the ground in an open space with one tree to manoeuvre around if charged) when I heard a twig break close by – intense excitement for about half an hour when out walked, about 15 yards off, a cow bison and calf. Of course I was at her at once but hit a tree with my first and no result. She, curious to say, stopped and looked at me, and with a steady aim I hit her with a shell just under the ear and rolled her over quite dead. That was the only animal killed on that beat, but on the next Powlett rolled over another cow with a single bullet. No one else got shots. For the next two days we did the same sort of thing, but killed nothing, and we returned on the Wednesday to Meligi. Staying a day or two longer we started on the 14th to Tirthalli en route to the Falls. We went by Hoonishee (15 miles) Anantapoor (15 miles) beat there, and Powlett killed a boar. Bye-the-bye I was wrong in saying that nothing else was killed at Hoolical, as the last day we were out when the beat was just finished, a man came and said he could show a chietal lying down in dense jungle. I started and went about 100 yards, cutting my way, when the man pointed to something about 5 yards from me. I thought it was a log of wood, and told the man I should shoot him if it did not turn out to be an animal. Through the bamboos I pointed my rifle, and let him have it with both barrels at once straight into what proved to be the shoulder. Very glad was I to find that I had killed him as he turned out to be an immense wild boar; for, as I could not have moved in the jungle, he must have ripped me if I had only wounded him. From Anantapoor we went to Sagur (14) and thence to Talgoopa (10) where we found Grant and Anderson. All there are N.I.'s in the Mysore Revenue Survey. On the 19th we started, four of us, to Bangalode on another shikar trip; beat small jungles the first day, when I shot a jungle sheep – splendid eating. Next day having news of a tigress about 4 miles off, we started. First eight nil. She came close to Grant, but would not break, so we took beaters out and moving our line of guns to exactly the opposite side of the jungle, made them beat back again to us. After about an hour, bang, bang from the gun on my right, and I moved facing round towards the shot, being in a tree so as to be ready if the

191

beast came my way. I had hardly turned when in the grass I caught sight of the tigress cantering past. I waited until the shot became open, and firing through a space in the tree, killed her with a shell in the body just behind the shoulder. She jumped up and fell on her back, never moving again. I gave her the second barrel as she lay to satisfy myself, but she did not move. Reloading I got down from my tree and walked up to her, and of course you can imagine my pleasure when I found that Grant had not fired at her at all, but had killed a panther. It was a lucky kill, as she was 45 yards off. Of course we carried them home and skinned them next morning. The skin etc. are mine, and I got 60 rupees from the Mysore Government as a reward. Next day but one news came of another tiger. Off we started 12 miles; began beating about 2 p.m. and the tiger came to Grant. When within about 10 yards of his tree he fired and hit it in the ear, turning it over at once, but not dead. Two more shots from Grant and then two more and up he got and walked away. Two from Anderson then followed but still not dead, but lying down in the jungle between Anderson and Grant. Powlett and I then went to Grant and together we walked up to the animal, Anderson directing us from his tree whence he could see it. Of course Grant had the first shot and this luckily finished him. It was an immense tiger, 9 feet 4 inches, and had all the eight bullets in him, five of which were in the head. Next day we returned to Talgoope, having had we considered a very successful trip. The following day we went to the Falls and such a sight I hardly think it possible to be seen anywhere else. We lay down on the rocks and put our heads over the precipice, and there is a sheer fall of 890 feet – nothing to interrupt it – into a pool. The top of the Fall is over loose rocks in the shape of a horseshoe, which is covered with water in the rains, but now is dry, except where the main beds of the stream lie. There were four running when we were there, and it was a glorious sight. We fired a gun into the abyss and millions (no exaggeration) of blue rock pigeons flew from the crevices. We went back in the afternoon, and next day started for Tirthalli, where we were to meet Macintyre again. At a place between Anantaoor and Hoonishee Cutty we had a beat but only took our guns with bullets; thinking these would be sufficient, very nearly cost Powlett his life. The beaters were close up. He had fired, as

192

he thought, at a jungle sheep, and, hearing something in the bush, he walked up the path. He had not proceeded more than 10 yards when, with a 'hoof' (the sound they make) a panther jumped straight at him. As luck would have it he shot him straight through the head quite dead, and then found that his first shot – as he thought at a sheep – had gone through the animal's body. During the march all through the jungle we shot geese, duck, red teal and cotton, so we had plenty to eat. We arrived at Tirthalli on the 30th, safe and sound, and as well as possible. Staying a couple of days, Barker and Beatham joined us, and we went to Malloor for two days. First day, beating – saw nothing. Second day, when the beat had been going on about two hours, a panther came down about 40 yards. I could not stand his looking at me and fired, knocking him over. I fired again at him on the ground but he got up and went back, and although we traced him about 50 yards by his blood, we could not find him. We have had no other sport yet but hope to get plenty here when the rain is over as the old footprints will be all washed out, and we shall go out stalking for a change. As for the country, it is beyond me to describe it. No level plains as at Bellasy, but continuous hills covered with thick jungle and trees, plenty of nullahs, streams etc. intersecting them; and splendid bathing improved by the excitement that a mugger may eat you at any moment. We stay here about a fortnight and then go to Shemogat en route to Mysore and the hills.

Mysore June 15th. Have had no more shikar, only hard travelling, and am now at Mysore, having passed through Seringapatam and slept in Tippo's Palace, visited his tomb, which is very well kept up by Government, and start tonight for Shamrajmuggur, about 36 miles. The Government Shikarree has captured 35 elephants in a space of 40 acres and wants European sportsmen to go into the jungle and drive the brutes into a smaller corral, where they can fasten them up to trees. It is a thing we shall never have a chance of seeing again, and is extremely dangerous, as if the brutes try to break back through our line we shall have to use our rifles and very likely get trodden on; but if they take things quietly and go into the smaller enclosure, we shall go in on Government elephants and see the fun of tying up.

Bangalore July 31st. We have had a good deal more knocking about and are now at Bangalore. I think my last told you of our intention of going to the elephants. We started from Mysore on the 16th ult., and arrived at the camp next day alright. All that day we inspected the keddahs. They were two in number – one large one, about a mile round, with the river running through it, and surrounded by a ditch, partly artificial, for irrigation purposes. In this keddah were the elephants. The second, or small keddah, was another complete circle of ditch about 300 yards round. The ditch itself was 10 feet deep by 9 feet wide at the top, all artificial; the interior was dense jungle. This was where we wanted to drive the elephants; it was only joined to the larger keddah by a small neck of dead land, and was closed by a gate. All that night we were up, as now everything was ready and the drive would take place on the morrow. Hundreds of fires and about 1000 coolies round the large keddah, together with the roars and trumpetings of the poor brutes enclosed, formed a scene that not many Europeans will ever witness. I assure you it was very exciting. Every now and then as we walked along the banks we could see an elephant moving through the jungle looking for a place to escape, but finding none he invariable retired with a roar, crashing the trees and jungle in his retreat. In the morning, all being complete, and the ladies placed in a position close to the gate to see as much as possible, about 10 Powlett Sanderson and self with 50 beaters entered the large keddah. We all had our rifles of course; and I took a lot of shot to fire at them to frighten them. We had not gone 200 yards in when we three on the right of the line came on the herd; now was my time, and I walked up as close as possible to the nearest and let him have both barrels, and away went the herd straight as a line, breaking everything, hardly a tree escaping. We got them close up to the gate, but owing to the noise and to some excited coolie letting off his gun, back they came straight on us. I fired off my shot as fast as possible and loaded with ball, as now was the dangerous work. They stopped short of our line where we were for a little. At last one immense female, who had a young one, charged down. She came, ears extended, trunk curled, head well up, and tail erect, as hard as she could – a sort of trot as an elephant cannot gallop. Sanderson, in front, let her come within 10 yards and gave her his first barrel in the head, dropping her on her knees; up she got and lucky for him his second killed her, hitting her in the heart, as only one step more and she would have been on top of him. We then had to retire, as the rest of the herd had broken back amongst the beaters. Thus the first drive failed. Seeing our defects we cleared the natives away in front and made all keep quiet; then, getting more ammunition, we started again with a deal more certainty of success. We entered at the same place, but instead of going together I went on the left, Powlett took the centre, and Sanderson the right. The beat was the same as before, and we got them up in front of the gate when the tusker of the herd got in front and kept the others back. This unlooked-for delay put us off a little; we were unable to account for the block, but the ladies informed us. However, we were soon alright again, and with a happy thought we all got torches, running forward and scorched them a derriere – not much chance for the tusker in front, the herd very soon sent him out of the way, and forward through the dead land under the gate they trooped in fours and everyone went in (53 elephants). Down came the gate with a crash, and with shouts of any and every description they were all secured in the small keddah. All was now over, as there was no chance of their escaping, except by falling into the ditch, but I doubt whether this would have made much difference. It was a grand success for Sanderson. Our camp was pitched within 200 yards of the small keddah. The whole jungle round was a sort of scrub jungle, and now we hoped to get shooting, as the tying up did not commence until about ten a.m; so we had the morning to ourselves, but somehow we never went out as we had to superintend the getting chains and ropes each morning for the day's performance, and what with watching the elephants, and with one thing or another, we were very busy. But the tying up must keep for another letter.

Edward's diary for the rest of 1874 and early 1875 reveals his increasing enjoyment with Army life in India – its military demands – its social pleasures – and to his especial liking an abundancy of hunting.

Ferdinando, a year junior to Edward, was closer to home serving in the Royal Engineers in which he embraced each new scientific duty with all the enthusiasm of a most devoted student. On the 31st August 1874 he was posted from Chatham to Portsmouth which abruptly closed his brilliant career in amateur cricket. Writing of him in *The Royal Engineers Journal* dated September 1830 his biographer recorded:

> His meteoric career as a cricketer chronologically calls for notice first. No record exists of his having played at Woolwich, but after joining at Chatham his play rapidly improved until for one season, that of 1874, he was the best bat then in Corps, if not the best bat ever produced by the Royal Engineers. In that year he made 889 runs for the R.E., with an average of 44.4 per innings, whilst also doing good service as a bowler and in the field. Amongst his biggest scores were 165 not out against the R.M.A., figures which sounded more formidable in those days than at present. And this was when Renny-Tailyour, then known as the best bat in England against bowling not of the very first class, was at his prime. The game which stood out beyond all others in Bennet's memory was when he played under the captaincy of W.G. Grace for Kent and Gloucestershire against All England, making 47 runs. If my recollection is trustworthy, he was for a time at the wickets with Grace, scoring equally rapidly. It is also reported that Bennet was asked to play for England against Australia. After 1874 he seldom played again.

During 1874, the year in which he played so well, he was quartered aboard H.M.S. *Hood* anchored in the Medway near Gillingham Pier. His draft to the Submarine and Mining operations of his Corps in Portsmouth closed this chapter of his life. A former Chief Engineer, Addison, writing in later years about Ferdinando's brilliant exploits as a cricketer had this to say:

> I have made some search in the bookcases at Lords and found there Lillywhite's Cricket Annual of 1875, with details of 1874 cricket. He gave a list of R.E. matches and the averages which confirmed that Ferdinando was at the top. As regards Gents v Players and Princes (where Cadogan Square now is) Lillywhite only mentions W.G. and one or two others who made a lot of runs. In reviewing the amateurs of 1874 he mentions Bennet as a good bat and very fine field.

Throughout 1875 and 1876 Kathleen, then twenty-seven, Ferdinando, twenty-five, and Edith aged seventeen, kept up a lively correspondence with their mother. Gully devoted more and more time to his judicial duties and at the Midsummer Sessions again presided in the absence of Sir Colman Rashleigh who was unable to leave the side of his seriously ill daughter. In 1875 Ferdinando began a correspondence with Leonard Darwin, an Army contemporary, which was to last for more than half a century.

> Royal Engineer Torpedo Office
> Fort Monckton
> Gosport
> Portsmouth
> 2nd February 1875

My dear Mother

After the usual amount of railway accidents, perils by land and perils by sea your loving son reached this beautiful spot last night – so now you're happy. At Bishop Stoke I met Chemside who after having been telegraphed for all over Ireland had been sent to Chatham and then ordered to join at Portsmouth immediately, so now we are three with nothing to do. Of course he talked incessantly and has continued to do ever since, hence I could not write this morning to allay your anxiety a day earlier. It has been snowing incessantly all day and now there is about 3 inches of it – got up tolerably comfortably by the aid of foot warmers and my Ulster but it was beastly cold. Our house is being painted and getting the fungi encrustation taken off, but in a week we hope to be settled especially as Chemie goes on leave tomorrow till the end of March. But it will be more cheerful to have two to quarrel with than one. The chances are much in favour of our being turned out of the new quarters just as we get settled; and after having spent so much in painting and papering the rotten old walls it will be a nuisance – Government only paints once in eight years so we have to pay it ourselves of course. It is getting dark and I can't see clearly what I am writing.

> FWB.

> Strathallan
> February 18th 1875

My dearest Mother

I have a bit of news that I know will delight your heart. This week I have been drafted off to a place next to Miss E at dinner and the first evening I was there we were talking of cooking and

Miss E asked if I should like to learn and of course I said Yes and she promised to ask Miss Theresa if she would teach me. I hardly thought she would remember to do so but sure enough the next evening she told me that Miss Theresa would!! Miss T has said nothing to me yet and she will not be able to have me yet as she is disabled in one wrist sprained it six months ago and now has blisters and not able to use it at all. Will it not be splendid as you said you would like me to learn. I am being laughed at now for my short frocks and Miss E trotted me out for inspection the other evening to show that they are too short but of course as she said that Miss T was just the opposite and said mine were much more sensible than having them sweeping on the ground. Of course I shall have to have my summer dress made longer.

We are not having washing dresses for common on account of the washing but some kind of alpaca. That wretched Annie laughs at me so for looking 'strong minded' with my short frocks, spectacles, bag and apron and Miss Entich is delighted at the idea and takes it up unmercifully. It is great fun. She wants to get more *style* into me!! Miss E told me to make all apologies for her forgetting about the banker. Bank of England Western Branch Burlington Gardens – now remember for next time. Carrie sent me a splendid valentine one of her own. Ought I to write and thank her? 'As you like it' was *very* good and Mrs Kendal as Rosaline was inexpressibly nice, pretty and very good. I have got the cold into my heel much in the same way as Kathleen I should think as it is neither a chilblain or a gathering but a funny little 'place'. I am afraid I shall have to get a pair of buttoned boots as the elastic sides make it bad. It is nothing serious so do not think I am laid up at all. Tell Kathleen Miss E wants to see her so she will have to come to London some time soon. Of course *you* will come some time before July. Certainly *do not* send my other muff, I do not want one at all. I hope you do not think I am sorry to have been at school at all I would not leave a day before July 26th if I had the chance and am very glad to have been but I do not want to stay on for ever and so am very glad to have the prospect of leaving in the summer to look forward to. I do not think there is a single lesson I really dislike. I am *very* fond of drawing, singing, English and music and like French and German very fairly but certainly less than the others but please do not talk of talents for I have none in the common meaning of the word. 'Tastes' are the utmost I can boast of. However I do not wonder you *dread* the time when I shall come home for good. Mr Bodda gave me such a difficult song yesterday called 'A Daydream' by Blumenthal words by Adelaide Proctor, a splendid one really worth learning but very difficult. Will write to Kathleen on Saturday. Had a pencilled note from Mrs Retallack on Tuesday to say the shawl arrived alright. Was it not good of her to write?

   Your own loving
     Edith

I send the specs. My others will not stick on so I shall send them to HE for a stronger setting as soon as you send back yours for use while the others are being done. Miss E is going to take me to the City for a pair of clips some time so when I get them I will return yours for good. I think clips cost about 6/6 so that is not ruinous and I want something of the sort until I get my gold ones!!

Strathallan
February 27th 1875

My dearest Mother

How very careful I have to be in what I say to you! Who would have dreamt that you would send specs without using them. I could do quite well with my own only I wished you not to keep yours longer than you wanted them I nearly sent them back by return of post only thought you would not appreciate my doing so. I do not want either white-bottle or shoes, thank you all the same for your trouble – felt laced boots lined with flannel 4/9 have almost cured my heel and mustard liniment is good for chilblains and Sancto makes a round with the latter every evening. I think it has not been cold since I got my boots and my heel and chilblain do not hurt a bit whereas before I could only hobble! Today it is a rapid thaw, lots of snow yesterday and not a vestige now. I should be sorry to think that the years of education I have had only result in a '*smattering*' and do not see how two or three terms longer would quickly change that into '*perfection*'. One's education is only begun on leaving school remember and here we

are taught how to instruct ourselves we are not supposed to leave off everything and rust on leaving school. I like my drawing lessons *immensely* and have such nice little copies – I shall learn to do flowers from nature by doing French ones sometime. Miss T suggests my wearing out my grey in the evenings. Do you not think I had better? Miss T says it will be up to my knees by the holidays!! Ferdie's drawing is splendid. The likeness is so perceptible. Nothing to say today so with heaps of love to you all
    Believe me
        Your very loving
           Edith.
What is Carrie's address? And am I to write to her as 'Carrie'?

                     Strathallan
                 March 4th 1875
Just been seeing patterns of summer dresses my dearest Mother – every day ones are to be a pretty quiet light brown with just the simple finish of dark brown it is some wool material and 1/- and something a yard. I have forgotten exactly what. The Sunday dresses are 4/- a yard, Yokahama. It is not yet at all settled about the dresses for common but we have been talking them over. We go on the 16th April and come back on the 3rd of May as we cannot have three weeks on account of the Confirmation which is to be on the 16th June in a Church close by but not the one we go to. When will Chaytor arrive. I *want* my broaches, I do! I return E's letters. There is nothing to say and no time in which to say that nothing so please excuse a scrawl. Confirmation Class in a few minutes. I told Miss Theresa I should be very glad to see my grey dress up to my knees but she was cruel enough to say that growing *broader* would help to get it there as well as *longer*. Was it not unkind? I cannot send Ed's letter yet though I have begun it I ask for a long notice!! If you like I will send it next week instead of your writing to him. I will tell you when my muff is found. I am so mad with chilblains to go on now and really have nothing to say.
    Your own ever loving
        Edith.

Fort Monckton
5th March 1875

My dear Mother

It has been snowing and freezing and thawing ever since I came back, but as the sun has actually appeared today and it is not so cold I feel able to write to you. The ham is much appreciated by Collings who begs you will send another at once, a leaner one that we may not have to waste the fat. We have eaten very fairly but there is no chance of the two ends meeting. We have heard nothing as yet about the awful fire you so graphically described at Gosport Station. I intend going that way next week when the smouldering embers will doubtless meet my eye. I went up in the train as far as Exeter with Rashleigh who told me about Brune, £6,000 a year being left him, I daresay I told you this before. Our furnishing gets on slowly, got some remarkably fine pictures for the drawing room yesterday from a blackguard for a pair of old bags and a few other little things like the skipper's tunic and so on, he wont want it much down here. Chemside has brought three forks (one has only two prongs) and a bit of a looking glass which will make the room much lighter I think but it is a bad fracture. The conservatory is nearly ready as by the time it is we shall be turned out of course. The cheese has arrived, a white one, not an atom of green. Not much news, very little doing, I am designing a pier and a nice safe structure I should think it would be when finished, I guess terra firma will be solid enough for me to walk on.

F.W.B.

Strathallan
March 6th 1887

Dearest Mother

Only a scrawl today as there is nothing going on and nothing to say in consequence. Finished my letter to Edward and will post it next Thursday. Bought half dozen new collars and marked them so respectably that Sancto says she shall instal me as her chief marker! Been given the pleasant duty with Annie F of looking after the five little ones ages 12 to 14 who have been very cheeky and so we have our hands pretty full. Mind you do not let Mrs V ask me there again if she says anything about it to you. If I am not

201

asked out Miss E will take me out more herself on Saturdays and that is ever so much nicer. I could see last term what a bore it was to Mrs V to have me though she was very kind.

Your own loving
Edith.

Thank the Father for his letter.

Strathallan
March 11th 1875

My dearest Mother

I am afraid my letter today will not be very long as it is a great scramble to write at all tonight but still I will do my best. On Tuesday Annie and I went with Miss Theresa to the Albert Hall to hear the 'Hymn of Praise' and the Slabat Mater. The former was not at all well sung but of course I enjoyed it immensely as I have never heard it better. On Saturday Miss Enticknays is going to take me to the 'Midsummer Night's Dream'. If it is acted as well as 'As you like it' it will be *splendid*! Please do not write to Miss E about my muff I will stir up Sancto again.

Your ever loving
Edith.

Strathallan House
March 18th 1875

My dearest Mother

Last Saturday was splendid! Phelps as 'Bottom' simply killing but no! I do not think I shall contract a taste for theatres. They do not come up to my expectations! It is too evidently '*acting*' and does not have any great fascination for me. Besides there is a girl here who does more harm in the school than all the others put together and the only topic of conversation which she has is theatres and actors etc. enough to disgust anyone with going off it. Happily she leaves at Easter but she is very *dangerous* and can make herself very nice to win over new girls and she gives us much trouble. Not that we can say anything to her only we have to keep others away from her as much as possible. We three monitoresses have not an easy life of it by any means. But to return to Saturday – we had seats in the front row of the dress circle (but of course being in the afternoon it was not 'dress') and saw splendidly. We simply roared at Phelps and Miss Entic as much as anyone. As a good many are going to have their dresses made in the house I told Miss Lean I would rather not go to Mrs King again as I like my dresses made more simply and she says she will have them made more simply more durably and much less expensively than Mrs K. Only three are to go to her for best dresses and all the everyday ones are to be made in the house. If I am not to take a hat to Cheshire what shall I wear in the train going up? We should not be allowed to take our new things for the holidays if we wanted to. Have you used the waggonette yet or is it kept to be looked at? Are you going to Cheshire this spring? It is beautiful, bright, sharp, sunny weather now and quite inspiriting! Only 4 weeks tomorrow before the holidays and next Thursday we leave off lessons till the Tuesday after so that will be a nice little break. Madame Bodda has bronchitis so Mr B did not come on Wednesday. Nasty little man it is the second lesson this term I have missed but happily you only pay by the lesson!! Goodbye my dearest mother. Heaps of love to you both.

Your very loving
  Edith.

Strathallan
March 25th 1875

My dearest Mother

The reason my letter was a day behind was because the servant did not take them in time for the post but it will not happen again! We are in a horrible state this afternoon with a lot of them going away till Monday and having had our callisthenics from 2.45 to 3.45 have now nothing to do until 5.30 when we go to Church. We have been going twice a day this week at 12 and at 6 – with a heavier lunch in the middle of the day and a hybrid meal (as Miss E calls it) at 7 between tea and dinner. We shall only be eleven here until Monday afternoon when they come back in time for dancing. The hats for everyday will be neat, pretty, shady brown ones to match the dresses. I have been measured for my dress and I think it will be very nice. I thought I might have it done as they must all be done before the holiday. The everyday ones are all to be done before the Sunday ones are touched. Where is Edward's photo? I must have my brooch sent here when it comes may I not? Ferdie has sent me a photo of the 'dearest dog' but it is to be returned. He is a beauty and no mistake. I had better wait till next term to be photoed and there is no particular hurry is there before then? Kathleen must doctor my poor hair before I care to be immortalized!! Ought not the Malabar to be in by this time? *Please* let my brooch be sent me when it comes. I cannot wait till July to see it can I?

    Very best love
        Your own loving
           Edith.

                    Strathallan
                March 27th 1875

My dearest Mother

  Here we are eleven of us muddling along in a lazy sort of way! Yesterday we went to Church morning and evening and tomorrow shall do ditto and I am going out shopping with Sancto this afternoon to get some fineries for Kathleen and a belt for myself as the bind of my serge has come to pieces. In fact the whole dress is gradually disintegrating and how it will hang together for 19 days longer I cannot think! However Sancto has patched it up 'beautiful' and put the pocket in another place so I suppose it will last on somehow. It is most exquisite weather today and indeed has been for the last week and I do hope we shall have a bright Easter. I am going to get a book called 'The Great Tone Poets' for Kathleen's birthday present and shall take it up with me. It is a very nice book all about the great musicians and as I want to read it myself it is killing two birds with one stone!

    Your own very loving
        Edith.

                    Fort Monckton
            Wednesday 17th March 1875

My dear Father

  I return Edward's letters – it will be probably alright about Edith's thing you know – it begins with br- but I cant trust myself to spell it at this early hour of the day. The Malabar will not be in for a fortnight or three weeks at least. The 48th Depot is attached to the 58th hence Chaytor's movements are intelligible enough.

We were very nearly getting the 48th Depot in here but think we have managed to stave them off. Had the dearest dog photographed last week, four attempts, the man very keen to take him, only one was any value and he was not in the proper position then so I expect he will have to be done again and perhaps his good master also. All sorts of rumours flying about, 100 Marines and 100 Blue Jackets to be added to each company of Submarine Miners R.E. The Hood to be done away with. Some quiet spot in Ireland to be chosen for two months' manoeuvres with the torpedo battalion. I think the Hood is doomed. Our Mess has the appearance of being the most ruinous affair and yet we live very economically but meat at 11d a pound runs up butchers bills. I am not going to Cheshire which I think is a relief to Kathleen.

Love etc.

F.W.B.

Strathallan
April 1st 1875

My dearest Mother

Are you prepared to see Miss E in Cornwall in July or rather August? She cannot find anyone to go abroad with her and if she does not go is thinking of a tour in Cornwall so of course I have told her she must come to us for a few days. You will not mind it will you? For you see she cannot stay more than a week at most as she is going to do Cornwall and Dartmoor and the coast of Devonshire. When you write next do invite her properly as of course she will not take *my* invitation!! She is so jolly and talkative you will find it very easy to get on with her. They know I am to leave in the summer and it came about on this wise. On Sunday at dinner they were saying that I ought to learn to make Miss T's plum puddings and she said 'Yes, it is a great pity she will not be here to make them next winter'!! I stared so she tried to bluff it over and saying she did not know why she should say that as she did not know so then Miss E asked how long I was going to stay and I had to say till the summer. They evidently expected it and did not say I ought to stay on longer. Miss T says I shall not get much cooking on account of the hot weather but I shall make her give me her recipes to copy and *will* pick up *some* new dishes at all events. I had such a nice singing lesson on Wednesday. Mr

Bodda gave me an hour to make up for the missed lesson and took me up a note higher. He says my voice is much stronger and altogether it was a good lesson. The decorations at St Peter's were lovely. Just what Mr Murray describes as what he likes, the Chancel one mass of lovely exotic, camellias and azaleas and heaps of other flowers. Of course the rest of the Church was not much done except the font (white flowers moss and ferns) and the windows. The services were very nice and we had a very good sermon in the morning from the Vicar. When will that wretched old 'Malabar' come in!!

    Ever your own loving
      Edith.

                      Strathallan
                      April 8th 1875

    No, my dearest Mother, there were no questions for you to answer except that about the hat, but as you said I was not to take a hat to Cheshire I was naturally anxious to know what I was to wear on my head in the train. However, I suppose I had better send Kathleen an inventory of my wardrobe and she can tell me what she thinks I shall want – is not that businesslike? So the 'Malabar' has arrived at last! and I suppose I can look out for my parcel any day now though for the matter of that I have expected it by every post for the last fortnight. I hope Ferdie will be quick. I wrote to him to send it immediately he could lay hands on it but have not heard since. I suppose my 'funds' will arrive *some time* before next Friday. How frabjous if you are in Cheshire while I am. I shall be able to see your first impressions of dear old Comberbach! Of course after you have paid Kathleen a visit you will come to London for a few days to see the school and far more important business! to get my watch! Miss Theresa is downstairs today for the first time since Saturday having had a bad bronchial cold, a very near escape from bronchitis to judge from the cough, which is still very bad. Miss Entichnap has a very bad cold too. I am glad you like my dress. If we all get one (K as well) we shall be taken for three sisters all with specs too! No more now as there is nothing to say.

    Your own loving
      Edith.

Strathallan
April 10th 1875

My dearest Mother

At last my tiger's claws are arrived and they are splendid – set in gold which is all chased and such a lot of it, but it does not make them look *showy* or *vulgar* but only *handsome*. You must come to Cheshire and see them. There are two sets of earrings which will make a lovely necklet on black velvet. I suppose you will bag some of them will you not. I am quite mad at the thought of next Friday and at my brooches too. Oh you must come and see them! Why have you not gone to Trethill? I shall not write again until next Saturday unless you want anything in particular. Must write to Edward before Thursday.

Your own loving
Edith.

Fort Monckton
11th April 1875

My dear Father

I had a letter written to you yesterday when I got yours so I burnt it. The Malabar arrived last Sunday and Edith's things were sent off and I have her acknowledgment this morning. What was your public dinner for, is it an annual thing? I don't remember hearing of it before. Chaytor gives a very good account of Edward who was alright and just off for another shoot. The Regiment moves to Secunderabad this autumn. I have let the Chatham business slide as I think it better to remain here. I shall have to go up for a few of their best matches and expect a heavy season for the pocket but it will or may be the last as they can't keep me at home much longer. We are beginning to be busy again but the weather bothers and delays us much. Had an afternoon's fishing near here last week and caught one trout, a very difficult ditch to fish anything under 10 inches being turned back. When do you go to Cheshire? I should have liked to hear cousin John's speech and am glad he is himself again. The papers are very warlike, I suppose they will be at it again shortly.

Yours etc.
F.W.B.

Comberbach House
April 17th 1875

My dearest Mother

Your dear child arrived safely yesterday at Crewe a minute or two before I arrived accompanied by three companions bound for Liverpool so I had an opportunity of talking to them and was not very much impressed but Edith herself is looking very well and of course in tremendous spirits. I have only had one evening to judge but we had a good deal of music last night and she seemed to me to show good teaching. Her voice is not at all powerful but there are two or three very sweet notes and she has pretty pieces which she likes and seemed to play easily. To return to the singing – clear and good enunciation. Miss Theresa wants her to write to you to know if for the next term she may have two hours music lessons instead of one but she does not wish it and I do not think it would be good for her. I do not think she would be able to arrange sufficient practise to profit by such long lessons. Do not write to Miss Theresa but only tell us what you think about it. Now about Edith's watch. We fully hoped to be in London in June for a fortnight and I should think (but will ask Willie) that it would be better to get it there than in Manchester as the latter is a very dear place and I feel rather disposed to devote the money you would not let me spend on her drawing lessons in getting her a gold bracelet or a good locket for a birthday present as she is to leave school soon and I will find out about a book for your present and order it. But you will be coming here yourself and then we can see about it. We expect you the week after next. I hope I have told you all you wanted to know Edith would have written but I preferred doing so. We are going into Northwich to fetch Willie presently.

Much love to you both
Ever your affectionate daughter
Kathleen.

Comberbach House
April 20th 1875

My dearest Mother

At last I am going to write to you but I am afraid I have been rather a long time. I had a very pleasant journey on Friday, the only drawback being the *dust* which was *dreadful*. We have suddenly jumped to summer here and of course I did not bring the right clothes thinking it was far too cold and now have only my old serge to wear for routing about in dusty places! However this heat cannot last and the country is dreadfully in want of rain. I certainly think it will require a great deal of resolution on your part to trust yourself and *that portmanteau* by rail again! Could you not take it in the carriage with you? I am not going to take my tiger's claws back to school and I do not think they are safe in this nasty Cheshire so you see it behoves you to come and fetch them as of course they must not be sent by post again. My black and white skirt for the black polonaise is being kilted and it looks so nice. I am not at all sure that I would not as soon wait till next year for my watch if that means Father getting it, but Kathleen seems to think she may as well get it in London so if you would rather I did not wait she is quite ready to do it. She says, and I think so too, that I had better get a plain gold bracelet with Aunt Edith's £5. I do not know yet what I want for my birthday. We did fix on a pair of little gold or silver 'solitaire' studs, but Kathleen got me such a nice pair of plain pearl ones in Northwich that I do not want any better ones. We drove to the station yesterday in the pony carriage to see the children arrived alright and brought Nelly back with us while Alice and Sarah went in the fly. They seem very nice girls but Nelly is too affectionate always hugging Kathleen until I get quite jealous!!! They are both of them taller than either of us! and now I really must go and make myself agreeable. We are going to pick primroses this morning and 'tea' with Aunt H this afternoon and tomorrow we are going to see Tabley Old Hall.

Best love from us both to you both
  Ever your own loving
   Edith.

         Comberbach House
          April 24th 1875

My dearest Mother

As your son-in-law prettily expresses it 'your intended coming gives me unutterable felicity' and I do hope the portmanteau will not be lost. You had better go in the guard's van with it!!! I want you to bring up my 'book' book, the one for putting down the books I have read in, also all my white silk ties (that means about one I think!). It is past eleven so I cannot write much as we are to meet so soon it is not worth while to write a description of our wild doings this week! Willie is able to stay until 7.15 tomorrow morning and it is very nice to have him although for so short a time.

Sunday. Such a fog this morning though now it has cleared off nicely again and the sun is shining. Kathleen is playing some of Sankey's hymns. Do you not like them? I think some are so pretty. I think you will like the pieces I have and I am so glad you are coming before I leave. Miss Shakerley is coming down this afternoon to go to Church with us. I do not mind them separately but it is quite too much for my equanimity to go up to Belmont and encounter all the party. We all went up on Friday to tea and Miss S and the two Miss Maxwells walked up with us so we were four couples one behind the other just like a school!! I am sure people will say Mrs Fox has set up a young ladies seminary!! No time for more as it is time to dress for Church.

Your own loving
Edith.

Douglas Hotel
Aberdeen
Sunday April 25th 1875

My dear Mother

On Friday at 2.30 p.m. I took myself by train from Stokes Bay and after travelling many miles arrived here at 12.30 yesterday (midday). I think I told you I was here as Acting Inspector for the Kensington Science and Art Schools people. My duties being to visit the schools at which the examinations are held between the hours of 7 and 10 every evening in Aberdeen.

Aberdeen is built of granite and a good clean town what I have seen of it, of course the people are Scottish and they talk incoherently when they do talk, as a rule they are silent and never laugh. Of their manner the less said the better, their Sunday customs are going to Kirk and they mostly carry prayerbooks and then walking up and down Union Street for ever and ever by sexes, never the sound of a horse or the whistle of a train on the

Sabbath, up and down, up and down a continuous stream, the men smoke and spit on the pavement and the womens' dresses mop it up. (this will probably disgust you as it did me but I am writing facts so it must stay). There are a good many red heads about and black eyes but the faces as a rule if homely are dry and uninteresting. The Scottish cap I am glad to see is very fashionable but I am disappointed in bagpipes and kilts, scarcely anybody but English tourists wearing the latter. This place is chockfull of commercial travellers and they prate and drivvel and lie to their hearts content and I have the coffee room to myself. Tomorrow there is another fellow coming down to help me so we shall divide up the county and then gang our ain gait I suppose. I shall start from here next Saturday week and if I can get there pass Sunday with Kathleen returning to Stokes Bay on the Monday. I hope to get some fishing some where but the rivers are very low.

Yours etc.

    F.W.B.

Douglas Hotel
Aberdeen
Sunday May 2nd 1875

My dear Father

Here I am back again for another Sunday in Aberdeen. I have been north as far as Frasersburgh which I found dull and the country as tame and uninteresting as anything I have yet seen anywhere, nothing whatever to relieve the monotony of an intolerably slow railway journey. I had a couple of days at Ellon about an hour northwards from here where I managed to catch the wily trout in the Ythan. This week I go to Kintore I expect for a day or two and then on to Alford where I expect to see finer scenery and have some more fishing, starting southwards on Saturday morning and hoping to reach Manchester that night. I shall not be able to do Edinburgh, and intend to pass Sunday at Comberbach. If there is no getting on from Manchester on Sunday morning I shall have to give it up as I must be at Stokes Bay on Monday. Of course this is a change but one finds oneself looking anxiously about at times in the hope of seeing a face one has seen before and a feeling of boredom now and then supervenes, however it will be all over in a week and when I get back I shall wish it had been a longer trip I suppose. Spaight another of our fellows on the same business has been with me a little during the week but he has gone now and besides a few commercial friends I am alone, we meet on the way South and the fellow has just been in to say the mail is going so I must shut up. Love to all. I've managed to catch a hearty cold, the East wind I suppose, but its better today.

    Yours in haste
       F.W.B.

                              Strathallan
                            May 4th 1875

My dearest Mother

I got on alright yesterday, met Nina at Crewe and got to London about six as the train was late. At Euston we found two of the servants on the platform as there were three different parties arriving about the same time. Miss Theresa has been ill again in the holidays and looks very white and 'pulled down' but does everything as usual. The dining room has been painted green and it looks so clean and cool. We have been for a walk in the Gardens today and it was so hot and close but notwithstanding the heat I should not like to have left for it and come back again after. I am in a different room this term with different girls and I am not quite sure if I approve of the change or not. The English governess Miss Jefferson looks tolerably nice but as yet is dreadfully shy and nervous I think. Fraulein seems very cheery and nice and I should think an immense improvement on Frau Boese. Only one new girl has arrived yet and she looks bright and nice but is only 14. Mr Green comes this afternoon. I have not found I have left anything behind yet!

    With love to you
       Believe me
          Your very loving
          Edith.

                              Strathallan
                            May 5th 1875

My dearest Mother

Thank you for your nice long letter which arrived this morning.

We have had our calisthenics today and are to have two lessons a week (instead of one dancing and one calisthenics) for five weeks so tell Kathleen that the last lesson will be next Monday month so if she wants to see them she will have to be up by then!! Miss Theresa is going to get Confirmation dresses for most of the girls and my pique is rather too grand and bunchy I think so if she will get me a nice soft plain lawn or anything soft (I do not know what material) would you like me to have a new one? I will not have *muslin* it is far too dressy and I only thought I had better have a simpler one than my pique. I do not care I only want to know what you would like. Of course if Miss T says I ought to have a new one I must, but I do not think she would make me. Now I really have no more to say and I have written every day since Monday! Please give the enclosed to Kathleen and Miss Gyp for me!!

Your own loving
    Edith.

Strathallan
May 15th 1875

My dearest Mother

Just going to hear Verdi's 'Requiem' at the Albert Hall. A friend has sent Miss E the tickets. Must post you a note before going as I did not write on Thursday but will write again and post on Monday. My hat is only a guinea and I enclose a pattern of my dress. Only just knew I had to go – am rather vexed as I wanted to write but daresay it will be nice.

Your own
    Edith.

Comberbach House
15th May 1875

As no letter has come from you this morning my dearest Mother I've concluded you had a successful and satisfactory journey reaching Plymouth in time to get a night's rest. But we were so lonely and dull last night and have never ceased regretting your departure – it was too short a change to do you as much good as you wanted. I hope you will feel more benefit from it in a few days be sure you tell me whether you get a tonic that does you good. Willie and his baggage have gone off but we rather fear it is blowing up for rain, it looks threatening, the heat is not nearly so oppressive and there were a few spots of rain this morning. Do you see Emily Molesworth has a son?

Much and best love

Ever your affectionate daughter

Kathleen T. Fox.

Strathallan

May 15th 1875

My dearest Mother

We have just come back from hearing the Requiem which I liked very much. Fraulein did not like the crowd at all but we got on alright and went to the Albert Memorial. The Duke and Duchess of Edinburgh were there and one of the little she 'Waleses' who was a naughty little girl would not sit down till her governess had told her several times. I had to wear my best toggery but do not think I have damaged it yet. My dress is a *perfect* fit and very prettily made with a very narrow piping of grey satin instead of the orthodox pink. My hat is trimmed with grey silk, lined with pink and two pink wild roses behind, no feathers and only a guinea. I am so pleased to have got it plainer. Next Saturday we may go to Bushy Park to see the chestnuts but of course we may not. I will write to you on Thursday as usual for the future but as I did not know for certain where you would be I thought I would not write to you until today. It is furiously hot here already and we have begun ice and are hoping for thunder. All the seats are out in the garden and it is quite furnished. I have not asked Miss T about my dress yet but I do not think I shall have another. Would you like me to get anything in the way of a black cape? *I need not.* I am sorry you did not stay away longer but of course you did not like to let Father go home by himself and I hope you are all the better for the change. No more to say. Please tell Kathleen I will write to her on Saturday not before.

Best love to you both

From your own loving

Edith.

Strathallan
May 20th 1875

My dearest Mother

Yes, you did pay me for the book alright and I think that was the only business question in your last letter. I am so sorry you did not go to Aunt Lily and that you have had so short a holiday. Never mind next time when we all go to Cheshire together you shall stay behind with Kathleen and I will keep house for Father! It would be fun and I would take such care of him. Do not trouble to write to me on Sunday and I suppose you will write for Thursday, and two letters so close together will be rather difficult to fill. I did a lily of the valley from nature last Tuesday and do not care about copies a bit now. I am so longing to get a rosebud to do from nature but unless I get a flower by chance I have to be content with artificial ones which are just the same practice. Have you noticed a misspelling in Ferdie's letter? Tell Father I have an Italian song and it is very pretty. Miss Theresa is going away tomorrow until Monday. I am very sorry as it is rather slow without her. Besides we always have our places at table changed on Sunday and if she is not here I am afraid we shall have to stay in the same places for another week. I am by Fraulein and she is such a pig (excuse the word but no other will do) that I do not know how I shall stand it! I never wish to go to Germany, *never* this Fraulein has come straight from there so has not got a scrap of English manners and German ones are disgusting. Just every vulgarity that one has been told not to do, she does, and it makes me ill to see her! All my good impressions of her are getting replaced by bad ones which I know is very wrong but it is hard work not to be angry.

Heaps of love to you both.

Your own loving
Edith.

Strathallan
May 26th 1875

Wednesday is to be the letter-writing evening in future my dearest Mother, as the two days will not be so close together. Tomorrow I am going to a concert in St. James' Hall to hear Sims Reeves!! Does it not come beautifully on my birthday! Mr Bodda

215

has given three of us such a nice trio called 'My Lady the Countess' and it is a most snappy conversation between two young ladies, one of whom has got the husband they *both* wanted and is a 'Countess' and someone else a Governess I should think who scolds them both. I believe it is Italian in reality from 'The Secret Marriage'. It is very pretty and good and we have to sing it at a little 'swarry' (see Pickwick) which Mr B wants to get up. I am the Countess and am grand and disdainful at the other girl's spitefulness! It will be too ridiculous to have to sing – I think we shall all laugh in the middle! I look forward to July, much as I like the school itself and mistresses. It is very difficult to know how to act for there are some girls who do much harm and hardly a day passes without little worries and complications which come a good deal on us three monitresses to settle. There is nothing *bad* by any means but still any amount of little worries such as I never had before last term. Very good for my character I expect and do not think it is any bad thing!! Miss T has seen my cloth jacket since I wrote last and says I do not want a cape at all so that is alright as I did not want one. I shall ask her about my Confirmation dress at the first opportunity. I believe we are to have 'mulled muslim' if you know what that is but I will ask if I may wear my pique.

27th. Thank you both for your nice long letters and the lovely roses which arrived quite fresh and I am now going to paint one. Had several presents but will tell you on Saturday.

Heaps of best of love
  Ever your very loving
    Edith aged 17 years!!!

              Strathallan
            May 29th 1875

My very *dearest* Mother

I wish there were some other way of expressing 'many happy returns of the day' but as there is not I wish you *very many very happy* returns of your birthday and please accept every other good wish that can be thought of. Kathleen tells me we are to get your present when she comes up and I hope we shall be successful. I hope Monday will be a brighter day is for it has been raining and is quite cold. The concert on Thursday was delicious. Henry

Leslie's choir is most wonderfully well trained and sings so well. Sims Reeves actually did not disappoint us and sang 'The Message' and 'Tom Bowling'. He would not be encored though the people did their best to make him and hissed when he would not! Thank you very much for the promise of sleeve links, they will be very useful indeed. Do you not think I could have a single watch chain? Kathleen says she has asked you and I can hardly explain what I mean but it ought to do just as well and would not be so expensive. Also I like one with a cross piece for the buttonhole and this combines that advantage and the eyeglass piece. I may go out at nine in the morning the day Kathleen wants me and I dare say might stay till Monday but she has not room and I want my watch more than anything else!! I believe we are to be dressed alike for the Confirmation in white muslin (I hope not *clear*) made very simply. Do you really mind a veil? Because they are only net and it will be much nicer to be covered up a little and as to its being finery, really I do not think it likely I shall be thinking about how I look. Mr Byng gives us such nice classes and I like the questions he gives us to do. We always go into the gymnasium on Sunday afternoons and do them. It is very nice here altogether and Miss E gives us very nice classes too. It is getting very near the time now; only Wednesday fortnight. Oh! I had quite forgotten about my presents. I had a carved wood bookslide, two frames, a travelling ink bottle (Russian leather) a 'Christian Year', a little double scent bottle and a beautiful little Russian leather prayer book and hymn book in a case with a chain to hook it on to the belt – all from the girls here. Then I heard from Kathleen, Ferdie, Edith Hayhurst, Elsie and Miriam so I was well off was not I? I must write lots of letters this afternoon so with best love to you both

Ever your most loving
little daughter Edith.

Comberbach House
Northwich
Cheshire
May 29th 1875

My dearest Mother
I am writing before my time to wish you (in the ordinary

phraseology) 'very many happy returns of the day' for this ought to reach you on your birthday – and you must please understand the commonplace words in their very fullest meaning. You know we have no birthday present yet for you but I hope those candlesticks may be forthcoming in a short time and that they will be what you would like. Willie took me such a pretty drive yesterday in the pony carriage to see an old Cheshire House and we found some curious marsh plant. Can you tell what it is? The weather was very showery (in fact has been all the week) and we were pursued by a thunder storm but got home a quarter of an hour before a deluge of rain. Willie having nearly killed poor Gyp by making her run after us! She slept the rest of the day!

    With much love to you both

        Believe me

            Your affectionate daughter

            Kathleen T. Fox

P.S. Tell me if there is anything else you would like me to do in London for you.

                Fort Monckton

                June 2nd 1875

My dear Mother

    Your feelings must be very much hurt by my not writing to congratulate you on your birthday before now, the only one of course who allowed his mother to pass unnoticed and forgotten, but my many and important duties have so engrossed my time I haven't been able to write before. Please accept my good wishes now. I send back Edward's letter and I've nothing to say. The best rackets I can get and the only ones from the Co-operative Stores are 12/6 each. I shall be happy to present you with a couple, I don't think my old rackets are light enough for ladies to use but you are welcome to them if you think fit. A full set of lawn tennis would be about £5 but the other fittings you can manage for yourself. I will write at once when you decide and order the rackets to be sent you. We have a new section here which completes the Company and adds another officer, we could easily have got on without these additions, as we are only in each others way. I go to Chatham for four days next week and shall not be here till Saturday, Brompton Barracks will therefore find me till Thursday night. Friday and Saturday I shall be in town and may see Edith if she likes to get up very early on Saturday and come to the Academy.

Yours in haste

F.W.B.

Strathallan

June 9th 1875

My dearest Mother

Well I ought to get out on Saturday certainly. This morning a letter arrived from 'the dear boy' asking if I could 'take him to the Academy on Saturday to see the pretty pictures'! Well! happily Miss E had heard from Kathleen also this morning and so I wrote to her at 42 Duke Street Grosvenor Square (where she will arrive tomorrow) to say that she must let him know where to go as she is coming early to fetch me and I told him that in case he did not hear from her to go to Duke Street. It is a fearful muddle but I hope it will come straight and if we all meet it will be *splendid*. If Ferdie wants to go to the Academy I do not know if we can get the watch but I have sent your letter to Kathleen so that she may take it in before Saturday. Last Saturday eight of us (all who had not gone out with friends) drove to Richmond Park in the afternoon, had dinner there and got home to tea at 9.30. It was a lovely day not too hot and we enjoyed ourselves immensely. It was all kept quiet until after lunch on Saturday and Miss Theresa had arranged everything so nicely. The Confirmation dresses are very simple and pretty, mulled muslin at 2/- a yard and the skirt is to be of a thicker material at 1/6 a yard as that will come for an under petticoat afterwards. Miss T told me all the prices carefully and I was so amused! I think you must forget that I got my cape *two* years ago wore it the first summer at home and at Putney last summer in best and *common* all the summer and now it is getting all brown and frayed and really I think has done good service. I do not want one here, it is only a question of wanting one when I come home. I think we are to go down in the crypt soon for dinner and lunch for it is furnished all in readiness for us but the heat is not very great now. There was a little thunder and rain this afternoon but very little. Only six weeks more so you must please excuse me tonight if this is too short but I have only an hour to get my Saturday letters written. I shall be dreadfully sorry to leave the girls here, some of them at least but oh! I shall not be sorry to leave school though I daresay these 'little worries' *are* very good for me. I cannot tell you about them by letter but am looking forward to telling you about them when I come home. I have already been thinking how to arrange my furniture. I may keep my little room may I not? At any rate for a little while.

    Best of love to you both
        From your own loving
            Edith.

                      42 Duke Street
                    Grosvenor Square
                    June 19th 1875

My dearest Mother

No! I know you do not like short notes but I really could not write more on Wednesday and I do not suppose you will mind another little note today and then I will try not to be guilty of any more such irregularities! I will not ask any questions! Well, Kathleen has given you a sketch of our doings today so I must only fill up a little. When we got to the Park after hearing the Band play at the Horticultural Gardens we met Mr Wise and Gertrude (to our great disgust) *riding*! The horses were fidgety and so we only saw them for about two minutes and Miss Wise was too tired to come. It was very *horrid* of Mr Wise to insist on Gertrude's riding for it was his doing and not hers. Miss Cooper and Mrs Puzey were very 'jolly' and as there is no help for it, it is no good being unhappy about it, so I am quite excited over the *bonnet* and the train! I decided after all to have a lovely little £20 watch which I hope will be what you and Father like. I like it better than any other and chose it quite myself and without any idea of having it 'because you would like it' but at the same time I think you both will like it for it is English and very good, and also a very pretty ladies' shape and *thin*.

    20th. Today we have been to the Temple Church and heard Dr. Vaughan in the morning and in the afternoon to St. Saviour's (the Deaf and Dumb Church) where we heard Mr Holland preach. It

220

was so curious to see it all being translated by signs by a clergyman who evidently belonged to the Church. John arrived just before lunch and stayed to go to St. Saviour's with us. Miss Connell came in just as we were starting too but we only saw her for a few minutes. Kathleen is going to take me back to Strathallan in time for calisthenics at 8.30 tomorrow morning and she is going to stay and see our performances and then Miss E has suggested our going to the South Kensington Museum afterwards as she will give me till lunchtime. Best love from us all.

Believe me
　　　Your ever loving
　　　　　Edith.

P.S. Please send me the date of my Baptism on a postcard.

　　　　　　　　　　　　　　　　　　　　Strathallan
　　　　　　　　　　　　　　　　　　　June 21st 1875

My dearest Mother

As Saturday seems to be what you chiefly wished to know about, though I suppose Kathleen has told you all about it already, I had better begin with that. Kathleen came to fetch me at 9 and when we got to Duke Street we found Mr Ferdinando there before us. Then we went to the Academy (where F left us about 12 to go to Lord's) and we had lunch there and then went about the watch. Back to Duke Street and then the Christy Minstrels and dinner finished the day and they both brought me back here at 9. I am going out again on Saturday for the day. The service this morning was such a beautiful one I wish you had been there. The Bishop was so nice and kind and it was not a very large Confirmation. We are going to Church this evening so I must write now and have not time for a long letter but I am sure you will not mind just this once. I should be so much happier and so much more glad to come home if I were sure you did not think that I do not love you as I ought. I know you think so from what you said in your last letter and as a proof it is not true I can tell you that those two lines hurt and grieved me more than anything and you do not know how many things have happened to trouble us this last week. But do not think I am unhappy about that now for I feel happier than I ever did before and I do hope that I may be a better daughter to you and Father for the future. It is post time so with best love to you both.

Believe me
    Your own loving child
        Edith.

                 London
                 Monday

My dearest Mother

The way you and Edith take things to heart about small expressions in each others letters is perfectly incomprehensible to me. She never alluded to the subject to me nor showed me your letter so I really am quite in the dark about that and it seems to me those things should be passed over as molehills grow into mountains on the smallest provocation. As to her having had so much to 'trouble' her it is utter nonsense and I most sincerely hope you will *not* write to Miss Enticknap. It would do a great deal of harm. Because some of the answers to Confirmation questions were written badly and without stops (hers were alright) and naturally commented on by Miss E and because some girls in *another* bedroom do not get on as well as they should do and others do not keep order as well as for their age they should do and because Miss E and Miss Theresa told her so she did not talk enough do you think that enough to make yourself miserable about? That literally is all and it is the most absurd nonsense I ever heard to make so much of it but she broods over things and fancies she has real troubles and sorrows. When they really come she will see how foolish she is and I have talked to her about it. She ought to be perfectly happy and I can see no reason why she is not and to tell you the truth from always having had an early happy life I do not think she realises the force of the words she uses and that she makes you fancy she is much more miserable than she is. She looks perfectly well.

In great haste
    Ever your affectionate
        K.T.F.

Strathallan
June 23rd 1875

My dearest Mother

Kathleen has been here today to say goodbye and bring my bonnet and watch. The former I think is very pretty especially in front and is just the shape that suits me. My chain was not quite finished when Kathleen was there so it is to be sent this evening. My spectacles are to arrive tomorrow. I have had to manage two pairs before now so shall get on alright I expect. Are you going into mourning for Emily Pepper? Kathleen quite frightened me by coming in black today. How very sudden it seems to have been. I should think everyone was glad for poor Miss Ley. Had she been worse lately or was the end unexpected? Everyone here is in a great state of excitement over the Lawn Tennis which has arrived this evening. I have not seen it played yet. We have sung our trio together for the first time today with Mr Bodda, it is such fun to see the little man's faces!! I have such a pretty song 'Living Poems' the words by Longfellow, music by Sullivan. Mr Pinch the Cambridge examiner is coming on the 7th and 8th so everyone is working very hard except me! I am sure you will not be sorry I am not doing them when I tell you that accomplishments and languages are allowed to be put aside for the English cramming! My little watch is such a beauty! I shall be afraid to wear it!

Best love to you both
Your own loving
Edith

Fort Monckton
June 27th 1875

My dear Mother

You must think I neglect you awfully I'm afraid, I have just seen a letter from Kathleen or rather with her writing outside and 'to be returned to M J B at once' on the envelope dated June 14th, of course its one of Edward's letters, and what the hurry about returning them is I could never find out, but still its bad not paying some attention to one's immediate relatives' wishes, however, I send it now. As usual I haven't had a moment to spare to write home. We have an inspection coming on and that gives a lot of early risings and extra work, then I play cricket once or twice a week and have to make up the time other days. Next week we are going to start the electric light business and that will keep me up to one or two every night for a month, so they say. They have paid me for my Scottish trip and I notched about £20 by that transaction so it was worth the fortnight's leave. I expect to go to Chatham for three or four days in a fortnight from this for a little cricket, I can't make any runs here.

Yours
    F.W.B.

                          Comberbach House
                          June 28th 1875

My dearest Mother

Only a few lines today for I have been so long and busy over blankets and linen with Agnes. I can tell you no further particulars about E. Pepper. We *imagine* it to be apoplexy but know nothing and we have not seen the Rector who went to the funeral; nor has Miss Pepper written to Carrie, nor Mr Pepper to Willie; and the servant who announced it to Aunt Harper spoke of her 'falling asleep in her arms' but no real particulars. Edith's mind is much disturbed now (and no wonder) by poor Nina being telegraphed for on Saturday her father having died suddenly in Scotland. I like the way Miss E spoke of Edith's work. Why she gave up English for her and made her devote her time to accomplishments as she knew she would have no opportunity of getting masters. And she said Edith was the one girl in the class who showed any intelligence or interest in her History reading. So she believes she will take that up afterwards but I quite agree and Edith now says that she is leaving school too soon. However we shall have to see what we can do. Consider Edith is better now but she seems to have been suffering from indigestion. Now I really must say goodbye.

    Much and best love
        Ever your affectionate daughter
        Kathleen T. Fox.

                              Strathallan
                           June 30th 1875

My dearst Mother

This has been rather a sad week for last Saturday a telegram arrived to say that one of the girls (Nina) father had died that morning. He had been ill for a very long time but she had not heard of his being worse and he was in Scotland *without* his wife when he died. Nina went off directly and they only told her he was very ill as if she had known the truth she could never have gone that long way all alone. She is coming back on Monday but I am afraid only to say goodbye as they will not be very well off and there are 11 or 12 children. She is the most popular girl here, so bright and sunny and so *nice* altogether, and we all miss her terribly. I have been in her room this term so know a good deal about her and it is very dreary without her.

It strikes me forcibly that I shall never get all my belongings into my present boxes, much less my train! What am I to get if I want something more? I have 5 hats and a bonnet to bring! and two little deal boxes to bring them in and they will only carry two hats and a bonnet! You see I have my summer uniform etc and all my books! Oh dear! you will have to send a cart to the station or the hay wagon! By-the-bye I hope the hay is alright. My spectacles have arrived this morning so at last I believe all my affairs are collected. I suppose I am to be photographed or you would have told me if you had changed your mind and I shall ask to go next Wednesday or Thursday when the examinations will be going on here. Everyone is cramming hard for Mr Pinches I do not think it is such an idea to stuff everything into one's head at last minute for it always goes out again directly after and this cramming is very bad for them all I am sure. I shall ask to have an hour's singing lesson next Wednesday as the others will not be able to go and I missed one – Mr Bodda must come for me and if he comes he may as well give me an hour. Our trio will fall to the ground now just as we have learnt it for Nina takes the contralto part and she will not have the spirit to sing it when she comes back. Yes, write up for a new black silk and we will have our finery down together. I keep my watch going though I do not wear it and it has not gained or lost a minute, I believe, since last Wednesday, it is such a darling. The chain is most satisfactory also. Have I told you that the holidays begin on the 20th? At least I believe we shall all go on that day. I shall be *very* sorry to leave here as I like the girls so much. Thanks for Ferdie's letter. 'The dearest dog' seems to have come off with flying colours.

>With best love to you both
>>Believe me
>>>Ever your own loving
>>>>Edith.

>>>>>Strathallan House
>>>>>Wetherby Road
>>>>>South Kensington
>>>>>July 3rd 1875

My dearest Mother

Just a line to say will you send me 10/- over my travelling money as my funds are rather low, and gloves etc. have walked off with more than that of my money this term.

I have just written to Barnes the photographer to make an appointment for Thursday so if you have any particular wishes about it you must let me know before that day. I was thinking of only having my head taken but perhaps he will take me in two or three different ways and he takes great pains to do you well, they say, and the photos I have seen of his are *very* good and only 10/6 or 12/6 a dozen! Please ask William to put the boat in the pond a week before I come so as to launch her.

>With best love
>>Ever your own loving
>>>Edith.

>>>>>Comberbach House
>>>>>Northwich
>>>>>July 5th 1875

My dearest Mother

What was it made Papa ill at Bodmin last week? The closeness of the Court? Was it only faintness or something like what he had in January? When, if I remember rightly, he became ill also at the Sessions – and is he better now? Be sure you tell me. The weather has been close and oppressive or rather I should say, depressing – without being ever warm but, we had a day's rain on Saturday and now the glass is at 'fair' with lovely blue sky, haze, and fresh breeze. The very thing for the hay which here was all cut on

Thursday. I have just had a message that strawberries currants and raspberries all want gathering. Mrs Capper alas goes after luncheon and the new cook arrives – a teetotaller with very good moral character and 'a good worker' but we shall see what her cookery is! Age 34 – so I have done nothing but collect clothes, pots, pans and plates and shall have more to do but the new housemaid seems to understand her work tho' I do not so far care much about her. However, I do not grieve in the least about losing Agnes – she was not a very good servant and I think we shall get so accustomed to changing soon that we shall think nothing of it. I should like to see Edith's room – but there is the comfort – in Cornwall things will keep clean until I can come and see them – here it would be different! Were not the accounts of the floods in France dreadful? We doubt however whether we do not pity the islanders more – they are so far from help and may be starved before it reaches them. We have had some nice roses but everything has been so dashed by the continual rain that the margueritte alone seems to survive. Tell me how you as well as Papa are. Much love to you both

Ever your affectionate daughter
Kathleen. T. Fox.

Strathallan House
Wetherby Road
South Kensington
July 7th 1875

My dearest Mother

Those horrid Sessions! That is all I can say. I hope Father is better and that you have not knocked yourself up about him. If you do *I shall come home!* As after next Wednesday I shall have finished with the Masters so in case you want someone to look after you both *I can come*, remember! No, do not let him go again to be Chairman. Do you know Mary Brune has had scarlet fever? They have been shut up in quarantine not able to go to the balls etc., but I do not know where they are now. Miss Theresa does not like me to go to Marshall and Snelgrove's for a cape as there has been a report of scarlet fever in their house and besides it is all about – 60 cases in Portman Square alone I believe and we are not allowed to go out at all on Saturdays now for it is very much about on different sides of us. Still I do not think we are likely to get it here and I have heard nothing about it the last few days. I have had my first cooking lesson today and made lots of things. I am going to have a book like Miss T's and she will mark the recipes that will do for me. I have seen her make paste today and I have to do it on Saturday. The examinations are going on and for your comfort I think I am equal to the questions they have had if I had studied like they have. The questions are much the same as but fewer and I think easier than we had at Putney. I have had another Italian song and such a nice singing lesson from Mr Bodda today. Our trio has come to an untimely end owing to poor Nina. She came back yesterday but of course it is very sad to see her and terribly trying at first for her. Please excuse this short note but I have *business* to attend to.

    Your own loving
       Edith.

                                        Fort Monckton
                                      July 15th 1875

My dear Mother

    There I hope the enclosed please you, now take your pick and send them back, with the one you admire most, marked so that I can get some printed for you. Got back from Chatham last night, an unlucky match, they 451 and we 130 for three wickets. A satisfactory termination of a two days match. Floods of rain and a gale of wind on here, a yacht belonging to one of our fellows aground just outside, getting dashed to pieces as fast as she can, everybody performing deeds of valour such as swimming off in the sea with a rope to fasten somewhere in the hope of saving her, launching boats and getting them turned once on top of them, legs and arms surf and yells, except me, I do the thinking and do it well. I think she will go to pieces if she aint took off very soon. Sorry to hear the Squire is out of sorts and think he is quite right to give up Bodmin, hope he has had no relapse – send the photos back soon as I want them printed. I can't write more now the times are too stirring.

    Yours
       F.W.B.

Strathallan House
Wetherby Road
South Kensington
July 16th 1875

My dearest Mother

I am very glad you have decided as you have. I have been hoping you would say 'no' as it would have been rather uncomfortable however much I should like to have seen them. If Mrs P can come it will be much better. Miss T wishes me to go by the first train so unless I happen to miss it I shall be at G. R. (D.V.) by 6.24. I should like to go to the Confirmation on Tuesday if it is convenient. No more till we meet.

Your own loving
Edith.

Fort Monckton
Gosport
July 25th 1875

My dear Mother,

I enclose a photo of myself, Chermie and the dearest dog, please return it as it isn't mine and it won't give you much of a notion of the admirable qualities and breeding of the quadruped, still it is better than nothing. His own photo won't go into any envelope I have so you will have to wait for that till my next appearance when you will be able to compare the real and the picture together. We have the usual awful weather and at length by dint of great exposure to a burning sun I have succeeded in catching a fearful cold. We are once more with inventions of all nationalities and their electric lights and they succeed admirably in turning night into day in more causes than one. I shall probably turn up about the end of September but am afraid the late rains will have put an end to a lot of partridges. I hope it has not damaged the corn. Have you used your new carriage yet or is it still allowed to remain in the coach house? I have now told you all the news, see you send back the photos and tell me if you want to start lawn tennis. We have put it up here and make great progress by dint of hard practise on Sundays.

Yours
F.W.B.

229

New Granby Barracks
August 4th 1875

My dear Mother

Nothing could have been more unfortunate than the Ladies Day. When we arrived on the ground on Wednesday people were trying to collect the tattered remains of the tent which were flapping in the wind, it was blowing very hard and the tent, an old one, could not stand it and was done for. Well, then they decided, quite wrongly I think, to have the dance at Lostwithiel, there was another tent there which would have covered the floor easily as I proved by measurement, still they said there would be nowhere to put the supper and settled to have it at the Talbot, wrote to the papers and telegraphed or wrote to most of the people they knew were coming, so that on the following day the Ladies Day, tickets were sent back, people wanted their money returned, about 20 turned up on the ground and I came away by the 6.9 train so don't know anything at all about the dance but don't think there could have been once 50 people, as no one came up by the train, save one party amongst whom, I think, I recognised Bessie Bull that was, Bessie something else now, anyhow we chatted and I don't know who else it was, but certainly wonderfully improved in looks, quite nice looking in fact, and altogether I enjoyed it, stayed with Robins, no one else there, very bad cricket, but met people one knew by name, Charles Sawle, young Kitson, Carey and so on. Don't know whether I shall induce the Skipper to come home next Friday and Saturday, but there is a possibility as he is immensely excited by my accounts of the fishing at Newquay, he may go to Guernsey before.

Yours ...

F.W.B.

On the 4th July 1975 Ferdinando Bennet wrote one of his earlier letters to his life-long friend Darwin.

Fort Monckton
Gosport
July 4th 1875

My dear Darwin

I suppose you are so darned proud now you've been round the

230

world that you have quite forgotten my existence. When you do write don't say a word about your travels or your failures, they will keep till your book appears, so dry up – what I want to tell you is that I expect to be at Chatham next Monday Tuesday and Wednesday July 12, 13, 14 and shall expect to see you there on one of the days for a few minutes just to see what you look like as I have quite forgotten you. Poor old Cardew – shipped off to Bermuda about three months ago. I know you hate long letters and as all my news will keep just as well as yours I shall dry up also.

Yours etc.

F W Bennet

Fort Monckton
Gosport
July 9th 1875

Dear Darwin

I shall only be at Chatham Tuesday and Wednesday next so turn up on one of those days if you are likely to be civil. I don't want to see you if you talk like you write, you ain't a bit improved, I never saw such a slouch of a letter in my life and it ain't your writing, the spelling is all wrong and I can't make out half of it. I swear I believe you were drunk, you had much better start tomorrow for Fiji, no one wants you here in your present mood, so just sit down and see if you can write again a more cheerful letter. Come down here next year for a day or so. I have nothing to tell you about myself except that I play a good deal of cricket, and must now shut up as a lamp in the neighbourhood is making such a ghastly pooping noise I am in mortal terror of having my b ... y head blown off.

Yours etc.

F W Bennet.

Fort Monckton
Gosport
August 24th 1875

My dear Mother

I feel it is a long time since I wrote you a proper letter but it is so hot and sultry and the cricket season is so near an end that I have little time or inclination. I made 129 yesterday against Gentlemen of Sussex so have at last reached a century after very hard trying. Our fellows stayed in for two whole days at Chatham against the Zingari and made 724 and three more wickets to go down, an unparalleled feat. Our married subaltern Addison and Knight have started for 3 weeks yachting in a little boat. It has been dead calm ever since they started so they are probably about Ryde by this time. I'll send you an account or two. No peaches yet.

Yours etc.

F.W.B.

Victoria Hotel
Southport
Lancashire
September 16th 1875

My dearest Mother

We were very sorry to hear Mr Square's opinion of Edith's sight but it is such a good thing to know in time to prevent its getting worse and now the very fact of being allowed to read and write so little will develop her conversational powers. She cannot sit still and do nothing, she will be *obliged* to talk! After all it is not nearly so bad as though you lived in a town. She can drive about and get out a great deal and she likes that sort of thing and her mind will improve much more from a little read and well thought over than a great deal swallowed and nothing digested. But I am very sorry your eye is so weak. How I wish we were not so far away! And that I could read to you both. But poor Mrs Smith – I do pity her – and it seems to me that after all a trial which comes straight from God's hand like that of bad sight must be a trifle compared to a second sorrow of this kind. It is so crushing – how can people do such things, I am exceedingly sorry, more than I can express for them all and to Mr Smith with his delicate health and the shock might be very serious. Do not you think Cornwall must be a very bad place? Your letters contain such an account of scandal now we are quite shocked. They will become at this rate as bad as the Police news in the papers! May not Square be a pessimist? I do not mean that his orders are to be disobeyed or neglected but perhaps like Bowman he frightens people with a view to making them rather more careful than they otherwise would be.

This is such a wonderful place – the country near is perfectly flat, there is nothing like a hill nor cliff nor even a rock. Where the town stands Willie remembers nothing but sandhills and now they appear at each end of the houses which must extend for about 2 or 2½ miles in a straight line. There is a long esplanade facing the place where the sea should be! (but it generally lives just out on the horizon) then a fine row of hotels and houses then inside a sort of long boulevard with trees on each side and very good shops parallel with the esplanade and consequently perfectly straight also. At right angles with these runs a wooden jetty out towards the sea a mile long with a trainway worked by a stationary engine in the middle to take people out to the end or back, so that when it is high tide you may have the water around you. Last night (as it was full moon) I thought I heard heavy rain and looking out positively saw that the sea had crept up nearer but it is dreadful sea. The people are very rich, many of them, tho' there are endless 'cheap trippers' and mostly Manchester and Liverpool out of town but ladies and gentlemen are rare in proportion to the numbers. We are in a very large good hotel but we fancy one of the most expensive – dearer than the one we were in at Scarborough. However we go home on Saturday and the position is very good. We must bring Edith here one day – it would astonish her. The only attraction to us are a first rate band and the aquarium. The bandmaster has a salary of £500 a year and £4,000 p.a. for the band and expenses, programmes etc. It plays twice a day all kinds of good music and ladies take their work and sit in the great building. A weekly ticket of 3/6 admits you to two of these concerts daily and the aquarium and gardens whenever you please. The building is a huge kind of greenhouse with pretty flower beds and rockwork. In the evenings besides the band, including string instruments, there is a lady singer, a lady violinist and a man singer, all of whom are quite pleasing to hear tho' not of course first class and often on Saturdays they have grander concerts for which you pay more when the London artistes come – Albanie is advertised. Were it not that there is a season here which lasts all the year such things could not be kept up but the band and aquarium are admirable, the latter larger than that at the

Crystal Palace. There was a report circulated a short time since (not true) that the bandmaster was going to retire – instantly without enquiring into it they raised his salary from £400 to £500 and sent him £50 as a present. But he deserves it all, the band is *most* excellent.

Do not be surprised after all this if I do not write again on Monday. I am most anxious to hear how the dance went off and how Edith enjoyed it; what did she wear in her hair? and was her dress low or only open? Tell me all about it and please don't read your letters over again – I am sure I shall understand them quite well and will ask if I cannot – but it is by far the worst part of writing a long yarn and I would rather have to guess at some things than strain your eyes. What does Square mean by saying it is constitutional?

With much love to you all
Believe me
Your affectionate daughter
Kathleen T. Fox

Strathallan House
November 1st 1875

My dearest Mother

At last your anxious mind will be set at ease by hearing that we had a most successful journey on Saturday. We had exactly time enough at Exeter and the train reached Vauxhall at 5.20. Sancto was not there but arrived a few minutes after and we got here just as they had sat down to a six o'clock dinner as there were some tableaux going on in the evening. Miss Theresa came out immediately and looked at my frock the first thing and then Miss Enticknays came out too and was very nice. But oh' the ordeal of going into the diningroom! I got that nervous I did not know what to do and Miss Theresa said I made her quite nervous too and the personal remarks about hair etc. were too embarrassing! Then in the evening there were some tableaux and then the girls went to bed and Annie and I stayed up with Miss E. It *is* so nice being a 'Parlour Boarder' Miss Theresa is looking so ill and is about half her former size. She has been very poorly since her return from Kissingen but says she is better now. Miss Enticknays is not at all well and in very low spirits in consequence. Annie is looking

234

dreadfully thin and delicate, is coddled from morning to night, does nothing but music and is of course a great anxiety to them. Her brother is just gone to Mentone with one lung affected and they are afraid of the same in her as she has had a bad cough and seems too languid and easily tired to do anything. So you see I have to be the useful one! Miss E is going to the doctor today and I hope he will make her alright as it is dreadful to have her cross and ill. Poor Miss Theresa gets so worried. I am seeing the other side of things now and know how much is hidden from the schoolroom. It is very nice to know the other side of their characters and they are both so kind and nice. 'Parlour boarders' get lots of privileges and are kissed 'goodnight'! I have a dear little room upstairs to myself. I think there has been a lot to worry Miss Theresa this term as two girls have had to leave from ill-health and she has had to take care of them and Annie instead of herself. Miss Enticknays and I went to hear Don Stanley at Westminster Abbey yesterday and we got very tolerable places. Miss E is going to write to you to ask if I may go to Haines Walton as she has had personal experience of his cleverness and has taken girls to him too. She has been also to White Cooper but does not think he is nearly as good. You see Miss Theresa does not know how much I ought to do and want to know now. I would much rather go to him and then I should know just how much I ought to do. Miss Theresa was perfectly miserable at Kissingen with that horribly stupid little Fraulein – she is so empty headed and ignorant and yet so *awfully* conceited. She goes at Christmas! Miss T gave her notice directly they got back to England and everybody will be *very* glad. Poor Miss Jefferson who is very nice is so good and patient but it must be very trying for her as Fraulein is so touchy and they have to be so much together. I have to lead the sopranos in the class and there is lots to be learnt. Miss Theresa was to have sent me a copy but she forgot so I have it all to do now.

2.30 pm   Miss Enticknays has been ordered to go away for two or three days as it is overwork. Miss Theresa told me yesterday in case Miss E did not write to you today I had better ask you about Haines Walton myself as she wants to know as soon as possible. Besides being an occulist he is a most clever surgeon and cured Miss E's foot once when no other man in London could have done it without using the knife (I don't know what was the matter with it!) She has been to him about her own eyes and taken two girls to him and he was very satisfactory.

With love to you (and tell Father I thought of him on Sunday)
Your ever very loving
Edith.

Strathallan
November 5th 1875

My dearest Kathleen

I cannot write you much now as I must go and practise but Mother will send on my letter to her. We have been to Haynes Walton today and he says everything almost *opposite* to Square – I am not to wear spectacles for a fortnight except the weak ones for music and out of doors. Then I am to go again – I am to work and read in moderation and wear blue specs at night. Oh! I do think it would have been better if I had stayed at home. They will do for my eyes soon if everybody thinks differently about them. He dilated the pupil of one so that I cannot see well in it for two or three days and it is very uncomfortable. I am writing very grumblingly but I am getting so *tired* of occulists and I do think I should be better at home for though Miss Theresa is very nice, things are very uncomfortable sometimes. Miss E told me I was to be a parlour boarder and now Miss T does not wish it. I am only a *worry* to *everyone*! I suppose it will be better soon and now I must go and practise.

Best of love
Ever your own loving
Edith

Strathallan House
November 5th 1875

My dearest Mother

We have just been to Haynes Walton but I can hardly tell you much for certain. He took a long time about me and says I am to have a pair of blue spectacles for evenings and only to wear my *weak* specs for music and out of doors for the next fortnight. This day fortnight I am to go again and then he will be able to tell us more about it. I may do lessons in moderation, reading and writing *without* specs. He says the eyes are congested a good deal and that I have a 'stigmatism' whatever that maybe, as he did not explain. I am to be out for two hours every day and not to read etc. by gaslight. He has given me a prescription but he did not attribute anything to my 'general health'. It is very wretched without spectacles here but I hope after the fortnight he will let me use them again. You see he does not agree with Square and now it is rather open to discussion as to which is right. I suppose Haynes Walton is a very clever man so he ought to be right. He is not nearly such a nice man as Square – Miss Theresa has not time to write to you as Miss Enticknays is still away. Do you want me to learn French? I can go to the conversation class and of course I always talk it but I think I had better work most at German, music and singing. It is horrid to go into classes in the middle of the term. I have not heard from Ferdie. Why cannot he go to Girsby? The thimble is yours not mine. I have mine with me. I almost repent coming back if it were not for the music and singing it is very tiresome what with this man and all. Now I hope you will not get in a fidget! You ought to be very glad I am not to wear spectacles. Now I must send Edward's letter on to Father.

With best love
Your own loving
Edith.

Strathallan House
November 6th 1875

My dearest Mother
I think it is a great mistake always to make up cheerful letters to you for fear of your being fidgety. No! I am not going to tell you anything dreadful about my eyes! There is nothing the matter only I want to have a little talk with you about things here. I do not think I have ever been in a more uncomfortable position than during the last week. Miss Enticknays told me on Sunday that I was to be a Parlour Boarder and stay up till 10 with them. I told you she went away on Monday afternoon, rather unluckily for me. I went into the library in the evening and made Miss Theresa so vexed by not talking that she sent us off to bed early. Tuesday as I was going in after prayers feeling very uncomfortable Miss Theresa began a long speech – she said I must not think I might come into the library when I liked and seemed quite to look on it

as a liberty. She was very much surprised when I told her Miss E had told me to, and said that she had never intended it and that when she was so tired it made her very irritable to see me sit up and not say anything. She said if Miss E wished it she, Miss T, would have to give way. Now Miss E has just returned and I am so afraid they will be angry with each other. They are both so *ill*, so *worried*, and of course so *irritable* that it is a most unfortunate time for me to have come. They are very kind to me but I feel I am only an additional worry and the more my not talking worries Miss Theresa the more I get shut up. I do *wish* I could talk. Miss Theresa is *very* nice to me but I cannot bear to see her look so worried and ill. Now do not think I want you to write to Miss Theresa (I do not know what you could write about either!) as that would be worse than ever. I am very glad to get some more lessons in music and singing but for everything else I wish myself at home again all day long. I would certainly never have asked to come if I had known what it was going to be like – that is the grumbly side. Now for the other – Miss T has just come back and is much better so I hope better times are in store. Next week must be better after all this. I am going in extensively for cooking and especially 'appley' things for Father! I shall tell Miss Theresa that Haynes Walton must not want me any more after next time. After all it will be a good thing if I can do without specs and I shall ask next time if I may have a drop glass. I wonder whether anyone knows what I ought to do. I am most sorry to have come on account of the expense. It does not seem worth it though I really will work at my music. Everybody here thinks me even worse-tempered than I really am and I am sure that is bad enough. I cannot help looking cross when I cannot *see* anyone properly and being with a lot of girls makes me quite nervous still though I have been at school nearly 4 years. I do want to be better tempered for I know I am only a worry to everyone. I know from the way you begin your letters now, how signally I have failed since July. I think we both get in *despair* and then that makes things worse. I am horribly despairing and when I get so it makes me more cross. You do not know how I have 'wanted my Ma' this week! I wish I could be transported home this moment! Oh dear! this is a very incoherent letter. I wonder if I ought to send it. It is so hard to collect one's thoughts when everyone is talking. Now do not make me repent my writing this by letting it worry you. Next week will be alright.

Your own loving little
    Edith.

Fort Monckton
November 9th 1875

My dear Mother

I ought to have written you before to inform you of my safe arrival but I see you heard it somehow, perhaps I sent you a line myself but I have suffered from water on the brain and everywhere else so badly that the past is a blank. I hope if I have time to enclose, I mean if I remember it, to send 'Onward Christian Soldiers' for Edith, I copied it I know but I don't know where I left it. I went to Church on Sunday and the parson preached about vestments, real presence, Saints, and so on. It shocked me but I found it was to be his last sermon so did not report him to his boss. I amused myself reading a hymn one of the verses of which I don't understand, it was: Jesu, to thy temple brought, Whom, as them the spirit taught, Simeon and Anna sought.

It puzzles me much as I can't make out who was brought to the temple. In the evening I was rewarded for my inattention by a walk from Portsmouth with boots in water up to my ankles the whole way, the lightning was so incessant that I had no difficulty in lighting my pipe only I burnt my fingers if I didn't keep them in my pockets. The thunder appeared to be some seconds in advance of the lightning, a very unusual thing in this part of the world. I have quite given up all idea of going to Girsby as everyone wants to go on leave and I cannot get away. There is very little news – the Prince of Wales arrived alright the papers will tell you of course. I haven't heard from Edith. I hope you are all quite well as it leaves me at present.

Yours etc.
    F.W.B.

Strathallan House
November 11th 1875

My own dearest Mother

I am so *glad* I wrote that letter and must thank you very very

239

much for your *dear* answer. I think we *shall* get on alright and as long as we do not *despair* I am sure we shall. I know I am a naughty unruly little child but if people treat me with love they get things done much better than by desiring a thing to be done for that you know turns me stubborn. You may think that I do not do things any better when you ask me nicely but though I know I often seem just as cross, in reality I always feel remorseful afterwards though I will not show it. I care a great deal more for what you say than you think Mother mine though I put on such a cold outside but I will try not to do that any more. One thing, you must not think I shall be dull at home. I have never been that yet and am not likely to be. It is a very good thing I came back now for I shall not want to come back to school again and that is the only thing that would be likely to make me discontented. I am *much* happier staying at home quietly than going about as much as I did last holidays so do not trouble about gaiety for me. I have not lived on my own resources for so long without being able to amuse myself! Now for the business! First, the key of my box was just where I thought it was with the identical bit of string on it which I thought I saw you take it up!! Second the prescription is only some steel to take. Third Dean Stanley announced when we heard him that he was going to preach about Commodore Goodenough the next day. I should like to have heard it. Fourth I do not wish to go to Mrs Venables but suppose if I am asked I must. We are only supposed to go out once a month though of course I could go oftener. Fifth please, I want to come home on Friday or Saturday four weeks! This day four weeks I shall have had six lessons in music, singing, dancing and calisthenics so by Friday the 10th December 1875 I shall be *quite* ready to return to Cornwall – I ought not to be here really for I miss the outdoor life for my eyes. Haines Walton said I could use them for lessons but though I do not do much they soon hurt and of course I cannot get out as much as I could at home. I shall *have* to practise now for that is the only thing that *never* hurts them and it will be my chief occupation. *Please* let me come then!!

6th What about the white silk? If you do not think it had better be made up I will bring it home again.

7th I do not think I want a new jacket this year. Both mine look quite nice. I have relapsed into an ordinary school girl and

240

am much happier than when I was a Parlour Boarder. Miss Enticknap is better but still far from well and as I fear was very vexed with Miss T for not letting me stay up. She has not however said anything to me so I hope the matter will drop.

9th I hope Edith is not making herself *too* charming 'I am a jealous little child I am!' and especially distrust Hayhurst ever since May's visit!! Yes! I think you had much better take a little trip somewhere until Newlyn has shaken down again. Aunt Emily might as well invite you up and then you could exchange Edith. I am so sorry Father has been out of sorts but hope he is up to par by this time. Thank him for his letter which I will answer on Saturday if I have time. I am just going to Mr Bodda. Poor little man he has a bad cold in his head and nearly killed us yesterday at the class by producing a large travelling cap and after about five minutes' shaking out he put it on with the peak behind! By the bye I hope he will not be worse and stay away today. If he does I shall have to stay a week longer and that is just what I do not want to do. My blue specs have arrived and they are such hugh great things – not like Mrs Chudleigh's but very large. But now I must finish this long letter for I do not think I have any more to say. I *must* come home 4 weeks, I have had enough of school and want to come home to my Ma!

    With best love to you both
      Believe me
          Your own most loving naughty little child
            Edith.

                Strathallan House
                December 4th 1875

My dearest Mother

I must write you a few lines this afternoon but I do not think they will be very coherent as I have been downstairs cooking since 10 this morning and now it is 4. I even had lunch down there as I could not leave the mince pies in the oven. We have made the Xmas puddings and mince meat and I am going to bring home a big pudding and some mince meat so mind you do not make much! We must have a dinner party some day to eat the plum pudding! Miss Theresa wants me to stay till Monday as then I can make a cake on Saturday which I shall also bring home!

Fletcher came for me on Thursday in the morning when I had arranged to go in the afternoon. It was snowing fast so Miss T would not let me go so I hope they will take me on Monday. I should think if I go to Steeple Langford on Monday I could leave on the Friday as I want to get home to my Ma! You have found the right way to manage your naughty child! I had a lot I wanted to tell you but I am so tired and muddled I cannot collect my ideas. Thank you *very* much for your letter. I was half afraid what you might think of my naughty letter and the result of your answering like that is that I will do all I can to do your commissions though as we are apparently snowed up it is doubtful if I have a chance! It has snowed nearly all day, it is quite deep and the roads are fearful, freezing hard and the horses only able to walk. No church tomorrow I am afraid! Oh! it is nearly post time and I cannot remember the things I wanted to say. I wish Miss E could go away somewhere these holidays but she will not. She is coming to see us next summer at least I tell her she must! She wants to come very much and I think you will like her. I wish we could have her now but she wants to come in the summer.

    With best love
        Believe me
            Ever your very loving child
            Edith.

                                    Strathallan
                        December 7th 1875

My dearest Mother

It strikes me that it will be a case of 'snowed up' soon. Here the snow has lain thick since last Wednesday and the air looks full of it still. Sunday was the only day we could get out and then it was lovely! Bright sunshine and blue sky all day and yet no perceptible thaw. Slippery as glass and Miss T and three of the girls went down but no damage done. There are no cabs to be got except with two or three horses and double fares. How I shall get to the Station I do not quite see! I am to go from Paddington to Wiley and do you not think it might be a good plan to send my portmanteau home with dirty things, books, etc, as it such a lot of luggage to take to SL. I am afraid I shall not have a chance of getting out to do any shopping, my chief anxiety is how to get to

Haines Walton tomorrow! I think we shall have to walk! I am not sorry that we did not go about the hat. Miss Theresa says Heath is *very* expensive and that Clements in Regent Street (where we get our hats) would do it much cheaper and just as well. What am I to wear at the Truro Ball? It ought to be white, everyone says it must be! What sort of dress is the bridesmaid's likely to be? I am half afraid to bring the silk home unmade as it strikes me I want it for the ball! What was Kathleen's white silk like for she did offer me her low body. I could easily leave my silks behind to be sent to Miss Cooper's with written directions as she would not want my measure again. Anyhow, *I am coming home* the *Friday after* if there is a train on the line! I suppose if I leave here sometime Friday afternoon I might get to Paddington by Saturday at 12 which is the time I have to leave reaching Wiley at 4.20. My specs have come. They are perfectly round (so suit my face Miss Theresa says!) and I resemble an owl in them. I hope to get to H.W. tomorrow. Now I think the muddle seems a little clearer.

With best love
>Ever your loving
>>Edith.

>>>>>Steeple Langford
>>>>>Bath
>>>>>December 14th 1875

My dearest Mother

We were all so shocked at the contents of your letter this morning. I can hardly realise it, for I was there only a hour or two before (on Friday) and they were all so bright and gay. I want to come home on Thursday if it does not interfere with your plans as they are going to send to the Station to meet the very train I should go by on that day so it will be no inconvenience to them and I want to get home. B suggests that you may be going to Aunt E and in that case I *must* come and look after Father. I do not like the idea of being bridesmaid so I hope you have refused for me. *Please* let me come on Thursday, I wish now I had come straight home. There is a dinner party here on Thursday which I shall not at all mind missing. I cannot write any more for I am quite muddled but remember *I can come on Thursday* with no inconvenience if only you can meet me or if your plans are altered will come straight home. It is so *dreadful* just as they were thinking him better. Now mind you go to Aunt E if she wants you as I will take *great care* of Father, or if he goes too I dare say someone will take me in or I should be quite contented at home by myself. Goodbye my *dearest* Mother. I wish I were at home.

    With best love to you both
        Ever your own loving
          Edith.

                          Fort Monckton
                     December 15th 1875

My dear Mother

    Have I written to you for a long time or not? I quite forget, anyhow I can't have since your good wishes, so thank you for them kindly, tho its a terrible thing to find oneself nearer 30 than 20 – awful to contemplate. I was sorry to hear from Kathleen of Uncle Henry's death, I suppose you are very anxious about Aunt E. Will it make any difference in their abode? Edith is, I think, at home. I wrote to her when at Steeple Langford, I hope the last accounts of her eyes are more favourable. Thanks for the stockings. Kathleen sent me a cheese so I am very contented. The skipper has been away so the mice have been playing during the last week – going over to Ryde and shooting a good deal. He comes back tomorrow and we are quite sorry – I may get 10 days or a fortnight directly after Xmas but that will be all.

    Yours etc.
        F.W.B.

                     Comberbach House
                     December 23rd 1875

    Accept my dearest Mother our best wishes for a very happy Xmas for you all and many of them I trust. We were so glad to hear about Aunt Emily and to see her letter. What an inexpressible comfort it must be to her that he knew how ill he was and what was the matter and she may well say how thoughtful all the provisions of the Will are and the thoughtfulness about the presents seem to me most touching. I suppose the girls (of age) have each £7,000 *now* with the income to do what they like with and the younger £100 a year for the time – is it so? I cannot quite understand it. When we return to Cheshire from Tresillian with Edith you and Papa had better then go to London for a time. It would be a good time of the year to be away and you could come on to us afterwards. What endless work Xmas involves – I have such a number of people for little things, 'Aunt Sallies' and so on. For the maids we have a petticoat each. Aunt Anna seems very much pleased with the hamper and as I packed it entirely myself I am gratified by hearing that nothing was broken. But she does not tell me the cost of carriage as I asked her to do so shall I ignore it? Perhaps it hurt her feelings to be supposed she could not pay for she uses better notepaper and envelopes than I do! Willie is hunting vigorously. Mr Barry had a very bad fall on Monday – not able to move – but doctors from London and Liverpool seem to hope it may only be a strain not injury to the spine – but he is not strong and it sounds unpleasant.

    Ever your loving daughter
        Kathleen.

Gully and Mary Bennet with their youngest daughter Edith celebrated Christmas 1875 at Tresillian House. Kathleen and Willie were at Comberbach House in Cheshire. The two soldier sons, Edward and Ferdinando, spent Christmas with their Regiments in India and Portsmouth. Edith had put her school days behind her and early in the New Year went to stay with her sister Kathleen in Cheshire.

On the 4th January 1876 the General Quarter Sessions of the Peace were held at Bodmin under the chairmanship of Sir Colman Rashleigh, Bart, and the calendar shows that Gully dealt with four cases.

Elizabeth Solomon a charwoman aged forty-two was convicted for stealing one drinking glass, and one teaspoon, the property of William Trebilcock of the Parish of St. Columb and sentenced to two calendar months hard labour in the House of Correction at Bodmin.

Elizabeth French, described as a servant was convicted of stealing a sovereign from Samuel Piper at the Parish of Landteglos by Camelford and sentenced to six weeks in hard labour in the House of Correction at Bodmin.

Joseph Thomas, a labourer aged twenty-two, was convicted of unlawfully and knowingly by certain false pretences obtaining of and from Emma Chapman at the Borough of Liskeard Board, Lodging and Money amounting to £1:11s:0d. with intent to cheat and defraud her of the same and with a previous conviction for theft three years earlier was sentenced to four calendar months hard labour.

Edward, serving with his Regiment at Malabar wrote to his mother on the 25th February 1876.

My dear Mother

You need not have told me that the weather was so much milder as that is easily seen in comparing your present letter with those written under the influence of Jack Frost. Your present letter is quite cheerful in comparison and by summer time I have no doubt they will be as young as Kathleen's but if you had lived out here for 4 years you would appreciate a little frost! It is always my desire when out walking here to be suddenly thrown into a snow heap. No doubt it would kill me but still it would be very pleasant. You asked me whether I liked the officers here. Of course I like all the officers of the Regiment but they are not all men who I should pick as my friends. Of course Lynch has commanded the Company for some time and we know one another very well but then he has his bad qualities. If you like you may picture to yourself a man six foot 2, well made in proportion with a handsome hard face and a very powerful man. Natural consequence, fond of flattery. Thinks no one can do anything or knows anything but himself and as is usual can do nothing and knows no more than an ordinary mortal. Has seen shikar in Bengal and as those deluded creatures think no one who has seen nothing but sport in Madras can know anything about it so we get the benefit of his experiences pretty often. What follows? I ain't a man to flatter anyone. I don't believe a word he says about shikar as I unfortunately have seen shikar and know his experiences to be wrong. I also know on what he grounds his experience having of course heard in the Regiment and I have seen myself more shikar than he has and have had more success. He thinks anyone ought to be proud to accompany him in the jungle but he loses nerve – give me Powlett for a friend in a nasty scrape and we'll see one another through most, but I'd be sorry to be with Lynch. But then Polly and I began together and have always gone out together when possible so it is but natural we should prefer one another and he is a much pleasanter companion. Now take Hood the other sub here, he is only just out from sick leave (two years) so I don't know much about him but what I do know I don't care for him. He isn't a sportsman and of course being livery is generally crotchety so I don't interfere with him. We all get on very well together and that is the great thing. There are no troops here except our Company as Government find that native troops are useless against Moplaks the physique and fanatical ideas of the latter making them more than a match for the poor Madras sepoy, but really there is nothing to fear in a Moplak if it were not for their priests; they are the originators of all disturbances just as the Jesuit priests in English History as they had nothing to lose so if successful they had everything to gain and Moplaks being under the influence of their priests are easily led away. What a lot of duffers your bridegroom's party must have been. If 42 people can cow a bridegroom I should think the bride would soon be master and mistress both and I don't think a mother ought to be sorry to lose her daughter. I know it is the correct thing to pretend to be so but pretension aint facts always. You ask me to get a Rampur Chudda shawl, I will if I can, they cost about £7 and I shall have to write to someone to get it for me so I don't promise. They are made in the north and take about six months to get as they only make to order. That is the best sort of course. Now and then you may get them cheaper from a travelling hawker but they dont come here at all. The skin you had made into a muff for Edith is called out here a species of deer but you I suppose carried away by its pretty skin call it a dear. I am afraid you wont do to go in for the spelling bee that nice new English game. How charmingly domestic and how awfully hard up for something to display their ignorance on must the present generation be in England. I should have thought Edith was a trifle too old for Xmas stockings. What is the last skin you got from Stamwith like? It ought to be much larger and much darker coloured than the rest as it was a very fine animal for these parts. Mind you it is one I shot myself and one that took a lot of killing and afforded us all many an anxious moment in following when wounded. What does Mrs Polwhale amuse herself with? She owes me a letter of about 2½ years standing. We have a few books here but dont get anything from Headquarters. Before you get this of course you will have received my letter saying I had given up leave. What's done cannot be undone but if anything occurs to prevent my getting the Depot as often happens you may not see me for years.

However I dont blame anyone. Of course if I had chosen for myself I should have taken the 15 months leave as I don't believe in letting opportunities slip you'll see very little of me at the Depot. You cant get leave in England like you can out here and 60 days leave in the year is all I am entitled to at home. I hope you will not forget to answer my question in the last. Here's another long letter for you and should you be half so tired reading it as I am of writing it I shall be more than paid.

 Love to you
   Your affectionate son
    E. Gully Bennet.

           Comberbach House
           March 11th 1876

My dearest Mother

To resume the thread of the discourse from where Kathleen left it yesterday. We went to the Cathedral service but had not time to go all over it afterwards as the service was rather long. We saw a good deal however and it certainly is a glorious place inside. Everything so beautifully and richly finished. We were rather disappointed in the outside but it was quite made up for when we got inside. We looked in at the shop windows and wished we had a whole morning for the occupation. The rest of our journey was very satisfactorily accomplished, no bother at Birmingham or Crewe and we got here about 5.30. It is a wretchedly wet day today, rainy and windy but Willie has gone off to the meet and we have just seen Mr Shakerby drive by on the same errand. Kathleen got a note from Miss S yesterday to say she would have come in then only she could not so she is going to try and come this morning. We cannot think what she is in such a hurry for (unless she thinks we came on Thursday) and are prepared to hear anything from the announcement she is going to be married! to some frightful account of wrong doing among the domestics here in K's absence. I suppose the truth is she has mistaken the day of our arrival! Everything here is so beautifully neat in the garden in preparation for us but it looks and feels much more wintery than Cornwall. Oh! the 'black country' yesterday – it was too filthy. I feel a shade cleaner today by dint of a scalding bath last night but we felt perfectly grubby when we

248

arrived. Tell Father that my journey only cost £3:2s:8d and the hotel 9s:4d only £3:12s:0d altogether. So I am quite rich! Fancy we shall be meeting at Plymouth (D.V.) in about two months.

Heaps of love to you both
From your very loving Edith

Comberbach House
March 20th 1876

My dearest Ma

The chief topic of conversation to wit the weather is waxing monotonous. We will tell you when we have a change and till then think of us in snow and hail and all that is wintery. Suffice it to say that we walked home from Church yesterday with snow an inch deep which had fallen during Church time and the pools covered with ice and that ever since we came the ground has been as often white as green. We continue notwithstanding to survive and be cheerful and cook omelets and lots of things. We went to the school yesterday and I was shut up for half an hour with worse than wild horses – the 'infants'!! It has been on my mind since that I did not pat the little darlings only you see the girls had hats on and the boys were out of reach so I could not very well – I did not see myself striking symptoms of measles or whooping cough (one did cough once though I think) but of course it is only probable that some at least are in some stage of an infectious disease. Never mind dear Ma, I feel in my usual rude health so far and will let you know if I am 'took wuss'. We brought home a big big box from the Household Stores in Manchester on Wednesday. Beyond that nothing of any moment occurred on our journey. Kathleen says that this is a long enough letter and that I must send everybody's love to all and stop. My filial devotion thinks otherwise but as you have invested her with authority I must submit. Oh! Ma dear I should like to run away and come home. They do starve us here so now there is no cook we live on sardines and ham and have to slave all the morning in the kitchen besides I get so snubbed and put upon that really I can scarcely climb up into my bed when I go to bed. Oh me! such are sisters and brother-in-laws.

With best love believe me
Your own little crushed rosebud
Edith.

Fort Monckton
Gosport
March 29th 1876

My dear Kathleen

Many thanks for your letter and Edward's which I return. I am sorry such a mistake has been made by Edward, I mean in going in for the Depot, of course 15 months leave would have been much better in every way, I feel it is my fault too as I believe I must have originated the idea that we would only get 6 months leave, no doubt letters were written from home comparing the advantages of 6 months leave with two years at the Depot and so he got over persuaded. I should have been pigheaded and stuck to my own idea of what was best. I thought I had told you we move to Plymouth and Cork shortly I dont know which I shall go to. I have no news, the weather is better, love to Edith.

Yours etc.
F.W.B.

Fort Monckton
May 11th 1876

My dear Mother

We saw the Section off to Cork on Tuesday with Whitmore and Knight in charge so I dont go there, on Thursday next the Headquarters of the Company are to go to Plymouth with Collings and Chermside and I believe I am to stay here for a week or two longer to help put the new Company which arrived yesterday into the way of the work which will suit very well. Today the Prince of Wales arrives and I am to have the honour of standing in the streets for 5 to 6 hours to assist in what will be a very fine spectacle. I hope you will enjoy your trip.

Yours etc.
F.W.B.

CHAPTER 12

Winds of the World, give answer!
They are whimpering to and fro -
And what should they know of England
who only England know? -
The poor little street-bred people
that vapour and fume and brag,
They are lifting their heads in the
stillness to yelp at the English flag!
Rudyard Kipling. *The English Flag.*

After several months with her sister in Cheshire Edith returned to Tresillian and lived with her parents. Ferdi encouraged his mother and Edith to take up tennis and by midsummer 1876 had presented his mother with a set of tennis equipment, some ladies' rackets and a box of eighteen tennis balls. His letters from Fort Monckton spurred on Edith who had acquired 'an arrow hand', presumably a reference to a fast and accurate service.

In July 1876 Ferdi was transferred to Devonport where he remained until April 1880 engaged firstly with his submarine mining company and then from 1877 with telegraph units of the Royal Engineers to whom the Post Office had handed over the construction and maintenance of their lines in the south and west of England.

On 13th February 1877 Edward embarked in H.M.S. *Crocodile* to return to England – almost to the day five years after he first arrived in Bombay harbour aboard the same ship. His diary records that Aden was very hot and disagreeable and the Mediterranean was cold and stormy. The *Crocodile* arrived in Portsmouth on the 17th March 1877. Edward reported to his regimental depot at Northampton where he was granted leave and immediately made for Tresillian.

His diary read very simply: Went home and found all well.

Shortly afterwards he stayed at Devonport with Ferdi for a few days and then travelled up to Cheshire where he spent a week with Kathleen.

In January 1878 the two brothers joined a shooting party. Edward's diary for 4th January reads: On January 4th went home with Ferdi but owing to the mild season got very few snipe – 66 snipe, 61 wood pigeons. Had one or two good days at the Retallacks.

The *Cornwall Gazette* of 10th January 1878 records that the Annual County Ball took place at Truro and among the guests listed was a party of four described as: Mrs Gully Bennet, chaperone, Miss Bennet, Mr F.W. Bennet, R.E., and Mr E. Gully Bennet, 48th Regt.

Edward returned to his Depot on 4th February and Ferdi reported back to the Telegraph Units. The rest of 1878 and 1879 passed uneventfully until 23rd December when Edward received orders to go to India. His diary records:

> I sailed on 2nd January 1880 with the 2nd 5th in H.M.S. Crocodile. Fair weather to Malta where we stopped for 24 hours. Dined at the Club with Muggeridge and went to the Opera (Faust) – very bad. Left Malta in a gale and had a very bad time for 3 days, every one on board being ill and decks under water. Wind reached 11. Got to Port Said in the course of time, Sunday, entered Canal in afternoon.

At the Berlin Congress of 1878 Turkey had agreed to make certain reforms in Asia Minor and to permit the Great Powers to see by inspection on the spot that these promises were kept. Several military Vice-Consuls were appointed for service in Asia Minor one of whom was Lieutenant F.W. Bennet, Royal Engineers, then aged twenty-nine. The military Vice-Consuls had very limited powers, they gave advice and attempted to exercise a moral influence over the Turkish rulers. Appointed in April 1880 Ferdie was employed under Sir Charles Wilson, the Consul-General. The young Vice-Consul was given charge of Anatolia and set about at once with boundless energy to every duty. Ferdie's diaries were reflected in long letters to his parents and family commencing on the 20th April 1880 with the boat train from Charing Cross, embarkation at Dover and a smooth passage to Calais. Several days were spent in Paris before travelling on by train to Geneva and from there to Turin, Milan, Venice, eventually arriving in Constantinople on 11th May 1880 after a week at sea having stopped briefly at Ancona, Brindisi and Athens.

Ferdie received his first orders in Constantinople and repeated them in his diary with undisguised pleasure:

May 11th 1880

Colonel Wilson has left me instructions to proceed to Kaisarich by Brussa and Angora, right across Asia Minor that is, or a good part of it, and make a map of the country as I go, he hopes to meet me at Angora. I have to pick up a Drago-man who will be my sole companion practically and is a species of Armenian gentleman, well educated, when I have found him. I shall have a groom and a valet and a couple of soldiers. I shall collect at Bronssa a lot of mules and horses and commence my journey across the desert in due course. A week I hope will see me off. I dined at the Embassy with the young gentlemen of the Foreign Office last night, how they envied me, would give anything to be going. I aint going sightseeing, I am going to make my preparations, Constantinople can wait. Am in excellent health and spirits and looking forward to it thoroughly.

F.W.B.

Istrishehr – June 1st 1880

A few minutes leisure at last so I will write from here. I forget whether I described Brusa, I think not, but I have seen so many lovely places since I was there that Brusa has almost been swamped in my mind's eye. It was a treat to get away from Constantinople but Brusa would be lovely at any time. It rained for the first two days which landed us over Sunday after which I actually went two miles out of town up the slopes of Mt. Olympus and camped, actually did all this when I might have stayed comfortably in the hotel. They tried to frighten one about the dangers but I was fool-hardly I suppose and one gets so tired of being warned. It was charming up there among the grand old trees and away from the dust dirt and heat of the town and although the jackals howled at night and the shepherds high up on the mountainside fitfully discharged their firearms at night, and although our Zaptiel (policeman) prowled about all night by the tents challenging imaginary foes and making the servants restless by his own alertness, we slept soundly and enjoyed our four days immensely. Then Wilson arrived, detained by stress of weather and famine enquiries, and I stayed with him at the hotel until Saturday catching the words of wisdom that fell from his lips and getting horses and wagons for our journey east. Orders were given to start at 5 a.m. on Saturday and start we did. The Cortege consisted of -

1. Zaptiel on horseback armed – Turk.
2. Guide to bring back the horses – Greek.
3. The Chief – English.
4. Interpreter in Chief – Mixture.
5. Ahmet, groom – Turk.
6. Arabah No. 1 with Tartar driver.
7. Arabah No. 2 with Tartar driver.
8. Theodore – valet – German.
9. Zaptiel – Turk.

We were all armed, at least we carried weapons somewhere about in the baggage or horse trappings. I had enough to care about without firearms. I may say that I had the best horse of the lot and he carried me well and that as yet I am skin whole and haven't come off. The first day we covered about 30 miles and were 12 hours in the saddle. It is hard to describe the roads, tracks is the best name they deserve, to go over the ground you would say at once it was utterly impossible for any *vehicle* to get over the ground. Turks never repair a road, mountain torrents wash down rocks and carry away hedges, no matter they let things stay. The Arabah driver will overcome the difficulty somehow, they wont repair it or get the rocks out of the way but they will get through round or over the obstacle or go another way, if they break a pole or a wheel they cut a tree and make another. An upset is nothing, they rather like it, they will drive up the side of a house, bump, bump, bump all day long, no springs, they dont care, they sit on their sheep skins and the wiry little horses drag the rotten old carts along somehow and the day's work is done when they arrive at the place you want to get to. The scenery all along was superb and one got over the sad fact that all the baggage will be smashed to atoms by the time we get to Kaisarich. Trees mountains and rivers and rich land, dark green and light green, freshness, good spirits and a cool breeze. Off again at 5 next day away down the rich valley, terrible dangers had to be encountered and a Lieutenant and 12 mounted men

(Cavalry) were told off by the Mudir as escort – I never travelled in so much state before. We arrived at Kershomick about 9 and halted for breakfast and took buffaloes to drag the Arabahs up the hill. We got to the top in four hours hard driving. It was 2300 feet (I took the height myself) and wooded all the way and the trees grew larger as we reached the summit where we rested awhile in what I thought a paradise. Then we leisurely descended to Bazardchiki (I may as well tell you that it is no use your looking for these places, I am making a new survey which will point them out plainly), by my observations we are now close to Adana which we reached at 5 p.m. and camped sooner than trust to Turkish hospitality. Started next day at 5 a.m. Before us stretched a lovely valley or rather vast open basin surrounded by wooded mountains and undulating with lesser hills itself, flocks and herds and men ploughing or scratching up the ground with a thing they think is a plough. Away on the horizon tier after tier of mountains. At the foot of the hills we turned abruptly to the right down a narrow gorge – what a sight! High hills rising on both sides abruptly, eagles soaring at the top, trees everywhere, the track and a rushing torrent at our feet and a breeze in our faces, blue sky above and we swept down it at a hard gallop. I never enjoyed anything like I have enjoyed this ride of about the last ninety miles and I cannot help thinking there must be some great disaster impending because everything has gone so smoothly and well, something is bound to occur to make up. I hope to get to Angora by Saturday and rest on Sunday, not that I require any rest but I suppose the men want a wash. I think nothing of getting up at 4 a.m. and riding ten or thirteen hours.

Angora – June 8th 1880

My dear Mother

The events of the five days journey from Esdrishehr to this place will not bear chronology. I could get no horses for riding purposes and had to endure the agonies of Arabah travelling, the details of my suffering are already fading from my memory. The sun poured down on our devoted heads and all the way there was not a blessed tree only an everlasting gentle up and down through what is now a wilderness of wild flowers, locusts and poverty, so much for the scenery. It is six or seven more days from here to

Kaisarich. As I can't even get horses here I am going to have a mattress made which I believe makes Arabah travelling very pleasant. Here I am well cared for in the house of our Vice-Consul Gatheral, an English wool merchant, but as I want to get to my destination I shall leave tomorrow hoping to reach Kaisarich in six days. It is awfully hot, unusually so I am told, and yesterday I paid a lot of official visits in full uniform and had enough of it. I dont think Anatolia from what I have seen of it would ever be an engrossingly interesting country, fancy 150 miles without a tree to speak of! Here there are only fruit trees, full of fruit too and bye and bye it will make one ill no doubt.

    F.W.B.

Kaiserich – June 20th 1880

My dear Mother

You will be interested I know to hear how my settling down progresses. I find myself the occupier on easy terms of one of the most imposing mansions in this city. It is a stone built house with wooden partitions inside inlaid with rough pine carvings of the modern style of bas-relief, the grand hall is richly ornamented with a solid stone floor and hole leading down to a well. All the rooms open into this hall in the centre of which I have hung a tallow candle enclosed in an elegant tin mounted glass frame. Above is a flat roof with centre dome rising 10 or 12 feet into the sky and admitting light. The rooms I found in a highly satisfactory state round two sides of them low couches of elegant bare boards range themselves upon which ants and other insects disport themselves and in the cupboards remnants of delicate honey and cobwebs still hang in graceful festoons. Now however all is changed, old women have scrubbed and turned the place to a state of ordinary cleanliness. The marvellous Theodore with the assistance of my cheque book has conducted the whole of the furnishing in a luxuriant manner. Tables on uneven legs try to fit themselves into the inequalities of the floor. Hard cushions of straw cover the wooden slabs and coverlets of some stuff make them look decent. Outside in the hall a wooden coffin does duty as a tub for the Vice-Consul to perform his ablutions. It is marvellous how quickly all this is done and the settling down process goes on. We generally work during the morning rising early and receiving visitors and paying visits in the middle of the day. There is a mad Armenian Doctor here who runs in and out occasionally and talks broken English. Out at Talas about five miles from where the people go to avoid the summer heat there is an American missionary and his wife, married daughter and son-in-law, and a Miss Clossom who keeps a school, these I have visited, otherwise no English spoken. As yet I have no horses but hire in the afternoon and ride among the vineyards at the foot of the many spurs reaching down from Mt. Oquis. Things are just the same here now as they were not in Jesus Christ's time but back to Abraham's and the Old Testament is much simpler when read here. The Turks are difficult but the Armenians are worse as they get up awkwardly when one passes by and do obeisance then they grovel and cheat the Turks and appeal to me to get justice done them in their fraudulent transactions. I have visited the chief officials in much grandeur and received assurances that no lawlessness exists in the district and that such things as bribery and corruption are unknown. They dont mean to lie, they cant help it, besides they believe it's the truth but then they dont know what honesty is nor the difference between truth and falsehood. My kavass (armed attendant) is 6 foot 2 inches, stuck around with silver mounted knives and pistols, a magnificent spectacle and ready to die at a wave of my hand, so he says; he is a horseman such as one reads about but very seldom sees, he can pick his cap up off the ground with his hand going at full gallop.

    F.W.B.

Ferdie spent the next two years as Military Vice-Consul of the Adana District. He was constantly on tour covering many miles, often in uncomfortable circumstances, and performing a difficult job. One of his last letters home was dated 9th July 1882:

Although I have been travelling 2 months I haven't anything to write to the Ambassador about – there is no security, there is no justice, all is corruption, and when you have said that you have said all. But my topographical notes take a good deal of midnight oil. Had a letter from the Consul General this morning informing me that my work here ceases on the 31st October but does not know if the F.O. will give us leave on full pay after that date and

257

advises me to put in for leave at once and so get out of here about August, but I don't think I shall as I must go to Adana again and I want to make a good job of the topographical part of my work. However I shall see when we meet on the 15th and anyway I ought to be home by the middle of November. Stewart wants me to come back with him via Egypt and Chermside talks of the Caucasus but I don't think he will get through before the snow. Egypt and Brindisi sounds more my form from Adana.

He wrote again from Kaisarich on the 23rd July 1882:

If I am allowed to depart from this wretched country at my own convenience my present intention is to leave about middle of August go to Adana and sell up and embark at Messina about beginning of September and come home via Beirut, Alexandria, Naples, Rome, Florence etc., but goodness only knows what may happen in Egypt. I don't look forward to Adana in August much but it will only be for 2 or 3 days perhaps, if the Ambassador don't keep me humbugging about waiting for my leave. The Consul General and Ramsay leave tomorrow for Sieas and I shall go a day's journey with them though it's too hot and the country too uninteresting for pleasure.

By the next month, August, hostilities had broken out with Egypt and all military officers stationed in Asia Minor were ordered to Egypt. Ferdie arrived in Alexandria on 11th September and wrote immediately to his family:

Alexandria

September 11th 1882

Just a line to say I got here yesterday soaked in fever, it came on after leaving Jaffa so don't know whether Ambassador is responsible or no. You know much more about this place than I do, all I did yesterday was to drive to Headquarters to get my orders to stay here for the present and then to the hotel to bed where I spent the most miserable day, beastly hotel. Chermside here as military attache, Colonel Wilson gone to Ismailia on his own and will probably go back to bring Turkish troops if they come which isn't likely. The General here received a telegram

from C in Chief to keep me here, yesterday, so Chermside says. Heavy fighting expected this week. Wood in command here, but I know absolutely nothing, all our news comes from London!
    F.W.B.

Alexandria
September 12th 1882

R. Gully Bennet Esq.,
Tresillian House
St. Columb Minor
Cornwall

My dear Sir
    I am desired by Lieut. Bennet to inform you that he received orders this morning to proceed to the front and consequently left this afternoon by the 'City of Lincoln' (hired transport) for Ismailia. He has quite recovered from the fever and was quite well and in good spirits when I left him on board. He also desired me to say that he will write to you by first opportunity.
    I am
    Yours truly
    M. H. Geo. Werndel
    Late Interpreter to Lt. Bennet.

S.S. City of Lincoln
September 13th 1882

My dear Father
    I was ordered up to Ismailia (correct spelling) but I think I shall catch a mail this morning at Port Said and so write to say I am considerably better and highly elated at being sent forward so quickly, though I have not the slightest idea what I'm to do when I get there. Yes, yesterday morning I thought I'd go down to Brigade office and report and so climbed into uniform – anything is called uniform on service – and they told me to go on board at once and go to Ismailia, at once meant 2 p.m. and I managed to get off but am miserably equipped but hope to pick up something at Ismailia. Drafts on board this craft very much like myself, don't know what is going to happen to them as they seem to be drafts of regiments in Cyprus, Alexandria, Malta, and anywhere,

but at Ismailia I don't suppose it matters.
    Yours
        F.W.B.

Lieutenant Bennet's war service lasted until November 1882 when he returned to Britain having been awarded the Egyptian Medal and Bronze Star. After leave over Christmas he was attached to the War Office in London from the 16th January 1883 to the 15th May 1883 and worked there in connection with his service in Asia Minor. On the 4th January 1883 he was promoted to Captain at the age of thirty-three. In August 1883 he joined C Troop at Aldershot where he remained for the next twelve months.

During Ferdie's service in Asia Minor and Egypt, his brother, Captain Edward Bennet, had returned from India and from November 1880 to July 1884 he was stationed with the 48th Regiment in Ireland.

During September 1884 Ferdie returned to Egypt to serve in the Royal Engineer's Telegraph Department in the Upper Nile expedition. He was appointed brevet Major on the 15th June 1885 and on the same day was mentioned in dispatches from Lord Wolseley, Commander of Forces in Egypt. Ferdie returned to England in September 1885 and took up duty with the 1st Division Telegraph Battalion at Falmouth where he served with his Corps until June 1888. From then until May 1891 he was second in command of 1st Division Telegraph Battalion at Aldershot and also served in Edinburgh; he had been appointed substantive Major in May 1889.

CHAPTER 13

'Wisdom does not show itself so much in precept as in life – in a firmness of mind and mastery of appetite. It teaches us to do, as well to talk; and to make our actions and words all of a colour.

Seneca.

Aldershot Camp
July 28th 1889

My dear Father
The oracle has again spoken and this time says Edinburgh is my destination in September where I am to take up the duties of Staff Officer to the Commanding Royal Engineers North Britain. I like the idea very much the only drawback being the distance from Cornwall, I shall get plenty of golf and an entire change in professional duties and as these will include a kind of superintendence over the Volunteer Divisions of Submarine Miners at the Tay, Clyde and Forth I hope to be able to see something of North Britain during the year or two which have probably to elapse before my turn for foreign service arrives. I shall probably live in lodgings and frequent a second rate civil club as only Commanding Officers are admitted to the swagger ones. My own fellow officers are all married and so uninteresting to me. As you know I have a penchant for Scotch Whisky and a fine eye for a kilt so expect to have a very good time. I only wish I was going this week instead of in September or October. I must try and run down for a week before I go north but shall be busy now till after the 7th so there is not much chance before the 20th when the peaches should be ripe. Randolph quite to the fore in the Queen's allowance debate as also the G.O.M.
Yours affectionately
F.W.B.

48 Melville Street
Edinburgh
March 7th 1890

My dear Father

I am afraid I have been rather remiss lately in letter writing but want of exciting incident and running about the country inspecting science schools must be my excuse. These latter have taken me as far as Montrose where I came in for a snow storm and played golf at St. Andrews on my way back. St. Andrews is the golfer's paradise and certainly the best links I have played on by far. In summer they are crowded but now no-one is there. Yesterday I went to Pitlochrie on the Tay away up in the Highlands. When the summer comes and before the trippers infest these parts I must arrange to go off on Saturday and return Monday morning. My new boss has arrived, Colonel White, a benign looking old gentleman of affable demeanour across whose shining pate, the story goes, a fly once slipped up and broke its leg, I don't think he will be much of an anxiety, loves a quiet life and sketches, writes also I am told most beautiful English for 2nd rate magazines, so can't see anything ahead to disturb the even tenor of my way of life. How de Beers have fallen and for no reason. The ways of the Stock markets are wonderful! If there was an absolute certainty it is that de Beers will be at 25 before June consequently they will most likely be at 11! I'm afraid Retallack is in a bad way, haven't heard anything from him for a long time but things are very dull in S. Africa. Sorry the ewes have been dying – what is the cause?

Yours

F.W.B.

Scottish Conservative Club
Edinburgh
20th July 1890

My dear Father

I have just had an offer of Garrison Instructor to the Australian Army at Melbourne for 5 years, £1000 a year which I am considering. Time too long unless they give me six months in the middle but many advantages. Pay fair, first pre-foreign service – I must go somewhere and may fare worse instead of better. Work may not suit but then it cant be more distasteful than what I am doing now, local rank of Lt. Col. It's a long way off and very suspensive but one ought to be able to keep the wolf from the door with £1000 a year. I am temporizing and trying to get better terms. So sorry for your hay troubles, it cant be much use after lying so long, here we have had endless rain but last two days fine and looking a bit more like summer. Pensylvania Railway Ord Stock safe as Bank of England, you wont touch I know, Canadian Pacific 5 per cent 1st Mortgage Bonds at about 113 are good enough for me. Egyptians also recommended, Union Steamship Co with its South African war increasing traffic should be safe to bring you in 4 per cent. If none of these suit I will send you others.

My love.

Yours

F.W.B.

Scottish Conservative Club
Edinburgh
22nd July 1890

My dear Father

I have decided that I won't go to S. Australia for more than 3 years, for many reasons, so the chances are that the opportunity is gone, but I have no doubt on the subject. They will now try elsewhere and if no-one will go may come back to me but that is not likely. Hope your hay is saved.

Yours F.W.B.

By August 1890 Edward Bennet was back at his Regimental Depot in Northampton when he accompanied his brother, Ferdie, on a tour of Scotland. Ferdie wrote to his father in glowing terms:

Scottish Conservative Club
Edinburgh
August 28th 1890

My dear Father

You will be thinking we have both been drowned or washed away in a flood or capsized in a brake, but no, we are alright and have had a very good time of it touring about Scotland since the 16th. We did exactly the round I contemplated, viz., to Oban, Staffa and Iona (lovely day) Oban to Gairloch via Loch Leaving,

263

a long day but sea quiet, a very crowded hotel at Gairloch, people sleeping all over the house 70 more than they had proper accommodation for and we had to wait over a day before getting a room. A terrific thunderstorm made us rather uncomfortable till we arrived at Inverness by rail. Hence down Caledonian Canel to Ballachulish and next day via Glencoe to Daturaly when we went a 20 mile walk. Back to Edinburgh on Monday via Loch Lomond, Trossachs and Callender. Edward has taken copious notes and promised to write fully so I will not forestall him, he left here last night for Northampton so you will hear perhaps on Tuesday. It was never very warm and uncomfortable crowds of trippers in places so that another time I should go earlier or later.

    Yours

        F.W.B.

    In the spring of 1891 Ferdie was still based upon Edinburgh but expecting his foreign posting at any time. His brother Edward was serving at Aldershot.

Scottish Conservative Club

Edinburgh

19th March 1891

My dear Father

    I have today received my orders for Hong Kong to embark about the 1st May, as you know I expected this, I am not disturbed by the tidings, on the contrary I think I am lucky to get a 3 years station, not bad when one thinks of it that I shall get through my 30 years service with only 6½ abroad, as I shall not be called upon to go again. Hong Kong too is not at all a bad station from all I hear and there is a Major R. E. here now who has just come thence so I shall easily get all information as to it etc. I have applied to be allowed to go out by Canada and I do not expect much obstruction, it will be much the pleasantest way as the Red Sea in May would be no catch. I shall be home about the 20th April I expect for a few days but I don't want to use up much of my leave as I shall want it to escape the worse of the climate in H.K. Hope the trees are looking better. In haste,

    yours

        F.W.B.

Scottish Conservative Club
Edinburgh
13th April 1891

My dear Father

The authorities having at last made up what they are pleased to consider their minds as to my movements I am in a position to decide details for myself. I am to catch a steamer which leaves Vancouver on June 6th and allowing for leisure time I think I shall do very well if I leave here on 1st May and England about 20th. I shall have to go to town first to order my kit and shall probably come West about 6th returning to complete my preparations in a week or 10 days. I shall do Canada at quite the best time of year and arrive in Hong Kong after the worst of the heat is over though it will still be bad enough for 3 or 4 months – so I am very well satisfied on the whole. Cold here still but we see the sun at times and there are distinct signs of spring about. Am golfing much.

Yours
F.W.B.

Junior United Service Club
London S.W.
May 16th 1891

My dear Father

I enclose receipt for Kings Norton and Hammond which please place with other papers. I attended Bankers meeting but was not much edified, the Directors got a little heckled and Micklem who seconded the adoption of the Report thinks that eventually when the S.American financial sky is clearer things will be alright, but when will that be? I don't think we are near bottom yet. Edward is laid up so I may not see him again. Went to the rottenest performance at the Court last night, the silliest trash, house crowded with elite who laughed themselves into hysterics, I don't know what the English taste is coming to. Leave on Monday 10.30 for Kathleen. Tremendous hail showers yesterday. The Mother and I had an uneventful journey, the Paynters must have avoided us. In haste.

Yours
F.W.B.

R.M.S. Teutonic
Queenstown
21st May 1891

My dear Mother

I was very glad I got on board so comfortably yesterday as there was a crush by the 4 pm boat by which time I was comfortably settled in with the knowledge that all my baggage was on board. We got away about 5.30 pm and by after dinner had cleared the mouth of the river and were passing everything down channel, there was no sea and the ship was like a rock all night. She is very comfortable and well ventilated throughout and if we have it smooth we should have a very good time. I don't think much of my fellow passengers, a very dull looking set, I played my first and I suspect my last rubber as the Yanks don't play the game as we do seemingly, don't count honours, game of seven instead of five, and play anyhow. Woke early and had a bath and then down went the anchor in Queenstown Harbour 7.30 am. Sun bright and calm but shan't get ashore to be annoyed by Irish beggars. My fellow passenger is an amiable Yank who will do as I tell him, the ship is not full only some 200 passengers so there's lots of room. I suppose you or K did not drop my hand luggage by any accident as my barometer seems to have suffered considerably and I don't think is working at all now, very annoying as I wanted it to play with going over the Rockies. We leave today about 2. Have already found a chap going through to Shanghai.

Yours ever
F.W.B.

R.M.S. Teutonic
May 22nd 1891

Well away from Old England and out on the billowy waste, it seems curious but all day we have not seen a sail, after coming down the channel with its hundreds of sail and steam craft on all sides, this strikes one as odd. Fellow passengers don't improve much on acquaintance, but one decent looking woman on board and she has visible gold in her teeth. Wind what there is ahead but we go such a pace that we make a hurricane by our rapid progress, I should say there was a mild breeze from somewhere to judge by the waves and the ship rolls sufficiently to cause many a gap in our previously sparsely filled tables. She is a wonderful vessel, we have 7-800 steerage passengers on board, about 150 second class and 220 saloon and a crew of 350 yet we see and hear next to nothing of anyone save our own 220. Since leaving Queenstown at 2 pm yesterday we ran 450 miles by noon today but that included 1¼ hours extra they put the clock back at midnight for the two days since leaving Liverpool. Had a rubber last night but have only so far found 3 men who understand the game as played in England, no gambling as yet in the smokeroom. One's day is bath at 7.15, hot salt, breakfast 8.30, lunch 1.30 and dinner 6.30 and to bed about 11. Already I have found 3 or 4 commercial gents bound to catch the Parthia at Vancouver on June 5th. Weather showery, fine in morning but now cloudy.

24th. Charming day yesterday, 468 miles run, moderate breeze. Found Miss Hale, friend of the Kembles, rather nice and not a bit of American twang about her. Today, Sunday, had enough strong wind from S.W. wet and disagreeable on deck and time spent mostly in library and smokeroom. The ship is ploughing through it grandly and we ran 483 miles to noon. We are more than half way across. Cradles on the saloon tables, no cards, and a short service in the morning. Most of the women and a good many men ill. Not too cheerful.

26th. Did 411 miles only yesterday in the teeth of what the Captain is pleased to call a moderate gale. I should say a stiff breeze at the outside. But it calmed down and I should not be surprised at a 500 mile run today. Found fishing vessels at anchor (only 60 feet they say) in mid-ocean, this surprised me as I thought the Atlantic unfathomable.

27th. Well I must finish this the first section of my journey as we are within sight of Long Island and expect to disembark about 4 pm. We made 486 miles yesterday part of the way through a fog so the foghorn was going dismally at times. Shall go to a hotel for the night and off to Niagara tomorrow morning by New York Central up Hudson River to Albany.

F.W.B.

May 31st 1891
Winnipeg

My dear Father

Just a line to let you know I am so far on my journey. On landing at New York the first thing I heard was that the Parthia had been put back 3 days and was to leave Vancouver on June 3rd instead of 6th. I was also told that if I got my baggage through the Customs pretty quick I might catch the train for Vancouver which I just managed to do and came through by Montreal having to give up Niagara and travel night and day across the Continent. This place is about 1200 miles out from Montreal and we left at about 8.40 pm on Thursday and arrived here 10.20 this morning (Sunday). Details must keep, we stay here four hours to give the cars a clean up not before it was wanted. I shall probably be unable to write from Vancouver as we have only about two hours there. They cant say I am losing much time. Hot on Friday, cold yesterday and wet and raw here today. Rather amusing this kind of thing but going too quick for pleasure. Horrid pen – no time for more.

F.W.B.

June 3rd 1891
S.S. Parthia

My dear Father

Well we have arrived at the end of our six days and nights rail and have just walked on board this old craft from the train and started, no time to see anything of Vancouver of course as we sailed under the hour. If it doesn't blow we shall do well enough on this old tub but she isn't a patch on the Teutonic in comfort. I have a large cabin to myself however and we are only 14 passengers all told. I wrote from Winnipeg on line and now shall not be able to say much as I post this at Victoria this evening and I cannot do justice to the occasion in short a time. Suffice it to say therefore that I was disappointed in the first 140 miles from Montreal to Winnipeg which traverses a stretch of broken burned country full of lakes swamps and rivers with of course good pieces here and there notably Lake Superior. The prairie 900 miles I was disappointed with as it is nearly an endless treeless prairie with very little cultivation or sign of life. The last 600 miles however through the Rockies simply overwhelmed me. The Canadian Pacific guidebook I left is very true and if you study it carefully you may get an idea of the wonderful scenery, it baffles description, I had no idea of what I was going to see, I thought it was going to be grand but it was far beyond my anticipation. 600 miles of ever varying grandeur – who could describe it? I must go back over it if possible. You might go over it 100 times and find new views every time. Our train was up to time all the way through but they allow a good margin. No more now.

F.W.B.

Hong Kong
June 27th 1891

My dear Father

Here I am at last after my long journey of 12,000 miles. The last two days on board were very uncomfortable, damp heat, a good deal of which I shall have to endure apparently. After Shanghai, all flat, Hong Kong appeared like fairyland almost, abrupt hills and islands rising in all directions several hundreds of feet above the sea, of course the peaks were all dried as the rainy season was just finishing but the lower parts were fair to see with grass covered hills and then Hong Kong harbour with thousands of craft. Hong Kong itself all clustered round the base of the hills with striking buildings on all the best sites, climbing up the steep slopes. And so to our anchorage and very shortly two R.E. officers appeared and took me off to our mess which is one of the best houses in the place, 500 feet above the level of the sea with a magnificent view over the town and harbour and Chinese territory beyond – all abrupt hills and islands, really a view hard to beat anywhere. That damned intolerable muggy heat I experienced on the Parthia when two days off continues here in a more intolerable form. The temperature varies but little night or day 81 degrees – 82 degrees up and about 84 degrees – 85 degrees down below, no great heat certainly considering I have experienced 110 degrees in the shade up the Nile but not day or night nor damp heat. I can safely say I have not been out of a perspiration day or night since I arrived.

French mail in with letters from the Mother and Edith which were very welcome. I am so sorry to hear of Willy's illness, he is too old to go out to camps, someone who knew him in Volunteers some years ago introduced himself to me but I forget his name. My present intuition is certainly not to remain out here for another summer – it is quite unbearable to my system, I am quite well but I cannot stand this climate to live in, however early days yet.

Yours ever

F.W.B.

Hong Kong
July 27th 1891

My dear Father

Now that I have summoned up energy to go down into the heat of the shops to hunt up some notepaper I must try and give you a more coherent account of life in H.K. than I have yet had the patience to do with that old flimsey stuff which has all become like blotting paper. Some day I will send some photos but I cannot do more shopping than absolutely necessary till cooler times arrive. Well, we live as I told you about 500 feet up the steep slopes that go to form this island and which rise to greater heights than 1800 feet. Immediately beneath (we face North East) among bright trees and gardens lie the suburbs and respectable portions of the town of Victoria, then you have the blue sea, covered with shipping, looking like a lake, as the mainland opposite, Kowloon, is only 3 to 5 miles away and the eastern entrance to Hong Kong harbour is very narrow. The hills opposite are wild and inhospitable looking but add to the picture immensely. We have a double house with 8 large bedrooms which just accommodate the unmarried R.E.'s, the Mess premises, large dining room, anteroom, balcony, etc. are on the ground floor and below is the accommodation for servants. The peak dwellers live in houses dotted about the broken hill tops wherever they can find a place flat enough to build on, they say it is cooler and I suppose they are about 3 degrees cooler than we are and we are 3 degrees cooler than the town below. But then we have the advantage of not living in the clouds, very frequently it is quite fine down here when there is a thick fog at the peak. There are two hotels up there but they don't do much business as the Colony (Merchantile portion of it) is stone broke and things are not as they were in the prosperous days. You get up to the peak by a cable car, a ghastly assent to look at and when you get up there you play lawn tennis. No-one does anything else but lawn tennis. Yesterday we steamed round the island and on the water it is much cooler and so was very enjoyable. I make myself go down to the Happy Valley 2 or 3 times a week to play golf but it is hard to keep up one's interest even in that fascinating game in such heat and on such a ground. We are terribly warlike here, have the heaviest kind of guns to deal with and some interesting forts just built to keep in order. I am building an emplacement and am deep in concrete and brickwork and water supply and a host of things which would not be bad employment in a decent climate, but here it is labour and trouble to take an interest in anything. Not much break in the weather yet save that the rain has ceased the last few days and there is more sun, consequently hotter and today it is 85 degrees up here and 87 degrees down below. The C.R.E. comes back this week from Japan. Well I must close this, mail expected today.

 F.W.B.

Hong Kong
December 20th 1891

My dear Father

Edith's of November 10th by last mail brought me great relief as I learned that La Grippe had run its course and left you if a weaker, a wiser man in that it had taught you the invaluable lesson of having a supply of good champagne to stimulate the system about 6 a.m. when all doctors agree the vital energies are liable to caught napping. I trust by this time you are out and about again and restored to health. I got the disease two years ago in Edinburgh, at least I caught it in London and unselfishly conveyed it to Edinburgh, it only lasted me a week but I don't want it again. Our new Governor, Sir W. Robinson has arrived and is settling down I hope – a fine looking middle-aged man, young wife and daughter about same age but by another wife, and I think there is a young family, also an aide de camp and a private secretary called Knaggs. They had a reception and we all attended along with the riff raff of merchantile society in our best clothes, shook hands and came away though Knaggs did offer me some soda water. Society, especially the military element is much exercised by the A.D.C. appearing in aiguillettes a badge only worn by

A.D.C.'s to Royalty, and also by the band playing God Save the Queen whenever he appears in public, so now everyone is truly happy picking holes in his habits which are somewhat eccentric. However I dare say he will harm little. Christmas is almost on us and I quite pity you in England as I bask in the sun of this delightful climate. I am nearly forgetting my original sufferings, we have regattas, dances and amateur pantomime and goodness knows what other troubles ahead not that they trouble me much. The regatta is, I understand, over. I should not have known it but that a cup appeared on the Mess table one night and I found one of our fellows had won a sailing race.

22nd. Today's mails brought yours, the Mothers, and Willy's scrap and all their dreadful details. Well well, it never rains but it pours and you do seem to be a pretty sick household, the only thing that remains is for Edward to get the disease (for of course you are all suffering from the same thing) I don't know at this distance that there is much for me to do except assure you all of my sympathy, one thing you could not be better than in Cornwall for a speedy recovery. The Mother, wonderful woman, of course is alright and doctors for two. Christmas just on us and no plum puddings to hand yet, but one is, I hear, signalled, so one's dinner is alright. We all dine here together. The Navy coming in from the North and many new faces around, a new Regiment is expected early in January.

My love to all.
Ever yours
F.W.B.

Hong Kong
January 5th 1892

My dear Father

Delighted to hear your good news of December 2nd that you are all progressing satisfactorily but I am still anxious about Kathleen and of course the Mother will break down, I have been expecting it the last letter or two but she still holds out bravely, by this time I hope she is sitting up again. Edith is evidently suffering from D.T. and I should stop the champagne as she has had more than is good for her. When one gravely tries to record on paper wanderings of fever the effort must be due to alcoholic stimulants,

I trust K has not also given way to the pernicious habit! Christmas is over thank goodness and things are settling down again, it is bad enough in England, in the company of soldiers here it is infinitely worse. We have the China New Year to look forward to however, when they go on the bend for a week, their only rest in the year so who could grudge it and yet I don't expect to see a single drunken Chinaman, I never have yet though the streets swarm with them – but many drunken Englishmen. And yet the Exeter Hall people get up and snort and want to stop opium for the Chinese. All your deaths are very sad particularly F. C. Lamb whom I should have liked to have met many times more. I think my chances of an exchange very doubtful and I don't very much care as I shall be in a very good position if I put in 3 years here, shall not have to go abroad again and of course one is serving in a place like this. It is difficult to imagine now that the heat is ever unbearable. I hear some of our youngsters sighing for the heat of summer when they can go to sleep after lunch, to me it is now delightful and I can actually walk up to the Mess without fatigue.

F.W.B.

Hong Kong
6th February 1892

My dear Father

Well I have done Canton at last and I don't think I shall do it again. Canton as you are probably aware is the largest city in South China, the Capital of two provinces and a busy commercial centre distant 98 miles from Hong Kong up the Canton River, a capital steam boat service takes you up in 8 or 9 hours. We were 18 hours coming back thanks to a fog. We were met by our guide who spoke English very well picked up chiefly during the English occupation 1857 – 1861 who took us off in chairs through the narrowest of streets to some shops when he bored us to death by things we did not want and which we could probably have got in Hong Kong without any trouble. The streets and crowds in the city are very objectionable and it is a marvel how they get the chairs along, six feet is about the average width and going round corners the chair poles grate against the brickwork and cut grooves in the soft bricks. The crowd is very orderly and get out of your

273

way somehow as best they can, there is no wheeled traffic of course, nothing but human beasts of burden, granite paving very rough as a rule and slippery when wet. A fairly good hotel in the European quarter which is shut off from the Chinese shuttered up for the night. Next day we visited a so called Chinese Club where some marvellous carvings chiefly wood gilded on coloured but no occupants as they do not come in from the country in winter. Then to a temple or two in one of which were 500 idols in gilded wood very dusty but religion is at a discount in China and what little they do now in the way of burning war tapers is down in their own houses. Then to a chamber of horror when various phases of torture are depicted in life size carvings for the benefit of the public. And so at last we escaped to the city walls out of the crowd where we got out of our chairs and walked a mile or so on the battlements which are by no means formidable, rusty old canon you could not fire. The walls go round the city and are 6 or 7 miles in length with several gateways. A most uninteresting city of squalid houses of black brick with tiled roofs, little to break the level anywhere, a Roman Catholic Cathedral the most striking looking feature and a few enormous ugly square buildings something like a grain elevator one sees in America which they said were pawn shops the people store their winter clothes in during summer. Then to the High Court of Justice when I was much edified at the behaviour of the judges, 3 or 4 sat at a table in a courtyard, one interrogated the malefactor at his feet in chains in a most aggressive manner sometimes cheerfully as if he was the prisoner's best friend at other times seriously and even angrily, when the latter occurred it generally ended in an instrument of torture being produced to frighten him. All the judges smoked and chatted pleasantly to each other, to a post near the centre of the hall was fastened a Chinaman with his arms tied back straight by his thumbs his pigtail tied back so as to keep his head up and his knees on the ground with the feet suspended by the big toes his body was quivering but he didn't die while I was there, it was not a pleasant sight but I have no doubt he richly deserved his punishment. Justice in China seems to me to be alright, the rich can buy it of course and the poor have to take their chances, but they never behead an innocent man so they torture him till he confesses, whether he is guilty or not, and then the law is satisfied with his head – there seemed to be no witnesses, only an interpreter, but during the hour we were there nothing was done, one man was put aside to think a bit about torture and another was remanded for 3 days as the judge got hungry. The river life in Canton is very curious and is no doubt the outcome of there being few railways and no roads to speak of in the country, consequently the teeming population transports itself and its produce to and from Canton in boats, thousands of which lie alongside the banks or moor up and down in the swishing tideway, the river is not more than 200 yards wide and very similar to the Thames at Westminster in size and tide; they have plenty of stern wheel ferry boats which work with their junks. The Chinese are wonderful boatmen. About 500 houses had been burnt down in one part of the town a month ago but they were busy rebuilding and had wisely decided to make the streets two feet wider. All Canton seemed nothing but shops and the awful things they enclose and sell – they seem to like everything we throw away. The races come off here on Thursday Friday and Saturday but as the Government had decided to stop the Chinese gambling houses some wiseacre read the ordinance as applying to every kind of betting and even a sweepstake was a very risky operation, consequently the Chinese who had flocked in thousands from outlying parts for their usual gamble finding it stopped left the ground about 3 o'clock the first day and never came back. The European enclosure was more like a funeral than a race meeting and everyone agreed it was the dullest affair. You will see by this paper that the damp season has come again and temperature increasing.

F.W.B.

Hong Kong
March 16th 1892

My dear Father

Yours dated Feb 9th arrived March 11th two days after the French mail which brought Edith's of Feb 3rd so now we hear no more for 12 days from 11th. I wish those steamers would divide the time a little better. I am so glad to hear the Mother has been induced to tear herself away and take a change at Bournemouth, t'will do her good. I am delighted to hear the pheasants are in the neighbourhood and I hope to hear of several broods around the

275

pond and garden. Yes the Bankers Investment Trust has gone to the dogs but the price is unduly depressed I think and I expect full dividends on the preferred and 1 or 2 p c on the deferred in May. Argentina seems inclined to repudiate her debts in toto and I don't see why not if she chooses to be dishonest who can make her pay? She will get no more money of course but that seems the limit of retaliation and the English money lenders have only to grin and bear it. This place keeps cold enough we seldom have a bright day generally dull and gloomy but much drier than in summer. I don't know where I shall go yet for my leave. The latest forecast of promotion in our Corps shows me retired at 48 as a Major but it wont come to that I expect. Had a line from Edward from M.C. He seems to have done no good at the tables and it goes without saying he will do no harm, a fascinating amusement and not dangerous to a Bennet. I hope Edith goes out if she gets the chance to the Kembles. Am amused by Edith's account of Greenwood's shooting affair, and fancy Polwhales ideas of hospitality as exemplified by a cold collation. Busy times with me now, the end of the financial year and so all work has to be completed and paid for before 31st then we are going to mobilise as for war and I shall have to go and live on an island and play at being soldiers for 3 days, 28th 29th and 30th. Fun but of a mild type. We lose Barker the next R.E. to me in a month or two don't know yet who succeeds but I should think most likely someone junior to me which will make me the Officer Commanding R.E. but not the Commanding Royal Engineer. As the former I have to weigh off prisoners and look after the two companies in a fatherly kind of way. Ellen James dunning me for a sovereign for her please tell Edith to give her one and I will repay.
    Yours
        F.W.B.

May 11th 1892
My dear Father
    Thanks for letters by French and English mails two from you and one from K, the last of yours dated 5th April. My plans unaltered and I leave here with Dumbleton on 28th for Vancouver picking up Dr Bourlay R.A. at Yokohama, never did a schoolboy

look forward to his holidays more eagerly? We (Dumbleton and I) think of finishing up by a run up the Alaskan coast in the ice region but there is time enough to mature our plans on the other side. I note a tendency more especially from the North to complain of the dullness of my letters, my only wonder is that I write at all, K had better come here for a year or two if she wants ideas, does she want to know how many I took to go round the golf links every day, or what the quality of cement is out here? Perhaps they will be more interesting from America. It is still not oppressively hot, about 80 degrees and no rain to speak of, about 30 inches are due this month. Last Saturday and Sunday I spent at Macau, a Portuguese settlement in a languishing state, not much more in fact now than an enormous Chinese fishing village, picturesque enough facing South with a strong wind but hotter than this place I think. It is on a peninsular at the mouth of the western branch of the Canton River, sea and colour, mosquitoes, priest ridden, islands all about. I found out poor Dicks grave in an enclosed yard out of the town with lawn tennis grounds just outside and one caretaker looks after both, a very painful spot with bamboo surrounding the place. Enjoyed the change – only 3 hours steam from here. The Hong Kong Regiment 1000 strong from India arrived on Saturday a welcome addition to our garrison 9 European officers and fine men, Sikhs etc from North India, it makes our DAAG quite important. Barker leaves shortly and is replaced by a Captain who should be here by middle of June, I don't know him, Stewart by name and a bachelor. Almost a year since I left England, it seems so long to look back on. Glad the gardener man seems likely to do, if you see Rashleigh you might ask him if he would care for any Hong Kong shrubs or trees, not much use sending them to Tresillian as they would require a milder climate and more attention probably than you would care to devote, his sheltered glens might give them a chance. I don't know the names but I could find out and he probably knows all about what grows in these parts. Tell K I see all periodicals thanks but she may send me Robin Hood or whatever it is to Vancouver – I shall have time to read it coming back I have no doubt. I forget if I sketched our route which is so far thus – Leave Hong Kong 28th May arrive Vancouver 18th June, San Francisco 20th, Yosemite Valley till 30th, back to Portland Oregon and thence via Spokane Falls to

Rivetstroke on CPR. Then dawdle about Rockies and possibly back to Vancouver by 16th July. Then for 10 or 12 days by S.S. Islander up the Alaskan coast having a week on return for Victoria. Leave Victoria 7th August arrive Hong Kong 29th.

Yours

F.W.B.

Hotel del Monk
Monterey, Cal.
July 2nd 1892

My dear Father

I wrote you on landing at Victoria and now you will be glad to hear we are still alive and flourishing. We stopped a couple of days in Victoria where I failed to discover any great signs of progress or anything to be particularly proud of and then started for San Francisco. A night's journey in a steamer through Puget Sound took us to Incoma and thence two days rail brought us to Frisco. The district traversed was interesting enough, mostly forest land with a sparse population and not much cultivation, here and there an attempt to raise corn or fruit but the soil did not strike me as very rich anywhere – the railway route is not difficult save near Mt. Shasta where it crosses a ridge of mountains about 4000 feet above the sea. Mt. Shasta is a glorious snowclad mountain rising 13000 feet not unlike Mt. Argeus in Anatolia. Frisco we found a fraud, but a wonderful climate has California near the coast, a fresh breeze and cloudless skies all the summer, never hot, a huge city with tramcars in every direction worked by cables under the ground as in Edinburgh. So we started off for the Yosemite about the 24th by rail for a night and then 60 miles by stage coach, a dreadful concern for a day and a half!

The Yosemite Valley so far as the scenery goes is wonderful and very like some photographs I will send by and bye and the big trees, seeds of which I will also supply, are well worth seeing but the discomforts were awful when we went in and at one time, the last night we spent in the Valley, we really wished ourselves back in Hong Kong, what with the heat and the dust and the jolting of the coach on the track which is often on rocks 6 inches deep in dust and the fact that you get nothing fit to eat or drink (except water) going or coming and the worst hotel in the civilised world when you get there are hardships too great even to endure even though you are rewarded by some perfectly unique scenery. It was really too awful at times but we may have gone in at an unfortunate time. We had one long walk when there, up to Glacier Point and around by some of the best waterfalls but we were glad to come away in 2½ days and now find ourselves resting in the most delightful and civilised hotel with such lovely grounds, our home till the 4th when we leave for the Banff. This is an awful country to travel in, western Americans are very odious in their manners and customs, they spit and chew and travel as one class, waiters are uncivil according to our ideas and their piggish way of feeding dumping everything around on small plates sweets and meats fruits and vegetables and giving you one knife and fork for the lot is very unappetising. Besides they don't know how to cook, except at the very best hotels you never get anything fit to eat or drink. It is certainly no place to travel in for comfort and so expensive, a dollar equals 2/- and you pay for everything. A room in Frisco was 4 dollars a day, boot cleaning 10 cents = 5d, a bottle of beer 3/- the Times 1/- a bath 2/-, one portmanteau 2/- railway travelling is about equal to third class and dear at that, the people one meets are not rude but they are not very interesting and the women are very ugly fat and ill mannered, overdressed, a nation of snobs I think someone has called them – not far wrong – though no doubt many exceptions. Agriculture in the Californian plains is conducted in a wonderful fashion. It was harvest time, the wheat and rye and barley all ripe. You see a huge concern drawn or pushed perhaps by from 12 to 18 or 24 horses, you see this passing over the field perhaps of 5000 acres cutting off only the heads of the corn and depositing a tied up sack of grain at regular intervals where it is carted off to the railway. Four or five men work this machine and they travel round with a movable house in which they live. Of course there are many descriptions of machines none however fitted for Tresillian House. Everywhere one sees economy of labour and no wonder when it costs 10/- a day. Time I have no doubt will soften the American manners and customs as it has done in the West and Chinese cheap labour would make a wonderful difference to the comfort of foreigners but that they won't have either here or in B.C. to a sufficient extent so the only thing to do is to avoid travelling in such a country.

3rd. We leave tomorrow for Banff, 6 days travelling on end about 600 people in this hotel and tomorrow being the 4th July they are rather fanatical and flaunt stars and stripes everywhere. No news from you since I left Hong Kong. I enclose seeds they will do anywhere, no heat necessary.

Yours
    F.W.B.

Hotel Vancouver
Vancouver B.C.
August 3rd 1892

My dear Father

Well here we are back from Alaska, a trip we all enjoyed after the long dusty railway journeys we have been making. The steamer Islander was very comfortable and only 35 passengers so we had separate cabins and a table of English people in the saloon. The rest of the passengers were unspeakable Yanks most of whom had never been away from their inland stores before and who were always in raptures at nothing. They ruin any market in the world giving all sorts of prices for furs and skins – $95 for a bear skin not worth $30 in Vancouver, they do the same in Japan, buy anything – a man gave £100 for two huge vases worth about £20 on a friend telling him they were too big to go in his house he said he knew it but he guessed they would look well in the garden. But – about Alaska – the Americans rave about the scenery, nothing like it in the world etc. Really it is a very pleasant inland sea voyage amongst densely fir wooded islands rising abruptly from the waters edge with occasional background of snowy mountains, plenty of whales, porpoises and salmon everywhere also acquatic birds. Salmon fishing which was just at its height is about all that goes on, population very small chiefly Indians who I was surprised to find dressed in European garments and evidently very well to do. We stopped at various places and had a run on shore, it was not cold but often wet and nearly always cloudy – in fact it rains on an average about 9 months in the year. No change in the scenery till we got to the Great Glazier when the trees stopped and the hills became very barren. The Glazier itself very impressive a mile in length 150 feet high, the overflow in ice of a huge inland frozen lake swooping down into the sea. We went close up to it and every now and then huge fragments kept breaking off with a tremendous roar as of thunder and plunging into the sea. The sea for miles is covered with ice floes making navigation in foggy weather very difficult, of course also it is cold in the immediate presence of the bergs. On our way back we went up the Gardners Inlet 100 miles into British Columbia and here the scenery was very grand, trees being replaced by plenty of snowclad mountains. We had a glorious day, any amount of waterfalls and it was nearly as grand as the Yosemite. Now we are off back to Vancouver Island where I hope to get a couple of days fishing before leaving in the Empress of India on the 7th. We have had a real good time of it all told. Your letters received until July 5th – excuse this scrawl but I have been much interrupted. May not write again till Hong Kong so don't be alarmed by a long silence.

Yours
F.W.B.

R.M.S. Empress of India
Vancouver
Sunday August 7th 1892

My dear Father

Since I wrote last week we have been over to Victoria again mainly to pick up the surgeon there but late last night we were informed that the ship would not touch at that port on account of smallpox so we had to rush on board the steamer which plies between Victoria and Vancouver and now we find ourselves and all our belongings safely on board this ship which is exactly the same as the one we came over in only a much better skipper. During our 3 or 4 days in Victoria we went up the Rail to Dunkins 40 miles where I did a day's fishing on the Cowicken R, exciting work in the rapids in a canoe. Caught one good fish about 3 lbs and a few smaller and so ends our 7 weeks journeyings in this country which I think we have both enjoyed immensely notwithstanding certain drawbacks I have alluded to. By the time we get back to Hong Kong we shall have covered over 17000 miles, not a bad record for 90 days and shall only have 2 months heat to endure which is a very comforting reflection. We have had charming weather throughout, here it is now hot by day but always cool nights.

Yours

F.W.B.

As Ferdie was settling back in Hong Kong his elder brother, Edward, following a two year posting to Aldershot, received orders to return to India. He sailed in H.M.S. *Malabar* on the 5th October 1892 and arrived in Bombay on the 1st November, almost twenty-four years since his first disembarkation as a junior subaltern. Ferdie, ever the regular correspondent, continued his letters home.

Hong Kong
5th January 1893

My dear Father

Yours of November 23rd and two from Kathleen and the latest home letters received on the 29th December, how lucky I am to have such correspondents. Now you have two sons abroad I shall not expect to be so well treated. No word from Edward yet, how long do his letters take to reach you? Here we have safely got through Christmas and embarked on the New Year without much trouble. I intend this summer, if I can get away, going off to Australia for three months, if I can only manage that I shan't have done so badly as no-one wants a better climate than this in winter, it was that first summer was such a sickener. A gay time here now, dances and theatrical dinners etc till you can't rest, but Dumby and I generally toast our feet over the fire and let the young ones go. We are going to give a small dance and dinner on the 18th when I shall play whist with the Governor upstairs far from the 'madding' crowd. It seems to me that there are more people about Tresillian than there used to be, you are always going somewhere, Newquay too will increase and if they only got golf would attract even in winter. The new horse venture will turn out well but you will never do much with Richard as stud groom. No wrecks to chronicle this time and somehow one never has time to write a letter in this place because there is nothing to do I suppose.

Yours

F.W.B.

CHAPTER 14

There's no sense in going further – it's the edge of cultivation, so they said, and I
believed it – broke my land and sowed my crop;
Built my barns and strung my fences in the little border station,
Tucked away below the foothills where the trails run out and stop.

Rudyard Kipling. The Explorer.

S.S. Changshas
Gulf of Carpentaria
14th June 1893

My dear Father

So far all going well. Left Hong Kong on 3rd at 5 pm in this
comfortable steamer 2300 hours, Captain Williams and 14 saloon
passengers. It was very hot for the first five days but now it is dry
heat and not at all oppressive, the cabins were unbearable at night
and so we slept on deck on the saloon table anywhere when there
was a little breeze. We started across the China Sea for two days
and then down the Philippian coast where we were quite close to
land and the considerable settlement of Surabaya. Thence through
Pitt Passage into the Baudac Sea and so across to Port Darwin
where we arrived on the 12th at 8 am, a very good passage for a
ship which only pretends to do 11 knots an hour. There is not
much to interest on the voyage, land in sight most of the time but
as a rule very remote, no ships or boats to speak of and not much
sea life. We were intensely lazy each taking up our own positions
on deck after breakfast and sleeping and reading through the day.
We are getting a little more lively now it is cooler and play whist,
sing songs in the usual ship style. The first sight of Australia is
very disappointing, a strip of yellow shore, a green strip of scrub
and above and below the blue of the sky and the blue of the
ocean. At Port Darwin we stopped four hours, we landed and

walked to the top of the bluff where the town stands 40 feet above the sea on a plateau enduring forever. Apparently 20 years ago they laid out the town after the American system in blocks with enormous roads but a more lifeless dreary place I have seldom come across. A few European houses built of a framework of timber covered over with white painted galvanised iron, a chinatown which seems thriving, a railway station whence a train starts to the interior for 100 miles to the mining country. Broad roads full of dust in dry weather and mud in wet. A few Aborigines loafing about all smoking pipes of strong tobacco, tall erect people, frightfully ugly, nearly black in colour, unkempt hair, thick lips, they seem very near the missing link. It is a poor place to live in and the Chinese seem to be the only people who can make a living, they seem to get plenty of gold which the Europeans cannot work profitably, we are taking on £20,000 worth, the Europeans (or Australians) are sick of the place which without being unhealthy is very hot for 9 months, they have few luxuries, no ice and until the Chinese came no fresh vegetables. We left at noon and are now getting a bit of a tossing in the sea so no writing. Tomorrow we get to Thursday Island where I shall post this in the hope that you will get it before my next from Sydney. After that the voyage is very pleasant going down the East coast to the Great Barrier Reef in smooth water. We shall likely not stop long in Sydney but go on in this ship to Melbourne and make the three weeks trip round New Zealand and back to Sydney. I expect to find the Australians very cut up by the financial crashes.

Yours

    F.W.B.

> Hadley's Orient Hotel
> Hobart, Tasmania
> 12th July 1893

My dear Father

I think this is my fourth letter from Australasia, last week's mail I missed I believe so it is a fortnight likely since you heard and a deal of country I have traversed since my last which was dated Sydney. Lloyd and I had then got back from our trip to the Blue Mountains which I described. We left Sydney on Tuesday 4th by slow freight for Melbourne, they mix goods and passenger trains in these parts and it was our only chance of seeing the country as the express goes by night. I should never do it again, however, as there is nothing much to see, just undulating ground with the eternal bluegums and grass and very little agriculture, just sheep and cattle grazing on scanty scrub. Still it was worth seeing for once just to get an idea of the ground which I must say is disappointing as I do not think the sod is any good for agriculture and the most it can maintain is a bullock an acre. After about 12 hours we had gone about 250 miles and were turned out to wait four hours for the express which came long at 1 am. The rest of the journey, another 201 miles about we did in about 10 hours, having to change carriages at 6 am as the gauge varies in the different colonies. Approaching Melbourne the land improves and then are great plains of grassland and the country is more cultivated and divided into big fields by fences. Melbourne is an astonishing great place, I never expected to find it half so big and the houses in the principal streets very fine and large, nearly every other one in the main street seemed to be a bank and most of the doors were open and going ahead as if nothing had happened. But they are in a rotten state in Melbourne worse even than in Sydney where there are thousands of unemployed one would imagine from the appearance of the parks and street corners where they loaf all day long. Australia is passing through the fire with a vengeance and I can see no possible rift in the cloud for five years. The average Australian is firmly imbued with the idea '8 hours work 8 hours play 8 hours sleep 8 bottles a day' but the time has come when he can't get 8 bottles a day, he has tried strikes and been beaten, funds are exhausted and now he is sulking and refusing to work for less than 8 bottles a day, expecting the Government to feed him and provide labour. They need to do that, they need to send these beggars off up country in hundreds to make roads and give them 7/6 a day! They need to feed them royally on beef and vegetables and bread and possibly beer but those happy days are gone and now the Government has no money they will have to take to rioting or accept the bitter pill of less wages and go to work again. The golden era is over for Australia for a long while unless great gold discoveries are made when great cities like Melbourne may again spring up in their vicinity. I doubt if Melbourne itself will recover, it sprang into splendour suddenly I believe in the gold times and now it is tearing downhill and everyone has gone bung as they say. We had only a short 24 hours in Melbourne which was not enough as the melancholy ruin seemed to have more life in it than Sydney after all, but we had joined our young friend Stephens (globe trotter) and taken our tickets through by the S.S. Patina so off we went on Friday at midday with a lot of landlubbers as crew, for a general strike of seamen and firemen had been ordered on a reduction of wages from £7 to £5 a month which the ship owners had decided upon and so they had to ship anyone they could get and very little difficulty was found in getting substitutes of a kind in these hard times. We turned up about 60 for lunch that day but there was a bit of a sea on the outside and a steward told me there were only four at dinner, however at 8 am next day we were steaming up the smooth waters of the Tamar River 30 miles to Launceston the second town of Tasmania and very pretty the river was, any amount of black swans and a much prettier country than Australia, much more broken up and the hills running up to 4000 feet with snow on their tips. Launceston and Hobart are just like second class English provincial towns, no attempt at swagger, no big houses or ostentation, long may they keep out of it. At Launceston where we stayed one night we went to see the cataract where the river comes down through a fine gorge boiling grandly. Next day a fine frosty clear morning we left by slow freight again for Hobart and were charmed with the country which had much more variety than Australia, more cultivation, more hedges and sheep grazing sensibly in fields instead of wandering over the surface of the globe. We took all day to do the 120 miles but again we had to wait four hours and so had a good walk. On this day we saw a rabbit for the first time since we have been in these parts, we have seen several more since then but no sign of a plague. Hobart is pleasantly situated on the lower slopes of Mt. Wellington on the sea and is a great very straggling town of 40000 inhabitants, there is nothing much to be done in the way of sightseeing, a pleasant drive down the coast and a stroll round the park which is simply a bit of Australia all bluegum and grass. On Monday we went off up to New Norfolk the centre of the hop gardens, orchards and agriculture. A peaceful valley surrounded by picturesque hills with very good soil and well framed, quite civilised in fact but being the depth of winter looking its worst, of course. Next day we went to the end of the railway to Glenara 35 miles from Hobart and walked back to New Norfolk, a beautiful day and any amount of parakeets with wonderful coloured plumage. These must be great pests to the fruit growers. Everything does well up that valley, apples, pears, plums, peaches, strawberries, any English fruit in fact, hops corn etc etc and a splendid river the Derwent flowing along in the middle, they ought to do well I don't whether they do though. People are all civil and obliging and give one goodday but ignorant about their own affairs and district and very backward in the comforts of life, villainous cooking and no ideas beyond beef and mutton, you can't get a drink for miles and miles and the Inns are very ramshackle old places as a rule. We visited the Government fishponds which have been going for 30 years, trout have flourished but out of the millions of salmon fry they have hatched and turned out not one salmon has ever been caught yet though some people would have you think the contrary. The next day, Wednesday, we walked back to Hobart 21 miles and had a very good time along the river, a steamer goes up to New Norfolk as well as the rail and we intended to come back that way, but though advertised to come we found out in the morning she wasn't and so took to our hindlegs as there are only two trains per day, one about light and the other after dark. The scenery is nothing wonderful, bold hills and they make out there are waterfalls but they hardly know where they are or the distance so we gave up attempting to see them and I don't think we missed much.

13th. Had another walk today but there is nothing to keep one here so we leave for New Zealand on Saturday. We have been wonderfully lucky in our weather, it has been an exceptionally wet winter here but we always escaped and I am so enjoying the cold bracing air. I dare say we shall find it almost too cold in New Z. Ed. Chudleigh is in Norfolk Island, I don't know where that is but his name does not appear in the New Z directory. No letters since leaving Hong Kong, hoping to get some at Wellington in about 3 weeks.

Yours

F.W.B.

Northern Club
Auckland, N.Z.
August 20th 1893

My dear Father

Yours of 20th June and Edith's with enclosure from Amy of 28th I found here on my arrival on the 17th. My last was from Wellington I think about a fortnight ago, there I said goodbye to Lloyd who had to return to Sydney for Hong Kong and I continued with Stephens a very nice young fellow. From Wellington we made Napier, by rail to Ekatahuna coach thence to Woodville 35 miles and in by train over the Hawkes Bay plains famous for sheep. Travelling has been risky by rail and road owing to the extraordinary amount of rain they have had lately and for the last 12 months (such a contrast to your experience) land slips swollen rivers and fearful roads all hindering to rapid progress. We were tolerably fortunate but had rain between Ekatahuna and Woodville and so could not see much of the bush or forest country which however is rapidly disappearing. They clear the dead undergrowth and when dry fire it as it is, this burns the standing trees which soon fall, then they scatter grass seed about and turn on a few sheep and wait for 10 to 15 years for the larger logs which cover half the ground to disappear and think they are happy, I never saw a more miserable waterlogged outlook, but the cry is all for land (small holdings) and starvation in some parts and confiscation or rather extra taxation for the large land holders so as to starve them out. The Hawkes Bay district is all sheep and very fertile in grass, 3 or 5 sheep to the acre I dare say, large freezing works of Nelson Bros which we inspected and they are making a quite large harbour which will cost them about a million before it is finished, interest guaranteed by a rate on the farmers of course. From Hawkes Bay we drove right across the North Island to see the hot springs geysers blow holes etc and were vastly disappointed. They over write their things always and it was the wrong time of year, but anyhow the whole thing is a ghastly fraud and I wouldn't go near the North Island again I think. We started on a Monday from Napier and drove 50 miles, the first day over two mountain ranges in a wild storm of wind and rain outside and a confounded squalling baby inside, the roads were ghastly and dangerous here and there and we got horrid accommodation that night. Next day we were soon clear of the mountains and out on the ghastliest country in the world, nothing but manuka scrub and bracken with sometimes a little tussock grass and a cabbage tree, bogs took the place of precipices and swollen rivers and at last we got to Lake Tansu another 50 miles. The so-called coaches are uncomfortable – buggins of leather straps holding 4 inside and 2 on the top beside the driver, four horses when the roads are fairly level and five once in the mountains. Next day we went on 8 miles to Waraku and saw the geysers, boiling water in pools of all sizes, sometimes spouting up a few feet, sometimes boiling around, steam blow holes, fissures emitting sulphur fumes etc etc bore you to death waiting for the beastly things to start after you have seen half a dozen, it was a novelty of course seeing boiling water and watching the Maoris do all their cooking in natural steam ovens. Just a bottomless box over a steam hole, put in the food cover over with a bit of sacking to confine the steam and come back in 20 minutes and dinner is ready. There was a grand rush of water out of Lake Tansu which was higher than it had been for years and at one place a fine waterfall, not high but great volume. Next day we continued our journey another 50 miles to Rotorua, our only amusement being when we got bogged down with the wheels on our side sinking over the axles which caused the buggy to stop suddenly and shot a very uninteresting couple (honeymooners who had been annoying us all through) and the driver head over heels. Stephens and I sat tight and roared at the others picking themselves out of the mud. No harm done. We spent 3 or 4 days at Rotorua doing the sights which only bored us to death – more feeble geysers and hot springs and soaking ourselves in stinking hot water which we pretended to enjoy, they are supposed to cure all diseases, all they did for us was to bring on 3 or 4 days later distinct rheumatic twinges! Then we drove on to Onford and here by train and steam barge as the railway was flooded in parts and so ended a very poor pleasure excursion. The roads are simply clearings in the scrub so that in good weather it is possible to get a 4-wheeled vehicle which is proof against bumps along at about 5 miles an hour. In places through the scrub when the wind can't get at them they are a foot deep in mud, no attempt at metalling of course as there is no stone to do it with and no traffic to make it worth while, the whole way across 190 miles we only met one vehicle and that was the road man. This is a charming place quite the best in New Zealand, an unpretending town of 50000 inhabitants beautifully situated on low ground, sea on both sides, and any amount of estuaries and low conical extinct volcanoes from which one gets splendid views over the surrounding country which is very rich grassland very green and fresh, plenty of English fir trees and volcanic rocks which they make hedges of, there must be some drawbacks of course but I don't know what unless they be mosquitoes and rather a hot summer, but they say they always get cool nights. I don't know what you poor farmers will do now this trouble of no grass no hay has come upon you, I don't think prices of stock will ever rise again, New Zealand can supply 2 millions of frozen sheep a year and be content if they get 4s a lb in London, and mind you as good as the best English mutton, I am a very good judge as Sam knows and the sheep out here are of the best breeds, fed on the best of grass and any amount of it and freezing it for a couple of years only improves it. Mutton should never be above 7d per lb from any butcher as it is in the large towns I have no doubt they say 1/- a lb for New Zealand mutton which costs 5d Australia I don't think ever will produce decent mutton, the climate is against them and they have no good grass as yet but they mean to try. New Zealand is flourishing without a doubt but they have a detestable Government and are now going in for womens suffrage and the abolition of all public houses, the restrictions in the case of the latter to apply to clubs, I don't suppose they will carry it. We leave here on Wednesday 23rd for Sydney, can't do anything from here because the roads outside the town district are impassable, they have taken 4 million pounds worth of gums out of the soil the last 20 years and are now beginning to notice that if they had just a small export duty on it they would have been able to make roads with the proceeds. I shall probably be in Sydney till about 8th September when I shall catch the steamer for Hong Kong. Will write again thence. Weather here delightful.

    My love etc

        F.W.B.

Major F. W. Bennet R.E., returned to Hong Kong and completed his tour of duty at the end of May 1894 when he returned to England in the Royal

Mailship *Lucania*. His elder brother, Edward, returned from India shortly afterwards. Gully Bennet's two soldier sons were at home together. On docking at Liverpool on the 7th June 1894 Ferdie wrote to his father: ... I shall go to Comberbach on Saturday, London on Monday and hope to catch the 11.45 train for Newquay on Wednesday whence I will get a conveyance to take me to Tresillian. My love to all. F.W.B.

CHAPTER 15

I do not love my Empire's foes,
Nor call them angels; still,
What is the sense of 'atin' those
'Oom' you are paid to kill?
So, barring' all that foreign lot
Which only joined for spite,
Myself, I'd just as soon as not
Respect the man I fight.
Rudyard Kipling. *Piet.*

After a short leave spent with his parents and sister Edith at Tresillian Ferdie joined his Corps at Aldershot where he immersed himself in studying for promotion and conducting a correspondence with a young lady he had met in Hong Kong.

Aldershot
July 13th 1894

My dear Father
  You will be pleased to hear that I have passed my examination alright and you will be still more pleased, I hope, to hear that I am engaged to be married to Evelyn Palmer. It is high time for me to take a wife to myself if I intend to do so at all and I think Evelyn is quite the right sort for me, not too young very sensible in everything and I am sure will make me happy. We have been in correspondence since I left Hong Kong and last night as arranged I got a wire accepting me. I expect she will come home in November and that we shall be married early next year. I don't know that you have ever seen her, she is rather small, not pretty by any means but a very pleasant face, of course no money, but I have enough for both as our tastes are not on the side of

extravagance. Her address is Civil Hospital Hong Kong and I hope some member of my family will write her a welcome by next mail. The Queen's Review just over. I was only a spectator which is much the best place on such occasions, I don't care to go out with four general service wagons behind me. Tell the Mother I certainly wish to continue my subscription for Mary Greenwood and I enclose a cheque for £10 for her to put to my account which she tells me is nearly exhausted. To whom shall I write to know whether I am entitled to vote for Courtney, the election is on the 25th I believe and I might try and come down for 3 or 4 days if my vote is alright. I suppose Williams has no chance.

    Yours

       F.W.B.

Evelyn Mary Palmer was the daughter of Major-General H.S. Palmer, Royal Engineers, who died and was buried in Japan on the 10th February 1893 at the early age of fifty-five. General Palmer was born in England in 1838 and first went to Japan in 1883 as a Lt. Col, Royal Engineers. The General had earned a distinguished reputation in the field of water engineering. He had designed and constructed waterworks in Canton and Hong Kong before travelling to Japan where his reputation preceded him. The Authorities at Yokohama desperately needed a water supply system and engaged the General as a Consulting Engineer to design and build the Municipal waterworks. The work began in April 1885 under his supervision and was completed in September 1887 at a cost of over one million yen. It was recognized as the first modern water supply system in Japan. During his work in Yokohama General Palmer gave advice and constructed water supply systems for Osaka and Tokyo and was engaged in the planning of Yokohama Harbour construction. Fifty years after the completion of the Municipal waterworks in Yokohama the Mayor and civic dignatories of that city honoured the General's memory both at his grave and at the unveiling of a memorial stone constructed in his memory at the Municipal waterworks. The engraving on the memorial stone is moving in its simple dignity:

> Dedicated to the founder of our waterworks. A monument erected
> to the memory of the late Major-General H.S. Palmer, at the cradle
> of Yokohama's waterworks. To recall the eminent services of the
> Englishman, the late Major-General H. Spencer Palmer, founder
> of the Upper Water Supply, in which the international port-city of

Yokohama takes great pride, and which is the genesis of our modern civilisation, and also to commemorate the 50th anniversary of its foundation in Yokohama, the City has erected a monument.

Palmer was an outstanding civil engineer, surveyor and astronomer but he was also a very talented writer and journalist. When he undertook the construction of the Yokohama waterworks he also accepted the appointment as correspondent in Japan for *The Times*. Palmer sent over forty major articles to *The Times* and his accounts of Japan's landscape, culture, customs and social events, were written in an elegant and flowing style that reflected his perception and love for Japan. It was his pen that set out the arguments in favour of revision of unequal treaties signed with Western powers in 1858. His designs for the dry dock, pier and harbour at Yokohama were adopted but he did not live to see their completion three years after his death.

On 30th April 1987 a ceremony at Nogeyama overlooking Yokohama Harbour took place to celebrate the centenary of Palmer's waterworks. A monument was unveiled consisting of his bust on a stone pedestal bearing a tablet reading The Cradle of Modern Japanese Waterworks. This centennial year was also celebrated by the Yokohama Archives History in an exposition entitled H. S. Palmer: A Special Exhibition of his Work and Designs for the Waterworks and Harbour Works of Yokohama.

And so the daughter of a most distinguished Royal Engineer became engaged to be married to a 44 year old Engineer serving in her father's former Corps. It was to be a very happy union. At the end of 1894 there was another landmark in the history of the Bennet family. Gully, ever conscious of his civic duty and responsibilities had completed a half-century of service as Chairman of the Board of Guardians in St. Columb. The event was marked by the presentation of an engraved silver salver reading:

> Presented to Richard Gully Bennet Esquire by the Guardians ex-Guardians and Officers of the St. Columb Major Union in recognition of his services as their Chairman during a period of fifty years. 20th December 1894.

Ferdie's marriage to Evelyn did not take place in 1895 as he had anticipated. He remained stationed at Aldershot and passed a further Command course during June of that year. Evelyn had returned from Hong Kong and was living at 24 Norfolk Square, Hyde Park, London. They were married at All Saint's Church, Norfolk Square, Hyde Park, on 17th February 1896. Ferdie wrote to his father on his wedding day before the newly weds set out on their honeymoon to the South of France.

> Junior United Service Club
> London S.W.
> February 17th 1896

My dear Father

Many thanks for all your good wishes and blessing on the most important event of my life and also for the parental welcome you have accorded my bride. Though penniless I feel I have secured a comrade in whom I can trust and one who I know will do her best to make life comfortable. I certainly have no regrets or doubts as to the future. Evelyn also was delighted with your letter to her. You will of course hear from us during our rambles in S. France. We should be at the Grand Hotel Biarritz on Thursday morning and remain a fortnight at least. My love to the Mother. I shall think of you tomorrow. Tell Francis I was sorry to miss last week but was very busy and could not make an appointment.

In haste
Yours ever
F.W.B.

> Hotel Gassion
> March 12th 1896

My dear Father

Here we are settling down most comfortably in double harness and getting on exceedingly well. We came on here on Monday sorry to leave Biarritz where we were very well cared for and until the last day or so left absolutely alone by the other visitors who, I fancy, diagnosed our condition and were accordingly sympathetic and absurd. Here we have Col. Marshall and two or three others to speak to and golf links are much better than at B. It is a beautiful place and our rooms face the broad valley and the glistening snow-clad tops of the Pyrenees 50 miles away. We shall spend our time very pleasantly till the 25th about when we return via Paris.

Yours
F.W.B.

Upon return from his honeymoon Ferdie was posted to Exeter and within a week or two received a substantive promotion to Lt. Colonel. However a posting to Ireland was imminent and on the 27th October 1896 he wrote to his father:

My dear Father

You will see by the Western Morning News that Belfast is to be my fate, rather far off but an important sort of command, lots going on in the R.E. way I hear, a big district barracks and fortifications so we must hope it will suit. I have to report myself there on November 25th the chances are that Evelyn will go to Kathleen about that time and remain over the event, while I go over to Ireland, have a good look round and hunt for a furnished house not necessarily Belfast but somewhere handy and then come back to London on leave for a month or six weeks from about December 20th. One of these days you will have to renew your acquaintance with the North of Ireland. I think we ought to do very well there when we settle down. I enclose cheque for £22:3 being ½ Matthews rent which I reduced to £50 less outgoings which includes £3 for the man to clean up. I have told him he can have £5:10 this year towards rebuilding the pig houses provided it is done to my satisfaction. The estimates he sent came to over £6 and as he offered to do it for £5:10 I thought that the best plan. Edith now here for a few hours looking very fit. I hope your cough is alright. How is Edward getting on?

Yours

F.W.B.

(The event referred to was Evelyn's first confinement due in January 1897)

Ulster Club
Belfast
November 25th 1896

My dear Father

I arrived here early this morning after safely depositing Evelyn at Kathleen's on Monday and having a look at old friends at the Club. The journey from London was done very comfortably, you get on board the train at Euston at 5.30, occupy a good part of the time in having a good dinner on the train between 6.30 and 8.00 and arrive at Fleetwood at 11.20, walk under cover on board the steamer, go to bed and wake up in Belfast. Last night there wasn't the least movement of the ship and I could with difficulty hear the engines. I won't describe Belfast just yet, it has been very gloomy and moist all day which is typical Belfast weather they say. I am sorry about Edward. I suppose they were afraid that eventually at all events he would not be able to devote his whole attention to the work and no doubt his great age was against him! Tell him I got the gun alright, I forgot if I said so to him. We cleared out of Claremont very comfortably and the heavy baggage will begin to arrive shortly I expect. Curtis and the horse should cross tomorrow night and now I have enough to do to gather up the reins of Government for a bit, I shall still hope in the summer that you and the Mother may be induced to revisit Ireland especially now I know how easy the journey is on a calm day at any rate. I am afraid I have just missed the mail but I don't think you can get this before Friday anyhow. My love etc.

Yours
F.W.B.

Ulster Club
Belfast
January 23rd 1897

My dear Father

I arrived back here this morning after a good passage across the lake, I am lucky not to have postponed till tonight as a strong north easter is now blowing with sleet and intense cold. I am glad to have survived the last three weeks, the whole business is too ghastly for words, probably another time I shall be more callous but I am certainly not inclined to think that the whole trouble rests with the female portion of the community! All anxiety was over some days before I left and she was making steady and satisfactory progress, everybody says your grandson is a fine specimen and as I have seen nothing in the baby line for a good many years I cannot contradict them, it seems to me to cry for food periodically and then lapse into slumber when hiccoughs permit but I haven't had much conversation with him yet. Young Matthews writes that he is leaving Penhale at Ladyday and that a brother of his is

297

taking it on and all will be right. I have congratulated him on getting a better farm and regretted his going and also informed him that his responsibilities would not cease with his quit, I suppose this is right or is the old father solely responsible? I find a pile of work awaiting me which will keep me employed for a week, luckily the General is going away for a few days so I shall be able to deal with it without his assistance. I went nowhere when in London save to the Club for a few hours in the middle of the day and altogether spent a most miserable month but don't repeat this or Kathleen will think it was her fault whereas it was purely human nature to be anxious at such a time, now I have to search for lodgings or somewhere for us to live for a few weeks until a house turns up. How I long to get settled again and a few more things unpacked.

Yours ever

F.W. Bennet.

P.S. Matthews is only going as far as St. Germans.

Ferdie's letter to his father dated 23rd January 1897 relates to the birth of his first child christened Leonard Wallis Bennet. There can be no doubt that the first Christian name was chosen after the name of Ferdie's life-long friend Leonard Darwin.

Chichester Park
Belfast
June 12th 1898

My dear Father

Thanks for yours of the 1st received at Kathleen's, we are sorry to hear the gardener is tired of living so far from a town but you can hardly expect another William Cole. I found the Mother full of go of course and endured my own five days dissipation without much damage I hope. Saw Col Tremayne only of Cornish folk. Here I found a pretty state of affairs on my return, after allowing a nationalist procession on the Monday with the usual opposition on the part of the Orange folk the latter turned their attention to the Police, mostly South Irish giants who are very rough in their dealings with the public, and easily overpowered and cowed them, then of course the wiseacres at the head of affairs transferred the safety of the disturbed area to the Military and since then from about 5 pm to midnight troops are out standing ready for any emergency. The people are favourably disposed towards the troops and perfectly quiet but openly say they will attack the Police the moment we are withdrawn. There are over 100 magistrates in Belfast and I suppose they have all taken their oaths to do their duty and preserve the peace, one of their duties is to accompany the troops when they are called out and to read the Riot Act if need be, would you believe it that none of the 100 will do even this for fear of hurting their businesses! So they have sworn in 8 or 10 officers as JP's and we have to do it all which means that I have spent 7 hours in the streets for the last 3 days and go out again this evening, truly an edifying example of the modern Justice of the Peace. The whole thing now is hostility to the Police and I doubt if their authority is restored for a long while. Last night (Saturday) there were any amount of drunken folk about but that is thought nothing of in Belfast, however it did not make standing about any the pleasanter. The people are detestable. The Police hopelessly unpopular and much to blame and the civic authorities cowards. All quiet at our end of the City and there has been no lawlessness such as stone throwing and looting public houses since Tuesday. The boy gets more independent daily, walks firmly and I think improves in appearance but his mother is anxious still about his hair. She keeps well as possible. Kathleen comes at the end of the month for a few days.

Our love etc
F.W.B.

Chichester Park
Belfast
8th July 1898

My dear Father

I suppose you and the Mother were so astonished on receipt of my news yesterday that you were unable to wire your condolences. '*TWINS*' – isn't it awful and it seems so hard to realise that Leonard was ever that size. However they turn the scale at 7 lbs each so I suppose they may thrive. Everything going as well as possible. Evelyn quite herself, only 2½ hours against 14 last time and it could have been done quicker the doctor says if he had not been single handed. It was a surprise, nothing I believe in either family to account for such an irregularity. They seem perfect specimens, no flaws but sinfully ugly of course. You may put it in the Western Morning News if you like. I have sent it to the Times and local papers. Edward wires 'Bravo – do for both of us'. The girl arrived first. Kathleen of much use now she has something to do. Amy comes on 17th. Well, I hope you will forgive us.

Yours ever

F.W. Bennet

(The twins were christened Mary and Charles)

Chichester Park
Belfast
January 3rd 1899

My dear Father

Many thanks on Leonard's behalf for the latest guinea, new shilling and six pence which arrived quite safely this morning. I well remember what a feeling of ownership and real wealth my guinea gave me in years gone by and if his Mother doesn't appropriate it as she has mine I hope he will soon feel similar enjoyment. Fancy your having ours left after all these years, you should call for an account of the others. Today has been most ghastly a gale of snow and rain and no keeping the wind out of a house like this. Luckily we don't get the combination of this, the front door faces north. 'Uncle' William Palmer is dead at last and Fred thoughtfully has not 'invited' me to the funeral, I am afraid it would have required many and special invitations to induce me to cross the Channel this weather – a happy release for all concerned. At last Mrs Glubb has favoured me with a proper notice about the water, I have replied by asking when they are going to restore the supply they cut off, they must send me a second notice and then I have three weeks to show cause and then they can do it themselves so long as it does not cost more than 3d a week. I shall show cause if I feel inclined and then they can't do anything till the Local Government Board decide the matter. Meanwhile I am trying to get Matthews and Bourchier to do something.

Yours ever

F.W.B.

Chichester Park
Belfast
March 25th 1899

My dear Father

I hasten to inform you now that I am free to do so that in the quaint language of the War Office 'I have been selected for the appointment of C.R.E. Woolwich' to take effect from the 21st May. I was consulted on the subject strictly private and confidential about a month ago and we had no difficulty in deciding to accept the change notwithstanding the expense. It is no promotion but simply a change of station the authorities probably considering that it was only fair not to keep one in Ireland for the whole five years as Lt. Col. I get a good Government House and garden in lieu of lodging allowance which will be a gain of 5/- a day command pay instead of 3/- so in that way it is a gain which however will be more than compensated for by the extra expenses connected with living near London. The work I should say must be easier than in a large district like this, but of course will require picking up. No doubt this frees me from any chance of foreign service as they would not have moved me if I had to go abroad. Evelyn is delighted notwithstanding the proximity to her mother! Very considerate of them to give such a long notice as we shall have time to do everything comfortably and I hope to be able to let my house which is on my hands until 1st November next. Tiresome to leave the garden. Our love – hope Edith is better. New General arrived yesterday. Mrs Geary still here with bad attack of flu.

Yours
F.W.B.

Chichester Park
Belfast
April 9th 1899

My dear Father

Rashleigh may well ask me to *write* to him, it is quite impossible to make him hear as far as I remember. But what about? Here we have nothing but a succession of gales with sleet and every discomfort, quite arctic. I am reading 'The Secret History of the Oxford Movement' the first part of which is highly diverting as

301

showing the underhand means adopted to draw us all to Rome. A Revd Lyne is mentioned and an abomination called Miss Sellon who I appear to remember as friends of the Mother? in Mrs Chudleigh's time! The book is well worth skimming through but what temptation may not be placed in the paths of the young who show an interest in religion. No garden (kitchen) at Woolwich and no fruit but really picturesque grounds and a cow, incubator and goat and chaise if I like, a large house with a diningroom (we shant use I expect) library double drawingroom the house begins very large in the basement, good accommodation on ground floor and only five small bedrooms and a dressing room above which we shall absorb with day and night nurses and our own rooms. Servants will have to sleep in basement and the mother all alone on ground floor! We have just been dining with George and a most monstrous big dinner did he eat. He always has Sunday dinner downstairs. I hope no damage was done by the thaw though your trees are probably in leaf not much sign of spring here. I see you got the wreck you expected at Boscastle. I rather dread the shift to Woolwich and don't know how it is to be arranged exactly. Go to lodgings here I suppose about May 10th then send things over and Curtis and family with horse carriages etc about the same time, I about 18th and probably come back and fetch the family about 25th. Luckily it will be the last move before my time is up as Lt. Col. The infants are well. The under nurse does not go to England so we have to get another before we leave.

 Our love to all
  Yours
   F.W.B.

Chichester Park
Belfast
April 23rd 1899

My dear Father

 As I expect we shall begin soon to be occupied with our move I had better take advantage of a peaceful moment to write to you. It is rather an undertaking of course getting such a menagerie shifted let me see our two selves, three infants, two female servants, Curtis his wife and four children, horse, dog, two carriages, furniture and personal baggage. I have not got out definite orders as yet but I fancy they will run somewhat as follows. On Monday morning May 15th the inhabitants of Ormond will turn out and go into lodgings two servants leaving. Furniture to be parked on vans by a Liverpool firm on Monday and Tuesday and leave for Woolwich. On Tuesday also two carriages by Clyde Steamer to St. Katherine's Docks. Thursday, Curtis, family, horse and dog by sea and rail to Woolwich. On Friday self to London by Stranraer and Larne. Things should reach Woolwich and be put into house by Wednesday 24th and then the Colonel's wife, three infants, two nurses, two prams might come over on Thursday, I to meet them at Euston and drive to Woolwich in an omnibus. There are other things of course, cook and parlour maid to be got but I daresay we shall survive. I have let this house and got everything I wanted off my hands, my successor a man in the Royal Welsh Rifles. Very lucky as I had the house until November 1st. We are going into a large rambling house at Woolwich with good grounds and all sorts of accessories including an icehouse! The work must I should think be less than it has been here, besides I have had 2½ years experience as a CRE and know the ropes which apply everywhere. We shall do our best to arrange that the Mother shall have a room between the two night nurseries as she does not like to be alone. Still cold and wet here and spring is very backward.

Yours

F.W.B.

Chichester Park
Belfast
April 27th 1899

My dear Darwin

Just back from a trip out west and I'm hanged if you haven't let yourself in for I read your letter out to my wife without thinking and she, a woman who as a rule is all submissive and amiability, at once decided that she accept your offer for herself, three children, two nurses, two prams and an omnibus of luggage whatever I might do as she has no idea of my doing anything to the house without her interference. She was quite amenable before to let me do everything but your letter roused in her the spirit of womens' rights and I have to take a back seat and shall have to ask you to include me also! Whom am I to tell her to send her orders to about gallons of milk required and sterilizer, barley water etc. You will be the sufferer and it will be a lesson to you never to do a good natured action on such an extraordinary scale again. Seriously it is most good of you and relieved us of much trouble in ever so many ways and I shall try to forgive myself for doing what I really imagined I should never consent to do. Most likely if you keep of the same mind the arrival will take place on Saturday morning or mid-day May 20th but do reconsider your awful position.

Yours

F. Bennet.

P.S. The infants will have to sleep in a lump.

Mill Lane House
Woolwich
25th May 1899

My dear Father

Just a few lines to let you know how anxious we are about the dear old Mother and sorry for you in this time of trouble. I do hope she will soon turn the corner and begin to mend. If I can do anything please let me know but I need hardly say that we are full of worries for the moment. This is a disgraceful ruin of a house with large grounds utterly uncared for and unkempt and even the drains are doubtful! It will take a long time to put straight and having to take over a new District with a fussy General does not improve matters. Evelyn works like a horse and on the whole we are getting on well but it is uphill work and we feel leaving our little house in Belfast where all was in good order. Give the Mother our love. Kathleen is going down tomorrow I hear.

Yours ever

F. W. Bennet.

Woolwich
June 11th 1899

My dear Father

Glad the improvement has been steadily satisfactory and now I hope the Mother will get away for a change and finish up by coming here but I do hope she won't do too much. This place does not improve on acquaintance so far, my predecessor appears to have allowed himself to be sat upon and I am afraid I shall have difficulty in getting my position properly recognised. The society is entirely military and 9/10ths Gunners who one would think would go out of their way to be civil to an R.E. (as I am sure we should be to a Gunner at Chatham) but so far I see no signs of it. Then they make London their social centre and there isn't any amusement in the place itself. That she elephant Ellen Tanner wired she was coming down on Saturday and duly arrived at 12.40 to stay till she was turned out at 9 pm! I never saw such a lump in my life, took her out for a drive in the afternoon and just as we got back luckily her weight bent the arch of the wagonette and the hind wheel refused to move. Daniel Lambert is a joke to her. I think she would have stayed until Monday if she had had half a chance. You and Edith will be left alone to get through your spring cleaning I suppose for a bit, I hear Edward has arrived in London. On Friday we went to the annual gathering of the R.E. ladies at the Inspector General of Fortifications at home, I should think there were 600 there and such a lot of hand shaking and just saying 'how do you do' for 3 hours. Evelyn very smart in a new dress seemed to enjoy it much. Thursday to Lords to see the Australians so we are getting a little fun. It is curious wandering around the old 'shop' and thinking of 30 years ago. Thank Edith for the photos, they are very good.

 Yours ever
  F.W.B.
12th. Thank the Mother for her letter just received.

Mill Lane House
Woolwich
October 2nd 1899

My dear Father

 I have just been informed that in the event of an Army Corps being sent to South Africa (which seems pretty certain) I have been selected in the post of C.R.E. on the lines of communication of the Field Force. Confidentially of course but as there are many others here also warned in the event there need be no secret about it. What the C.R.E. L of C has to do will not be very easy to determine until the L of C is known but I take it there will be posts to defend and arrangements for water supply etc of troops going to the front and that I may have hard work with little chance of distinction and probably not much danger. I suppose I shall not be replaced here and that Evelyn will be allowed to remain where she is – anyway I don't suppose I shall go out for a month or so and of course if Sir G. White finds he can take the offensive and finish the business the Army Corps may not be wanted. But that is unlikely. Rather I look for British disasters at first and possibly soon, and that we shall all be wanted I have very little doubt. I go to London tomorrow to see about kit and try and find out more. I have a Captain detailed as assistant and I suppose they will give me a clerk or two but the whole thing is very much in the air at present. So no more, with love etc.

Yours ever
F.

Mill Lane House
Woolwich
5th October 1899

My dear Father

Events are progressing rapidly and from private information great developments are expected tomorrow so I shall possibly not be able to write. My appointment has been altered to Assistant Adjutant General Lines of Communication. It appears that they require a bigger RE than me to do CRE and as I had been warned for the latter appointment I had to be given something as a sop. So I am put from work I might have been expected to know something about to a job I am utterly new to and as a rule quite outside RE work. However, I dare say common sense will help one I don't think it can be very difficult. I have ordered my kit and they talk of our going about the 14th but I doubt it being so soon. We ought to make very short work of the Boers when we are ready to advance but I don't suppose that will be before the middle of December. They seem to be sending out everyone who has ever been on active service. The mobilisation and dispatch of such a force will be interesting to watch, 100 vessels of 5000 tons! A good thing those two ships beginning with a Z broke down, they will be more careful. Renny Tailyour has a job under

Guinness (Brewery) worth £1500 a year and as he has a large family and the employments lasts longer than in the Army has done a good thing for himself. Addison also goes to the same business, they are wise in their generation and lucky. You won't of course expect me to come down to say 'goodbye' if I go, only Edith would think of such a thing after our recent visit.

Yours
F.W.B.

Mill Lane House
Woolwich
11th October 1899

My dear Father

I was nearly forgetting to send your cheque. Please excuse in the hurry of the hour. My room is rapidly filling with camp kit etc and I am ordered to hold myself in readiness for an early departure which I hope will be by an ordinary passenger steamer as then I can go out in plain clothes. The whole thing seems very extraordinary considering that 2000 troops is the utmost we have put against the Boers heretofore. Why we should take 70000 for this job passes comprehension. I suppose it is to afford foreign powers an edifying experience. Evelyn remains here if the affair is a short one, I tell her to sit tight and not turn out if she is told to, whatever happens Evelyn will be equal to the occasion. I get 2 servants from Cavalry Reservists and have to provide myself with 3 horses S.A.! Or a bicycle in lieu of one, but I hope I shan't have much riding. Am about making a will and tell Edward I have put him in as Trustee with Evelyn and Darwin. I knew it was unnecessary to ask him to act. It is possible I go on Saturday but 21st is more likely, they will want L of C staff out early I should think.

Yours ever
F.W.B.

On the 11th October 1899, on the day Ferdie wrote his last letter before embarkation an ultimatum from Kruger delivered to the British two days earlier expired and war was declared by the Boers. Ferdie arrived in South Africa on the 21st October 1899 and took up his appointment as Assistant Adjutant General, Lines of Communication. In September 1900 he was made Brevet Colonel. He was mentioned in dispatches and awarded the

Queens Medal with two clasps. Throughout 1900 Britain suffered many humiliating setbacks. Senior Officers were anxious and concerned about the conduct of the War, if not critical of it but in true military tradition persevered against recurring Boer successes in the field. After a short period as Assistant Adjutant General Ferdie was appointed Assistant Inspector General of the Lines of Communications.

Queenstown
South Africa
December 9th 1900

My dear Darwin,

I was so delighted to hear from my wife this week that you were about to be married. Of course that is just what you wanted, someone to look after you and your house and to stop your eating too fast and to make you play golf etc. Well I *am* glad. This is a poor business this War, and I don't like the look of it at all. The Dutch of Transvaal and Orange River Colony are ruined out and out so are desperate and will go on fighting in a way for months if not years, the Dutch in Cape Colony were never more bitter and should they rise might prolong the thing indefinitely and cost us another £100,000,000! We are now pinning our faith on Colonial recruits at 11/- a day, as a rule an undisciplined rabble but better at the work than the Tommy stuck on a horse I dare say. I have seen none of it but I have had and am having an anxious time on what they call the Eastern system of L of C from East London to Bethuli and Aliwal all rebel districts. I am not a success, pitchforked into a position as AAG L of C and now an AIG, losing 12/- pay a day and mighty bored by the whole thing and every prospect of its going on another year! Of course they had only one thing to do and that was to defend the Southern portion of ORC so that no commandos could ever approach Cape Colony again. That they did not do with the result you see of everybody waiting to welcome De Wet with open arms and the Colony practically defenceless. Kitchener has now collected quite an army at Aliwal and with any luck should catch De Wet but a great risk has been run and we are not yet out of the wood. Hoping to play golf with you again someday and with every good wish.

Yours sincerely
F.W. Bennet.

National Hotel
East London
10th April 1901

My dear Father

I am afraid I am again late with my dividends however better late than never so I enclose cheque for £122.10, £100 being for Edith in payment of her loan, £15 for you and £7.10 for the Mother and Edith interest to June 30th so that puts us all square. I hope by the time you get this Evelyn will be down at Newquay with the children for a month or two, if I can't see them myself its as well you should. It is very hard being so long away just at the time the children are interesting at any rate to their own parents. This weary chase still goes on but for the moment the Boers seem to be lost in the vastness of their country. Everybody seems to be utterly sick of the whole show including the Boers so it would seem we ought to be able to come to terms somehow, catch the beggars we never shall. With all this flesh and blood coming out new life may be put into the proceedings but they seem a queer lot, some of the officers. I was talking to one tonight and had great difficulty in understanding him, he admitted he talked French and German better than he did English and yet said he had been serving continuously as a Militia Officer for over two years past. I wonder whether he can be a spy! You will now be beginning to find the garden interesting, I wish to goodness I could take a walk round. Almost 18 months since I left. Fancy your having lived to see both your sons finish their careers in the Army. Nothing will induce me to serve a day longer than I can help after 8th September. I have had a very good time but I am tired of it and have not been too well treated of late, but that is not the reason I am leaving. I want freedom for the rest of my life, one has been a slave long enough. It is not fair on wife and children to go on knocking about, besides I might not be employed again. So many thanks for your weekly letters which keep me posted in Tresillian details which of course I don't get from my wife.

Ever yours
F.

By May of 1901 Ferdie had completed over thirty years continuous military service. He was posted back to Britain, took leave from the 21st

May 1901 to the 18th July that year, and then returned to Woolwich as C.R.E. until he retired from the Royal Engineers on the 8th September 1901. He wrote to Leonard Darwin:

St. Brannocks
Newquay
26th May 1901

Dear old chap

I'm back again and have now completed my service. I've had a proper sickener the last two years and have no doubts whatever on the subject. I look forward to peace and rest at Westward Ho with no regrets. I have had a very good time in the service but having only one life and there being no necessity as far as money goes I leave with joy and gladness having done my best. Now I shall play golf grow chickens and watch my charming children develop into wild beasts no doubt. I am not too old to cycle. I have great and peculiar grievances to retire on which I mean to thoroughly enjoy, though half afraid they may discover they are genuine and heal them at once. I agree with you that I have not pushed myself sufficiently but that is a gift possessed of many which I do not envy. Sorry I had not time to see you but I had only a few hours in town and as you may imagine I wanted to see my family but I shall be up again soon and will see you. I have a great scheme to develop when I have an hour to work it out, a much better one than the skimming boat you would have none of. I never knew what it was to be happy before. My life is now a dream.

Yours ever
F.B.

PART FOUR

PART FOUR

CHAPTER 16

The cultivation of a hobby and new forms of interest is therefore a policy of first importance to a public man. But this is not a business that can be undertaken in a day or swiftly improvised by a mere command of the will. The growth of alternative mental interests is a long process. The seeds must be carefully chosen; they must fall on good ground; they must be sedulously tended, if the vivifying fruits are to be at hand when needed. To be really happy and really safe, one ought to have at least two or three hobbies, and they must all be real. It is no use starting late in life to say: 'I will take an interest in this or that.' Such an attempt only aggravates the strain of mental effort. A man may acquire great knowledge of topics unconnected with his daily work, and yet hardly get any benefit or relief. It is no use doing what you like, you have got to like what you do.

Winston S. Churchill: An Essay on Hobbies.

Following his retirement from the Army on the 7th September 1901 Ferdie, with his family, rented a property in Northam North Devon and having settled in immediately began to search for a property to buy.

Cleftridge
Northam
N. Devon
September 26th 1901

My dear Father
 They seem inclined to accept my offer of £6000 for Fairlea and I look on the matter as practically settled, they haggled for an extra £100 for expenses so that each of the three owners could have their £2000 a piece which I have agreed to, so I regard the matter as settled. One would never take any real interest in a place one rents by the year and I feel I want that. Give me a real house and I feel I should never want to move much, besides it is a sweet little place of its kind and if one wants a change it ought to

let well. I can find the money from investments only bringing in a little over 3% so shan't lose much while out of possession anyway. We were glad to hear you got home comfortably and hope you will repeat the visit after the winter. I doubt our being able to come down in October as the new nurse does not shape well I am afraid but perhaps she will improve. 16 inches of water in my reservoirs one night so I trust the water question is solved. Am busy building a pigsty with Curtis' assistance and odds and ends I find about the place. It already looks to me like a grand place for a pig to die in. Evelyn delighted with her bike which after riding on the lawn she is ready to face precipices on. A first visit to the dentist impending so no more.

    Love to all
        Yours ever
           F.

                        Cleftridge
                        Northam
                        N. Devon
                  October 4th 1901

Dear Darwin

    You will be interested to know that I am settling down in this part of the world and have joined the noble army of retired veterans of golfers and do nothings and have never been so well satisfied before. I have also purchased a ripping little estate called Fairlea hard by this place and so am now fairly committed to Northam. My only anxiety is lest the few remaining years or months should pass too quickly so I do nothing, not even study local Government so far, simply rest, that is play golf, bike, and settle down and build castles for the future with my wife as to what we will do when we enter into possession of Fairlea probably a year hence. One must have a place of one's very own, there is no joy in seeing other people's fruit trees blossom bring forth and the produce go to the birds or rot on the trees or as soon as gathered. I am built for the country, give me wireworms, caterpillars, sparrow et hoc genus omne and let me know that it is my own they are destroying. I want to plant my own fruit trees and feel that the American blight is my crops etc etc but really it is too lovely this freedom, this escape from worry, trying to make

20d do where £20 is required. A CRE's life is the most hateful of all jobs, Captains and even Majors may have a good time but CRE's never. Fancy never having to get on a horse again! Come down and play golf with me for a few days whenever you think well of it, if Mrs D can come too so much the better if she can put up with a drive here and there and a tea fight or two and a bike ride but on that point I must consult the Mrs as the great servant question is not quite settled yet and perchance your Mrs would not like the country in the winter and a house with children.

Yours ever

F.W. Bennet.

Fairlea
Northam
N. Devon
May 22nd 1902

My dear Father

You will be glad to hear that we are fairly well settled in our new abode after a very busy week and that Evelyn is none the worse for her exertions for it has been impossible to confine her to the sofa during these busy times. We are quite delighted with our home and the more I see of it the more satisfied I am with my purchase. Everything seems of the very best and although 25 years old not a crack or flaw anywhere of importance. Tresillian is pretty well built but this place is out and away the best built house in this Parish and will cost next to nothing to keep going. All is substantial and for external painting etc nothing but a small amount of iron work has to be done, all windows are in iron frames of course, internal painting and papering has now been thoroughly renovated and I expect a pretty heavy bill. The nursery arrangements are ample and give every satisfaction but you must really make a point of coming to see it all in the autumn. We are both delighted, of course much remains to finish, drawing rooms not habitable so far but we have lots of time before us as we cannot do any entertaining until the 'event' is well over. It really seems too good to be true that I should have such a home to cultivate and enjoy after my life of restlessness. I feel as if I never wanted to move again, no doubt an hereditary instinct. Ingeborg Muller was lunching here today and she will be able to tell you all about us as she returns on Monday. Thank goodness the wind has at last gone to the West and we may hope for rain and warm nights. I still have Cleftridge on my hands which is a nuisance but it is practically let and I left the new tenant and the owner yesterday squabbling only about internal decorations. Of course with all these distractions I have done nothing at golf during the Whitsuntide meeting; I have played but my muscles were distorted by other exertions and would not answer the helm sufficiently to hit the ball with any accuracy. I am not quite happy about my water, more as regards quality than quantity, otherwise I am more than satisfied with everything which is a great thing for me to say. We moved in last Friday but I have not been able to write comfortably before, but now the children are provided for I hope to be a little more at leisure. I find I have written on a rough sketch I made of proposed pond, orchard etc, I don't know whether you can follow it.

    Love from us both
       Yours
         F.W.B.

Fairlea: Northam

316

Fairlea
Northam
N. Devon
June 17th 1902 10 pm

My dear Father

All continues to go well. Evelyn had a baddish time for 3 hours before and after the event which came off about 9 am. Now she is quite comfortable and cheerful. A thumping girl I am told and judging by the noise lungs alright. I have only seen her head and hands. I am very glad of the addition, and especially that it is a girl. But four is enough. The nurse only arrived late tonight as the event was not expected so soon by a week or ten days but the cook and head nurse were good substitutions. I do hope now we are going to have some summer weather, it has been miserably wet and cold the last 10 days and my magnificent strawberries are rotting on the ground. Still we have had some very good dishes. Thinning grapes is nice quiet exercise but I am half afraid they have suffered. A peach tree in the vinery which looks healthy and bears a good crop declines to prevent the peaches remaining about the size of small walnuts for the last month. I shall clear those things and flowers out of that house. Vines should be kept alone. I am following your advice as to removing blistered leaves from peach trees but in some cases on large trees it means every leaf must come off, I never saw such a sight as they are and I think the trees will die. Apple trees white like snow with American blight in places. Vegetables looking well.

Yours ever
F.W.B.

The arrival of Evelyn Marjorie on 17th June 1902 completed Ferdie's young family. Leonard Wallis was aged five years, the twins, Mary Kathleen and Charles Hosken were four years. Richard Gully Bennet and his darling Mary still presided over Tresillian, he in his eight-second year and Mary then eighty. Ferdie with his entirely new life opening up before him was fifty-two.

Fairlea
Northam
N. Devon
April 2nd 1903

My dear Darwin

A long time since I heard of you directly at all events. I am so busy that I find no time for letter writing and grow more and more fascinated with this life every day. Now it is chickens, last month it was the new pond which is a great success or will be when it is a little grown over so long as the children don't fall in, then golf and new discoveries how to correct errors. I have become a regular country bore so much so that I have written to the Secretary JUSC taking my name off because they won't do anything for country members. I haven't been near the place since September 1901 and can't afford to go on paying 8 guineas a year for nothing. I think they are very shortsighted, lots of Colonels etc about here have given up their accounts for the same reason and if I had any time I would start a modest club for retired officers living in the country. However enough of that. How gets on your country residence? My new fruit trees are all alive and many even looking well, it does not seem to matter how you jam things in the ground they are sure to grow. We have had a sticky winter, very wet and I have done next to no golf owing to that and a succession of gales but not a slate moved in good old Fairlea. Dreadful thing H.M. He commanded at Aliwal N and interfered with me, never thought him fit for anything but a Sergeant Major. 'They are Lorrd Kitchener's Orrders and I'm going to carry them oot.' was his sole receipt when you did not agree with him. One would have thought he might have done something in the Turkish Army without making a mess.

Yours ever
F W Bennet.

Fairlea
Northam
N. Devon
30th September 1903

My dear Father

Whitford has duly paid me for Penhale, the proceeds I have

318

invested in shares which I think a better business than a doubtful £50 a year with outgoings for the farm. For the moment I fight shy of American Railways. The old horse has a fresh lease of life and took us 7 miles out and home again today as well as ever but I am firm in my idea of replacing the horse by a motorcar which increase and multiply day by day. The late trials are a good test of what they can do seven or eight days continuous running of over 100 miles. Having more faith in Chamberlain than any of the rest of Balfour's crowd I shall be prepared to support him in the future I think. Peaches won't travel and its no use trying to make them, flavour also wanting in the last the Mother sent us. Tell her to keep her pears until they ripen, her experienced eye will not fail to detect the signs of ripening. Dumbleton left us today, we played much golf and I went near winning the medal on Saturday last. I enclose cheque for £20 as usual. Infant a trifle out of sorts otherwise all well.

    Love to all
        Yours
            F.W.B.

                                                    Fairlea
                                                    Northam
                                                    N. Devon
                                                    June 7th 1904

My dear Darwin

    Right oh! and thanks very much for confirming me in my opinion to let well alone and not get mixed in anything which might cause me trouble and vexation. I believe in the future of wireless telegraphy for the Army and for public use but probably they will find something far simpler than even a pole 180 feet high. So whether it turns out well or ill I am obliged to you and shall never cast it in your gums. Phil was yachting – I had written to him – and today wired a very non-committal reply so thats alright. You ought to go and see Algy Hildebrand at the Stores, you know he is Secretary. The little man seems as nimble with his pen as ever, he and I have always kept up a sort of correspondence, but he talks and writes 10,000 times as much as I do. Board meetings once a week! Good Lord. Where would Fairlea be then and where my peace of mind? No thank you £300 a year and twelve journeys to London is what I want and I don't know that I particularly care about that if there is to be any anxiety attached. I am beginning to have fun with my District Council and frequently have to refer to 'Municipal Trade'. We are ruined as a District and my only hope to reduce the rates is to make something on the millions of tons of gravel that is shipped from here to Cardiff etc. But no-one knows whom the foreshore belongs to. Who can tell me?

Yours ever
F.W.B.

Fairlea
Northam
N. Devon
October 2nd 1904

My dear Darwin

Touching the removal of shingle from our foreshore which for years the Office of Works have allowed to go on wholesale, not to meet local requirements but chiefly for engineering works on the Bristol Channel, without exercising the least supervision or taking any steps to protect their rights or to derive a revenue for the public from the trade, we have now arrived at an impasse. As you helped to put the Northam District Council in touch with the Board of Trade I will tell you shortly what has occurred. The NDC applied for a lease of the foreshore and were offered one (excluding the pebble ridge the removal of material from which has since been absolutely prohibited by special order of the Board of Trade) for £1 a year and 4d a ton for every ton of material removed, or if the Council charged more than 8d a ton then one half of whatever the charge was. The Council thought 6d a ton the maximum they could charge without jeopardising the trade which would give them 2d a ton out of which they would have to pay all expenses. The terms offered are therefore impossible and notwithstanding urgent appeals and arguments the Office of Works remains obdurate and will not abate a jot. We offered them 25% of the proceeds but they won't hear of it. Don't you think this very extraordinary action on the part of the Office of Works. It seems to me a regular case of the dog in the manger which neither Parliament nor the public generally would approve. The removal of material from the foreshore is always a serious matter and not to be lightly undertaken (e.g. Hallsands) yet here we have hundreds of thousands of tons removed under the very eye of those responsible without their taking any notice and when the local authority tries to turn an honest penny for the good of an over-taxed district (rates 9/4 in the £ or 11/4 with water) they are offered terms which are simply preposterous. What do you think we can do now? I have no doubt Mr Soares our member would be delighted to take the matter up or we might try publicity in the Press. Meanwhile the removal of shingle continues to increase and no doubt in a comparatively short space of time our gold mine will be worked out. Perhaps you could interest yourself in the matter somehow.

Yours sincerely

F.W. Bennet.

Fairlea
Northam
N. Devon
2nd October 1905

My dear Darwin

The other letter you can send off to any pal of yours if you think it will do any good. I suppose you couldn't come for a few days golf to help me bear up during my wife's absence from 12th to 22nd. We shall probably be in town for a few days in November just when the fogs are on as a penance.

Yours ever

F.W.B.

Fairlea
Northam
N. Devon
February 1906

My dear Darwin

It strikes me that you will be pretty unspeakable just now in the heyday of your Free Trade triumph! I am the one blooming idiot out of the 100 that is all. How any sane man can contrive to see things in your light beats me. We make a motorcar to sell for £300 landed in America that becomes £420 exclusive of freight.

321

How can we compete with the American car of same value landed on our shores for nothing? Anyway I am sick of Balfour and hope the fragments of a party will elect Chamberlain. We are getting through this winter fairly well, it suits me and the children are alright but my wife has an obstinate cold. The motorcar is really coming at last, they say in 10 days. Horse and brougham sold and I hope never to be troubled with a quad again. An 8 hp Wolseley is all I could run to. Hope it will be a success, goodness knows I have been long enough considering the question. My poor old mother is going downhill fast, no suffering thank God but it can only be a question of weeks, she sticks on bravely and knows she has but a short time. I go down this week. I have great schemes on hand here but as they are only in the embryo I won't bore you with details. I mean things like the gravel question the income of which has been spent on permanent improvements and not gone to the rates. You haven't written a book on 'The Laws of Commons' have you? I want to get the Northam Burrows put on a proper footing. A very intricate question – what are you doing anyway and how is Cripps Corner, mind the birds don't pick out all your fruit buds as they are doing here.

    Our best wishes
        Yours ever
            F.W.B.

                    Fairlea
                  Northam
               N. Devon
        March 1st 1906

My dear Darwin

    I find I shall not have time for some months (now that I have a motor car) to fully expose the fallacies in yours of 6th ulto on Free Trade. You, of course, realise that taking the world at large you are in a worse position than the twelfth juryman who was unable to convert the other eleven silly ones to his views. It is all very well for the Spectator and you to say that the inhabitants of these Isles have definitely refused protection, time will tell, meanwhile I leave you to stew with the odd juryman! I don't know why people don't write in pencil sitting in a chair before the fire, I can only suppose that they are afraid of the shock produced on the recipient who would naturally imagine the letter came from the sickbed, to me however you may always write in pencil. I came down from Birmingham through sleet and snow in very bad weather in grand style and though somewhat afraid of the brute drove her 25 miles today in about 2 hours, my third lesson, now I am thinking of having my groom trained. All very well if things go right, but I don't feel very sure yet of tracing faults, I hope I am not too old to learn. Thanks for the information about Commons Law I see we are to have a R Commission on foreshores and Commons so shall have to drop that question also for a bit. My wife is at last bettering from a long bronchial attack which has caused me much anxiety. My mother is going slowly and painlessly down, a bathchair on fine days. April 18th will see my old folk wedded for 60 years! You are quite right it was not Protection but Slavery and a wish for a change from Balfourism that influenced the electors.

Yours ever

F.W. Bennet.

Fairlea
Northam
N. Devon
March 20th 1906

My dear Darwin

I have duly examined your commission save that the bill will only be presented on your next visit to Fairlea. I think I have told you before that you should not hang your trousers on your Golf clubs it is sure to make them warp. Motorcar going strong, I have driven it twice without assistance successfully and diagnosed an electrical fault with ease but others may follow when I may not be so successful. My wife is still coughing, indeed we all are more-or-less, it is the weather I suppose. I see you Radicals are making a fine hash of it SA, your unwieldly majority will soon be pulverized however much CB may bluster at first. Mind let us know next time you come this way.

Yours

F.W.B.

Fairlea
Northam
N. Devon
May 4th 1906

My dear Darwin

My wife tells me she looked you up but you were round at the Corner. She is up with Charles consulting various specialists for adenoids, eyesight etc. etc. So its a case of shell out and all I have to hope for that they will return me my beautiful healthy child no worse for all their humbug. These doctors make me sick. They all play into each others hands and what can a poor father do? These diseases weren't known in our young days and I am morally certain I have survived adenoids for 50 years and ain't dead yet. When Leonard was born they operated on him within a week for an adhesive foreskin, five guineas, when a Jewish man would have done it! Am going very strong with motorcar and all, the Council raked in over £500 last year for gravel dues, am on all committees at Golf Club, District Council, was even run for Church Warden and got well beaten I am thankful to say. Off to Newquay next week in the car 70 miles and more. My old mother still living but two nurses necessary and does not suffer much, the doctors gave her a year *two* years ago. My old people celebrated their diamond wedding day a fortnight ago only there was not much celebration about it. I hope you and Mrs Darwin will come and see us this summer. I have so much I want your advice about. Maintenance of main roads, keeping private roads in order also I should like to see whether you can play golf yet.

Yours
F.W.B.

Fairlea
June 10th 1906

My dear Darwin

Many thanks but I shall answer – yes she is gone – and no-one could regret it, not that there was any suffering, just a gradual sinking, weaker and weaker until the end without a struggle, simply a cessation of life, gradually the breathing ceased. Though conscious to the end it was as natural as death ought to be I suppose. They say it was cancer, it looked to me like senile decay anyway. She lived a year longer than the doctor gave her two years ago. My father bears it well but he also is near the senile decay stage and I think old folks feelings are blunted to a certain extent, anyway I hope so, 60 years of married life and never a storm, he says never a cross word, but that would be impossible.

Yours ever

F.W.B.

Fairlea

Northam

N. Devon

January 20th 1907

My dear Darwin

It is quite impossible to give any advice about motorcars, I spent some 3 years studying the question and taking advice and eventually decided on an 8-10 HP Wolseley which cost with extras £330, I have had that car nearly a year and it is now thoroughly out of date and not worth £150 to sell I suppose; side chains horizontal engines etc etc are out of fashion and I don't think the car is any longer made though mine was one of the first of its type. I have driven it 2000 miles, it has never given any trouble, the tyres look almost as good as new, and the upkeep has been practically the cost of petrol and a few sparking plugs and certainly not over £20 for the year, and I would not exchange it for any car I know of for this country with its hills and narrow lanes but I drive carefully and am quite satisfied with 15 miles an hour average. Any known firm is alright and the Clement Talbot have a good reputation I believe but of course I swear by my own car which has now become the Siddeley as I believe the so-called Wolseley cars are given up. It is the same firm but if you are not going to drive yourself or take any interest in the mechanism I give you up. The whole pleasure is in driving yourself and looking after it. You need never dirty your hands, any lad can clean it down and what he can't do could be done once a month at any garage for 5/-. There is nothing in it, as simple as ABC and nothing at all to be afraid of. The idea of going shares in a car does not commend itself, the car costs nothing and does not deteriorate while it is not working provided it is set going for a few minutes once a week or so, you might almost as well talk about sharing a wife! The other fellow is bound to do all the damage. A chauffeur will ruin you very likely and the car will never be fit to go unless he wants to go out. As usual the makers are spoiling the whole show by going for 6 cylinder £1000 cars and now for racing at this new track at Brooklands they wont cater for the modest motorists till the needs of the millionaires are satisfied. Dumbleton has just been here and my golf is very satisfactory my handicap now being 3! We are well except *between* ourselves my wife has a very obstinate cough which causes me great uneasiness. Hope you enjoy your trip and pay for your MC by lecturing in America.

    With best regards
        Yours ever
           F.W. Bennet.

Fairlea
Northam
N. Devon
8th May 1907

My dear Darwin

    We were to have left for Newquay this week but our dear little Mary who I always think is too good to live contracted some disease which of course defied the doctor and caused us great anxiety for 48 hours. For five days she retained nothing in the shape of food or medicine then she existed for two days on white of egg and water and today I am thankful to say that she has taken something more nutritious so I hope the worst is over and that we may be able to get off a week late as children are good at recovery. The gravel trade is bringing in £200 a month as I anticipated with practically little to go on so I should say 'guessed'. Now the question arises what to do with it? and of course I am moving to make it a part 2 service, i.e. pay off debt or on improvements in drainage which will benefit posterity but not on maintenance i.e. roads or immediate relief of rates. So we have a fight as my brother Councillors can only see as far as their noses and require much assisting. It is all great fun to me. I bothered you once about a flying ship skimming over the surface of the water now I am distressed by the harnessing of Niagara and in due course of the only spot on earth I have a hankering to see, the Victoria Falls. Of course it is inevitable that these things will be utilised unless we can *harness the tide*. In my simple way I have never seen any difficulty in this and I wish you could refer me to any author who has put the difficulty on paper as I think I could smooth them away. You have a constant and irrestible force easily transformed as one would imagine into mechanical power; why then is it not done? A heavy float must rise with the flood tide and must fall with the ebb; on such a thing you have working dynamos etc. electric light, traction etc. On the ebb the float being sufficiently heavy the same power is available by gravity. If I could only get 10 minutes or a quarter of an hour to think these things out properly! But my time is so fully occupied in trying to protect young wild ducks from the ravages of cats, playing golf, cutting grass, and trying to keep the District Council on the rails that I fear I shall be in my grave before I can do the world much good. If you ever see any of your friends in the Office of Works, scrag them, tear them limb from limb especially the man they call Jack Horner, if ever a man deserved hanging he does, allowing our foreshore to be taken away for nothing and then when the local authority steps in, demanding half the takings. Excuse the long yarn but my wife is with the invalid so I have no-one to be silent with.

    Kind regards
        Yours
            F.W.B.

PS Leonard is delighted we are delayed going to Newquay as he hopes his bike will arrive before we start, but I tell him it wont.

Fairlea
Northam
N. Devon
27th December 1907

My dear Darwin

    A long time since we have forgathered but you always were a poor correspondent. No time, I know all about it, next week, some time, never. Well how did your lecturing tour in America come off and did you pay expenses? I wish to goodness you would divert your attention from Municipal trading to the upkeep of main roads and say by whom should the cost be borne. I say by the County Council entirely for Rural and Urban Districts, except where in the case of urban districts the Council have got a stamped contract with the CC to maintain the roads for a fixed sum per annum. This is my hobby just now and as Chairman of our Finance Committee I am trying to prevent any local rates going to main roads as we have no contract and the CC pitch £500 a year at our heads which is at the rate of £70 per mile per annum whereas the average cost of maintaining main roads in urban districts in England and Wales is £225 per mile per annum. No wonder our roads are the worst in England. A treatise on this subject would be of great importance when you can find the time. There was talk of the golf championships being played here, consequently a great rumpus, the potwallopers or commoners who have always been obstructive gave the golfers a free hand to remove rushes and cut bunkers, the Club allowed the Committee a free hand, various experts were consulted with the result that we shall have the best links to suit the ideas of one man namely Fowler (no mean authority) in the world. We are all at home now, the cloud I spoke of in my last is not removed (probably you have forgotten it so don't allude to it) but I am sometimes hopeful that it will be but I am a pessimist and have not enjoyed very good spirits the last year. Leonard is at school at Burnham preparing for the Navy (I don't care a straw whether he passes or not) a dull but good boy. Charles at a day school here getting on wonderfully as he has a memory but the most thoughtless silly young idiot under the sun, I really think there is a screw loose, so impossible is it to make him understand the why and wherefore of anything, but quite wonderful in his Latin and French, anything he can remember, but ask him to apply his Arithmetic to any practical use and it seems hopeless. Mary his twin sister just the reverse, dull at lessons (but what matters that) but so thoughtful, painstaking and unselfish I have never met her like. Marjorie the youngest aged 5½ her father's darling of course and perhaps a little spoilt. Forgive this rigmarole, on the whole I am not sure you are not best off, education begins to pull and we have not been to London this year. A motor trip or two, a fortnight at Newquay otherwise a stay at home, life dull to most people but not to me. My old father

328

still lives though very feeble.

With best wishes for the new year to you and Mrs Darwin.

Yours ever

F.W. Bennet.

Fairlea
Northam
N. Devon
January 3rd 1909

Dear Darwin

Many thanks for yours, I thought the Geographical Society might upset your old stomach and you have got to endure it for two years haven't you? Here we are all well at the moment but all the children have been down at different times in the past fortnight with high temperature for 48 hours and then alright again. Doctor says 'flu' while I think sweets and Xmas fare more likely. I always think they are going to die when they get a tummy ache. We had to endure four days of 4 inches of snow, when it cleared off in one night and a friend who came for a week luckily got two days golf. I am likely to have to come to town in July to take Leonard up for his exam for RN, he is a duffer rather and I don't think will pass, I don't care a straw whether he does or not as it is a dog's life, 14 days leave a year and kicked out at any time. However, it gets a boy off one's hands early.

With best wishes from us both to Mrs Darwin and yourself for new year.

Yours ever

F.W. Bennet.

Fairlea
Northam
N. Devon
February 12th 1909

My dear Darwin

I feel like writing to you tonight on the anniversary of your father's birth 100 years ago. My! How old we must be getting. How well I remember my visits to Down about 40 years ago when we used to look down that old well surrounded by laurels

(?) about 100 feet deep and the sensitive plants in the greenhouse and the walk at the end of the garden through trees overlooking a landscape and the stately figure of your father, he sat on a high chair at mealtimes, and a deerhound I think. Your brother Frank was there and an infant, Bernard I presume. My old father is living still and he was born in 1820. Here we are flourishing, both the boys away at school and I play golf when it is not too cold or windy i.e. about once a fortnight. I am labouring to preserve the burrows from the inroads of the sea, to prevent the parishioners from having to pay for a new Church Tower because 3 stones tumbled down off it, to prohibit the Instow Beagles from hunting a bagged hare, and I believe I am to be appointed patron of the hospital next week to keep other more undesirables out of it! You have your Royal Geographical Society to keep you quiet and you had a difficult job to throw cold water on that Arctic man's scheme the other day. Leonard goes up for the Navy in July, I hope to goodness he gets chucked so I might see you then though not likely as I shan't stop longer than I can help and shall have to do the Tower, Madam Tussauds etc.

 Yours
  F.W.B.

Fairlea
Northam
N. Devon
March 1st 1909

My dear Darwin
 Excuse me for not having answered yours of 22nd ulto before. I cannot accept your very kind invitation for us to stop with you for Leonard's exam because I shan't know when he is to appear before the Board till well on in May I expect, but if I may I will leave it open (just what you don't want) and then if you can't have us I can always go to my sister's flat, so don't think any more about it. Leonard may have to go up twice at about a fortnight's interval, I certainly can't stand London for as long as that. This frost is becoming tiresome, I never remember such a dry February and the roads are like midsummer for dust and the hedges are white but we have no snow and fairly long intervals of sunshine and are better off than most places I take it including the

Riviera, I do but little golf and gardening is done up till we get rain, and I hardly know what I do but it always seems to be Sunday!

Yours ever
F.W. Bennet.

Fairlea
Northam
N. Devon
May 12th 1909

Dear Darwin

I am glad to say I have managed to put Leonard off the Navy, I was never very keen about it myself, so now we shall not bother you in July. I shall take him up to town later on as I want to see the White City or whatever they call it myself, before I die and do the scenic railway but this will be in August or September probably when you will be out of town no doubt. I hope you like the budget and are becoming reconciled to Reform. What a family yours is! Now I see Horace is coming to the fore you will all be 'Sirs' if you don't mind. Sir T Holdich has been down here and I golfed with him once or twice. How I pity you in London, this is the best time of year in the country to see things grow, to feel that summer is on us, to watch the fruit trees and flowers, but last week was beastly. I hope Cripps Corner is flourishing.

Yours
F.W.B.

Fairlea
Northam
N. Devon
May 29th 1910

My dear Darwin

Thanks for your nice letter, my old father failed the last few years mentally and bodily so the end was a relief especially to my sister who always looked after him, I suppose it was the perfect end, a gradual cessation of vital power. Poor old Phil, I never knew he was ill, cancer of course. Remember me to Kitchener and tell him I have just been reading 'How to save

England'. I have been thinking about our long silence and feel guilty but I always think you are such a busy man that you have little time for ordinary correspondence, I know you will let me know if you are ever in the west and would care for a round on the best links in the world. Bernard I saw when he was sampling them a few weeks ago. We lead the same quiet life but the family man is ever on the brink of a volcano and we have lately been indulging in scarlatina in a boy at school, German measles at home, and my younger daughter now in bed with a temperature. I fear she is delicate as she is given this way and as I always imagine the worst I am not always gay. I am a Guardian in addition to my other duties but don't pretend much interest in the job.

Our kind regards to your wife

Yours ever

F.W. Bennet.

Bennet Memorial: Parish Church of Saint Enoder

Fairlea
Northam
N. Devon
October 23rd 1910

My dear Darwin

I have been living in the hope that following your nephew's example you would have felt it a duty as a golfer to visit our new links in which case I felt sure you would have applied to me for board and lodging. By the way I have not seen his book yet. But no, you won't come and I, this year, have escaped a pilgrimage to London so we have not met for long, but if you and Mrs Darwin have a week to spare in November I need hardly say how glad we should be. Your obituary notice on poor old Phil I read with much interest, it was a very nice one and now today I see an appeal from you for the Bedford College, which reveals you in a new capacity and to which I do not respond for in these days of Form IV and schooling I have nothing to spare for the higher education of women. Besides they don't want it, if you would only learn them to cook how much happier we should be. Leonard has gone to Marlborough. I was horrified at the want of comfort in the Junior School house, they spend too much money on chattels, but it is a fine school in many ways and the boy likes it. How is Cripps Corner getting on? Fruit trees bearing yet? I suppose you are all in favour of the land taxes, I am quite unable to understand their equity but amused myself never-the-less in answering Lloyd G's investment queries. This I could easily do as I had two forms to fill up, one for house and grounds and the other for 3 or 4 fields, as I bought them together I could not say what I gave for them separately but I feel sure he will have me! Old Hildebrand has chucked the Stores in some disgust and gone off to Argentine for 6 months or so. Lewis Coker is here now, I played with him today, but much altered and indifferent golfer. Old Kinney who lives next door to me has a nerve collapse and won't see anyone for the last 3 months, sticks in bed, he ought to be sent to a nursing home as he is difficult and has only a sister in the house (a nurse) but she has a bad time. Are you still President Geographical? I have added Guardian to my other duties and don't like it at all and shall get out of it as soon as I can i.e. after 3 years. We are all well, boys at school, girls ditto close by at a day school so we have some life in the house. Garden going strong in the fruit line and I seldom play two rounds a day 'Anno Domini' but I don't admit it nor do I see that means old age but I hear it used in that sense.

Yours ever

F.W. Bennet.

Fairlea
Northam
N. Devon
August 15th 1911

My dear Darwin

I was reading 'BD' who writes in Country Life last Sunday and I wondered whether you were the 'venerable relative' he spoke of who was driving so badly with a wooden club that he took to a driving mashie and effected an immediate change for the better, though I noticed he was not hopeful of a continuance. 'Venerable relative' indeed! Where have you been all this summer? It must have reminded you of the few weeks foreign service you once did in Malta – about all you ever did do if I remember rightly. Here were it not for the want of rain we have had an ideal summer, two hot for me but seldom 80 degrees and I pity Londoners. Holidays on now and the boys home, Leonard arrived with German measles out on him so we are boycotted as usual. At Easter we suffered in the same way, a maid servant contracting measles just as the holiday began. None of the children took it and in this later case they haven't either. What times we are living in, I think Harold Cox & Co are about our only chance of salvation, must send them a trifle. Any chance of your coming this way in October for that last game of golf?

Yours ever

F.W. Bennet.

Fairlea
Northam
N. Devon
July 25th 1912

My dear Darwin

I take in the Telegraph and I write to ask whether that is really you in today's issue. Of course I recollect that you are a Director of the 'Clove' Co and you are quite right, if correctly reported, in saying that the first thing to do is to get the public to understand the meaning of the word 'eugenic' but I fail entirely to recognise your features. You will undoubtedly not escape a Knighthood for long and I did think better of you. You said you would like to have another game of golf with me, I am still waiting for you to turn up, and I suppose I shall have to wait. We got through the championships alright, fine weather and an exciting finish but it bored me awfully and I hope we shall never see another down here though the scribblers did crack up the course! We are all well, boys come home next week, at least Charles does and Leonard goes into camp for a week with the Marlborough boys, how time flies. I am failing, a new motorcar is bringing my grey hairs etc etc and I can't eat, no teeth and little appetite though I feel alright but wasting away. H. Hilton was here about Easter and as he played with the Silver King ball there has been a tremendous run on them ever since which I believe ought to interest you. What a hideous state we are in as a country, when are we going to take a turn for the better?

Yours

F.W. Bennet.

At the outbreak of War with Germany in 1914 Ferdie's elder brother, Edward, was living at Tresillian having succeeded to Richard Gully Bennet's estate. Ferdie remained at Fairlea. His two sons, Leonard and Charles, seventeen and sixteen years respectively, were still at Marlborough. In 1915 Ferdie then aged sixty-five, volunteered for military service and was recalled for duty as C.R.E. at Plymouth, a post he held for almost a year.

Royal Engineers Office
Devonport
18th April 1916

My dear Darwin

This is not an invention but if there is anything in it you might be able to do something. I always imagine the Germans never hear the truth about anything and that the people as a whole are firmly convinced that the war was forced on them and that they are defending themselves against unscrupulous enemies. Now why cannot the Allies scatter broadcast over Germany by small balloons leaflets containing the truth as to how the War arose, in simple language, the inventions committee can no doubt arrange for them to be scattered while the balloons are at a height so that they would not fall in a bundle but drift all over a large area. Some might fall in good ground and the seed grow. This must have occurred to others but has it been acted on sufficiently? It should go on perseveringly, not always the same leaflet, but a variety bearing on different subjects but all truth and as convincing as possible. I never lived in a mess thank goodness with about 100 young officers but in the R.W.Y. Club. The weather here is perfectly beastly but it will keep the Zeppelins away at any rate. Leonard writes that he has fired his gun in anger and says that three of the enemy's small shells fell in his dugout without scratching him! which sounds curious!.

 Yours
  F.W. Bennet.

By April 1916 Leonard Wallis Bennet was serving in France as a young subaltern in the Royal Artillery. Charles Bennet joined the same regiment and followed Leonard to France where they both saw continuous active service until the Armistice in 1918.

Fairlea
Northam
N. Devon
July 8th 1917

Dear Darwin
 I doubt if I have written to enquire after your welfare since I was returned to store over a year ago now and this dreadful War still continues and if it goes on for another three years we shall hardly be able to get along without it. If they had only followed my advice and continued dropping leaflets in Germany explaining the real cause of all the trouble, I think by now the democracy might have understood and the end would have been hastened. As it is I quite expect it to last over next year at least, a great hope is that the Socialists will throw over the Kaiser and all his party, nothing else can end it now both sides have gone to ground. You will have 50 aeroplanes next time and then 100 over London if

Johnny French don't wake up a bit. I don't see any objection to giving notice of reprisals and then carrying them out. Leonard has been over in France with his Siege Battery for more than a year and we had him home once on Christmas day for 10 days. He is an acting Captain and has been commanding the Battery for two or three months and will be in the Gazette as Acting Major I expect any day. Though I don't think he will keep it, not bad at 20, we should have been 40 before we got such a command. Charles is still at Exeter, a fine fellow though I say it, he is just 19 and will be off shortly to France. I am devoted to gardening even to vegetables which I had to take up as my gardener made such a mess of it, I like it too and the difference is very marked. Luckily he will do what he is told and is a capital worker. As for fruit, I have never known such a good year, the apple crop is prodigious and I shant know how to get rid of them, must try and find a market in London. Mary lives at home and makes herself useful in the convalescent hospital and at Girl Guides etc. Mary is at school. My wife well but her deafness increases. She too is a very busy woman. I still try to play golf but going back.

Yours sincerely
F.W. Bennet.

CHAPTER 17

When I survey in the light of these reflections the scene of my past life as a whole, I have no doubt that I do not wish to live it over again. Happy, vivid and full of interest as it has been, I do not seek to tread again the toilsome and dangerous path. Not even an opportunity of making a different set of mistakes and experiencing a different series of adventures and success lure me. How can I tell that the good fortune which has up to the present attended me with fair constancy would not be lacking at some critical moment in another chain of causation? Let us be contented with what has happened to us and thankful for all we have been spared. Let us reconcile ourselves to the mysterious rhythm of our destinies, such as they must be in this world of space and time. Let us treasure our joys but not bewail our sorrows. The glory of light cannot exist without its shadows. Life is a whole, and good and ill must be accepted together. The journey has been enjoyable and well worth making – once.

Winston S. Churchill : An Essay. *A Second Choice*

Fairlea
Northam
N. Devon
February 11th 1918

My dear Darwin

Its about time for our annual letter isn't it? And how goes it with you? Still hoping to see the end of the War? It would have been over long ago if they had only followed our advice and gone in for systematically scattering leaflets among the enemy. See how they hate it, and give our chaps 10 years for doing it. What in the world they want to go and get caught at it for I can't imagine, with the winds we have been having lately if they went up 10,000 feet on our side the leaflets would carry 40 or 50 miles into their side which would be far enough. Everyone says it must be over this year but so it has always been and I don't see why any more than last year and even if it is I don't know who is going to end it. I only trust Sir D. Haig has not been letting the grass grow and is prepared for the attack we may expect. I have hardly left home since I returned from Plymouth in May 1916, just went to Newquay for a fortnight and then had to return for my wife to undergo another operation which went off alright I am glad to say. I am very thin but able to play golf still and do a bit of gardening. Such a good fruit year I never remember but everything this year is too forward, the late frosts last year gave us the abundance. Your godson is in England going through a course for a month at Lydd or Salisbury and comes home for a fortnight on Saturday. The other boy back 'at rest' for a bit too, they have both been close together for months near Ypres and never knew it. Leonard was 21 on January 3rd. How time flies! One girl at home, cooking at a hospital nearby and the younger one at school at Salisbury. We keep to rations but haven't come down to less than 2½ lbs meat, but the majority, the farmers and the workers pay no attention, one girl who has just gone into service at our Vicarage goes home every evening to have a meat meal. I see old Cautley and Lewis in today's obituary. Lets have a line sometime to say how it fares with you, hope they have not been dropping bombs about you.

Yours ever

F.W. Bennet.

Fairlea
Northam
N. Devon
2nd January 1919

My dear Darwin

A happy new year to you. Damn this pen! I am reminded of you by two things in today's Times, your letter and 'Propaganda by Balloon'. Are you the 'distinguished Engineer' or am I? Anyway I believe the leaflets did do something towards hastening the end of the War which I am thankful to have lived to see whatever the future may bring, and sometimes I think the clouds are very dark, though the election makes a rift. Both my boys came through without a scratch, thank God, and both have done good work I believe though no reward other than a Mention has been bestowed.

Leonard is a Captain in the R.A. after two years and 9 months service! Both are still in France and likely to remain there with their Armies, 2nd and 5th. I am doddering down to the grave with a golf handicap of 9 at which I fondly imagine I more than hold my own. I have to work hard in the garden now, even with a spade, and my wife has to do the same in the house with only two domestics and my elder daughter unable to help much as she has been cook at the VAD hospital from 7 am to 2 pm for many months, the younger still at school but thank goodness the bread is more palatable and we have always had enough butter and not had to eat the abominable substitute. Things will gradually improve no doubt and I look forward to getting a new motorcar some day. I sold my old one when petrol ceased. It will take some years to restore the roads which I hear are in a shocking state outside my boundary which is Bideford. Well how are you? Do you ever play golf? Never was such a bad apple year, but I sent up 30 Comice Pears to Covent Garden which sold for five guineas. 3/6 each to save you trouble.

 Yours
  F.W. Bennet.

After the Armistice Ferdie's two sons returned from active service in France. Charles, then a Lieutenant in the Royal Artillery contracted influenza on the journey home. He died within three months of the Armistice.

Fairlea
Northam
N. Devon
2nd March 1919

My dear Darwin

 Thanks old man, yes its a regular knock downer and I feel so sore about it. I should get drunk I think if I had any whisky. A most promising life absolutely thrown away, if he had only been killed in action the blow would have been lighter but its all over now. Watching him day after day and night after night through the fatal illness was awful. I gave up hope after 10 days.

 Yours
  F.W. Bennet.

Fairlea
Northam
N. Devon
October 31st 1919

My dear Darwin

I hope you saw 'Propaganda in War' in todays Times glorifying Northcliffe of course. I am going to have put on my tombstone the concluding words – 'He saved thousands of millions of money and at least a million lives' for you remember my writing you in 1915 I think about scattering leaflets! How are you keeping all this time? Full up with work no doubt, eugenics and the making of golf balls amongst other things, the old Silver King still holds its own in my opinion for I still play, or try to, but my handicap has gone up to 10 and I can't drive the length I used to, but I have a son (your godson) who hits a terrific ball, now a Captain R.A. You heard the cruel loss I sustained by the death early this year of my younger son from pneumonia. My elder daughter Mary is going to take up nursing and goes to the London Hospital for 3 years training at the end of the year when my younger daughter leaves school. We shall miss Mary much as she has been such a help of late years but the young must leave the nest. I still do a lot in the garden and have a wonderful year of apples and fruit generally. I hear poor Downing killed himself by working in his garden. My wife keeps well (away just now) but her deafness increases and I can't shout platitudes somehow. I hope you don't worry about the future of your country, I don't, it will last us out!

Yours

F.W. Bennet.

Fairlea
Northam
N. Devon
30th December 1920

My dear Darwin

A line to wish you both a happy new year and may the outlook at the end of it be brighter than it is at the beginning. What political party do you now adhere to? After Margot's extraordinary escapade I fear Asquith will never return to power, not that I want him to but they are all rotters and the middle class are ruined. Still

341

we exist, Mary at the London Hospital, home for a fortnight just before Christmas, she likes the life but I think the hours too long for anybody. Leonard on leave for a month or so from Larkhill, several dances on for him and my younger daughter, fortunately parents are de trop and may sit at home by the fire. I am well and my wife too but I don't play golf much as caddies are scarce and I am past 70, besides I don't seem able to hit the little brute. We had a cold snap back along, but the mildest Christmas I remember, about 52 degrees. I find much to do in the garden as I can only keep one man and no motorcar. Hildebrand is in a queer state, a Colonel and Mrs Watling late R.E. are living with him and conducting his correspondence so I have given up writing. If you are down Wimbledon way you might look him up. I suppose he's alright but he has heaps of relations. I trust you are still able to get about on crutches and attend your old eugenic feasts.

    Yours
      F.W. Bennet.

                      Fairlea
                    Northam
                 N. Devon
       23rd December 1921

My dear Darwin

    Once a year I think we correspond just to pass the compliments of the season and to prove that we still exist. I am very fit and going on much in the old way, growing apples very successfully this year and playing a round or two of golf a week when I can get someone to take me down and bring me back from the course. I can walk it but don't want to! My wife keeps well and is of course up to her eyes in working for others, just now making up parcels of food for 150 so-called unemployed. Leonard is home for a month or so hitting a prodigious ball in these gales, Mary still at the London Hospital doing well and liking the life, she comes home the end of January for a fortnight. My other daughter at home with plenty of dances ahead for her and Leonard. How are you? I hope well and able to crawl about still. I saw you got to Yankee Land and hope you enjoyed the trip. Was it your first visit there? Do you mind you, I and P Cardew going to Antwerp in '72'? I hear Hildebrand is very bad but a good many of our batch still survive. What a summer we have had! I suppose the Irish will now play the Kilkenny Cat game, what a bore the question is and all the other troubles the War has left us. The Silvertown blue dot golf ball holds the field still, I see by the way you are Chairman of that Company now and have to speechify at the annual meeting. Well goodbye and best wishes for new year old man.

    Yours sincerely

      F.W. Bennet.

Fairlea

Northam

N. Devon

21st December 1922

My dear Darwin

Once more I write to wish you well this Christmastide; the years pass away (I have just celebrated my 72 years) but I don't feel old and can quite imagine I could go into bat on Chatham lines and make 100 runs! I hope you keep fit also. I think our batch is reduced to 8 or 9. Cardew, Porter, White, Badgley, Dewing, Cook, Hildebrand, Kitchener are gone, poor Hildebrand died last summer after a long illness, he left the remainder of the lease of his house and the residue of his estate £45,000, after some legacies, to Colonel Watling, late R.E. who had been looking after him for a long time. I see you have given up the Chairmanship of Silvertown and I dare say are not quite so busy as you used to be. We are still much as usual, the only trouble being servants, my elder daughter is still slaving away at the London Hospital while the younger is content to remain at home, work with her needle, play golf and dance and act as chauffeuse as I found I could not tackle the Morris Cowley I bought last spring. Leonard my son is with us now on leave from Dere Island Bantry Bay where he leads a poor life with no amusements but a little sea fishing as they are not allowed to land. I still play a little golf, handicap 17, and garden, such a year of apples but no market. How is your garden, I don't think your tastes lie much in fruit growing, I find it a great occupation. Generals swarm about here, I don't think I ever met Harper killed at Sherborne a few days ago. My wife and daughter go to London occasionally, I never do and seldom get further than Cornwall to see my brother at our old

343

home where he reigns in solitary squalor. We have had it very dry here for the last 3 months and Bideford is out of water, however rain seems to have come at last.

Best wishes old man
Yours
    F.W. Bennet.

Fairlea
Northam
N. Devon
2nd December 1923

My dear Darwin

Sorry to see from the report of your Company that you were hors de combat on account of an operation. I hope it is nothing worse than having a tooth out or a corn removed. Really though I do hope that it is nothing to be alarmed about, but we are getting on! There is to be a wedding here on 22nd. My younger daughter and a Captain Ferguson (Indian Army) a decent young fellow as far as I can judge, so all is bustle and confusion in this house and I hope my son and elder daughter will be able to come and assist. My part of the show seems to be signing cheques. The old folk will then be left alone for a bit at any rate, but I hope the elder girl may give up nursing at London Hospital at the end of her 4 years (i.e. next October) and come home. Barring corns I keep very well and still play a little golf with young Generals and people of that class. And how about this election you old Radical? Personally I do hope they will give protection a run otherwise the old ship will go on the rocks, but I ain't taking an active part in it.

Yours ever
    F.W. Bennet.

Best wishes to you and yours for Christmas and the New Year when they come.

Evelyn Marjorie Bennet married Captain Ferguson of the Rajputana Rifles and after their honeymoon she accompanied her husband to India. Mary, four years older was still unmarried and nursing in London. Leonard, five years older than Marjorie was serving in the Royal Artillery and was also unmarried.

Fairlea
Northam
N. Devon
26th October 1924

My dear Darwin

I wonder whether you would convey a message to your nephew Bernard whom I don't think I have spoken to since he was in his pram at Downes about 1873, that we should be very glad to put him up for the amateur championship next May and if his wife accompanies him on these excursions, her also. You know how we are situated about a mile from the golf club, a motorcar, which has been laid up for a year since my chauffeuse Marjorie got married, but now to be taken into use again as my elder daughter Mary is coming home soon after surviving 5 years at the London Hospital and so she will drive it. We shall have plenty of pens and ink but I have no typist I fear and a very quiet time. We shall probably have Dumbleton here and if Bernard is not a Professor at the game a little bridge but no mahjohn! I hope you keep fit and have got that book off your chest. I keep well notwithstanding the ghastly summer we have had. If Bernard won't come perhaps you and Mrs Darwin would consider the invitation if you could tolerate a week's golf, spectacular I mean, that is sitting on a sandhill and munching sandwiches if it is fine and warm. Leonard had gone to Hong Kong and likes it so far. Bother this election, I can't take any interest in it.

Yours ever
F.W. Bennet.

At the beginning of January 1925 Mary Bennet was in London prior to making a journey to India to go and stay with her younger sister Marjorie. Ferdie wrote to her at the Strand Palace Hotel on the eve of her departure.

7th January 1925
My dear old Mary

Just a line or two to wish you God speed and a joyful time in India and to thank you for your very nice letter. The Bennets are reticent people and I am not sure it is not just as well that we are unable to gush which becomes tiresome. It took me a long time to do that crossword puzzle and I shan't try another. The short words are a nuisance to avoid repetition and the longer ones require a dictionary. I certainly did not know that word (I forget it now) meant throat, but it does. When things are settled out in India you must let me know and I will arrange for your return passage but that won't be till October, I mean I will send out the money. How glad you will be to be done with shopping and to settle down in your cabin. It has been calm here for two days so I quite hope the Bay will be amiable. Miss Whats-her-name came to say goodbye to you yesterday, they used to live at Westward Ho!, she is a nurse, you wrote to her at Christmas to London and all the time she was at Westward Ho. She said she would write to you. So goodbye my all too perfect daughter, I could never tell you what you have been to me all these short years and remember if you do happen across the *right* man out there, don't hesitate. Parents would much sooner see their children *happily* married than constrained to live at home – 'crabbed age and youth etc'. Been tea'ing today next door and tomorrow with the Burns. Mrs Boyle asked me to lunch on Sunday. Shan't go. Marple back.

Your affectionate father
F.W.B.

Fairlea
Northam
N. Devon
11th December 1925

My dear Darwin

How nice to get a letter from you telling me all about your shift to Granby Hall. Many years ago I used to go shooting at Girsby Manor, Market Rasen, I wonder whether that is near you? My sister married the younger brother of the then owner, Captain Fox, dead long ago. I wonder you can get on so far from London, you will have to take to hunting or shooting in your old age. My news is all good I am glad to say. Leonard is now shifting from Hong Kong to Karachi. My son-in-law, Ferguson has just completed his Staff College 2 years at Quetta and sent my two daughters and my grandchild home about 2 months ago and is now following them and expects to reach London on 26th. He has an appointment at Kohat in February so won't be long at home, he takes Marjorie back with him and probably leaves us the grandchild. Mary went out to India about January to see her sister through her confinement which took place in February and she will now remain here. As for myself I am very well but get a pain in the calf of my right leg after walking say 150 yards which has stopped my golf, indeed I do little but make rugs, play bridge and potter about in the garden when I never feel it. My friends keep nagging me to see a doctor, I say it is old age and I have had a good long innings and let it go as I am rather a sceptic about doctors. The grandchild 'Penelope' is a great amusement to us both. My wife is very well but hard of hearing like you and she quite enjoys the child and indeed we are very fortunate. I expect you have had it very cold in Lincolnshire. Even here where we don't expect to get much cold before Christmas we have had 3 weeks of frost, over now thank goodness. I shall look out for your stiff dull book in due course. I do a little J.P. duty but have dropped other things. I was sorry to see poor Frank's death. I met him once at Downes in? 74.

With best wishes from us both to Mrs Darwin and yourself for the new year.

Yours ever

F.W. Bennet.

Fairlea
Northam
N. Devon
28th December 1926

My dear Darwin

We generally write to one another about now partly to prove we are still alive and partly to pass the compliments of the season. Time is dealing me kindly but I can't play golf any more and haven't been on the links this year. Still I am fairly well can potter about the garden but can't walk any distance. My old brother is ailing and both my sisters feel the weight of years but I am another grandfather out in India and expect my daughter and her two children and my son-in-law and also my son all to be home for a time next year. And how are you? Still acting the Squire down in Lincolnshire or back at Cripps Corner as you half threatened last year. You will have to take to hunting or shooting in your old age! My fingers ain't good for writing so goodbye with best wishes from us both.

Yours
 F.W. Bennet.

Fairlea
Northam
N. Devon
July 22nd 1927

My dear Darwin

Years ago you were appointed a Trustee of my Will, well, if you are feeling like me, you will be relieved to hear that I have substituted the public trustee for all my time expired trustees. My brother was one, he is now lying very ill, paralysed and speechless. I am nearly in like condition.

Yours sincerely
 F.W. Bennet.

Fairlea
Northam
N. Devon
August 8th 1927

My dear Darwin

Many thanks for your kind letter. The old brother has gone and I succeed him. But I shall never live down there. Possibly my son may leave the service and try it with my daughter to keep house for him till he marries but I don't know how it will pan out.

Yours ever
 F.W.B.

Fairlea
Northam
N. Devon
4th January 1928

My dear Darwin

So many thanks for your nice letter. I saw the notice of your sister's death in the Times. I remember her as a girl at Downes. I am very well but can't write very well and my brother's death has upset me a bit and given a lot of work. You always chaff me about the pact we made 'never to write to each other'. However we must forget those things.

> With best wishes
> Yours ever
> F.W. Bennet.

Sadly that was Ferdie's last letter to his life-long friend Leonard Darwin. They had joined the Royal Military Academy, Woolwich, together sixty years earlier in July 1868 and were of the same batch to pass out on being gazetted to the Royal Engineers. Within a few weeks, in February 1928, Ferdie became very ill and after the amputation of a leg that year, his illness lingered on until his death on the 17th October 1929. Writing a week after Ferdie's death to Leonard Darwin, his wife Evelyn described her husband's last months:

> Yes it is true that Ferdie is now released from a life of absolute helplessness which he felt so terribly. Barely two years ago pain started in his left foot which was at first thought to be a trivial matter, but it became gradually worse and gangrene set in and after intense suffering for over 4 months the leg had to be amputated above the knee to save his life. He pulled through the operation wonderfully but it was a sad life for him afterwards as not only physically but mentally he was not as he had been. He was perfectly rational but could not concentrate and he knew himself that his brain was not what it had been which made it so pitiful. The end was so peaceful, he just passed away in his sleep but it came as a terrible shock to me as he had been unusually well for several days before and had been out in the garden in his wheelchair. Dear Ferdie, he was the best of husbands and we had spent 33 of the happiest possible years together and he was so devoted to his children and his four grandchildren. I am enclosing a local newspaper cutting which may interest you, it will show that he did not lead a useless life after retiring from the Army. I am trying to feel thankful that he has been spared a longer life of helplessness but I do dread the loneliness of the future. I came up yesterday to stay with my elder girl, Mary, for a week. Her husband is at the Imperial Defence College and I am hoping very much that when he goes to sea early in the next year she may come to live with me for a time.

Eight years later Darwin was to write this about his old friend in a letter to Captain Leonard Bennet:

> I have not read through your father's letters for some time. The language in some cases is rather strong, but in reading them at the time his friends could guess the expression which was on his face when writing them and they only raised a corresponding smile on the faces of the recipients. When writing to your mother please tell her that I well remember my pleasant days at Fairlea and that I was very glad to hear that she is so well. Your father's character was not an easy one to understand; for his rather strong expressions in speech and writing covered up much that only became gradually apparent.

A memoir to Colonel F. W. Bennet, R.E., published in the *Royal Engineers Journal* in September 1930, from which much material written above has been derived, concluded in this way:

> He was somewhat unconventional in his ways and cared little for society. For example, when staying in a country house when a dance was taking place for the entertainment of the cricket team of which he was a member, he was found tucked up in bed in perfect peace of mind. Bennet's was, in fact, a well-marked personality, but one very difficult to sketch in words, though endearing him greatly to his friends and the young officers who served under him. And this must be my excuse for introducing one personal anecdote. He and I belonged to the same batch, and when saying good-bye before all were scattering at the end of our course, he spoke to me somewhat as follows: 'Now don't let us have any silly nonsense about writing to each other; no-one does keep it up; let us make a bargain never to put pen to paper to each other.' On this we shook hands; but this was, in truth, the prelude to a correspondence which lasted with few breaks for over half a century – until he could write no more. His marked individual characteristics, whilst they may occasionally have surprised those who did not know him well, yet served both to increase the keen feeling of affection which he aroused amongst his friends and to give rise to many pleasant and vivid memories in the minds of a wide circle of acquaintances.

CHAPTER 18

'The play is done; the curtain drops;
Slow falling to the prompter's bell;
A moment yet the actor stops
And looks around, to say farewell.
It is an irksome word and task;
And when he's laughed and said his say,
He shows, as he removes the mask,
A face that's anything but gay.'
Thackeray. *The End of the Play.*

The death of Colonel F.W. Bennet broke the tradition of hundreds of years in that he was the first Bennet to be buried outside his native Cornwall. He was buried in Northam, North Devon, his home for more than a quarter of a century following his retirement from military service.

During his last and fatal illness Colonel F.W. Bennet gave his blessing to the marriage of his eldest child, and son, Captain L.W. Bennet, who, at his father's insistence, had succeeded to Tresillian House. Leonard Bennet took up residence following the death of his uncle, Lt. Col. Edward Bennet. Edward Gully Bennet of Tresillian House in the Parish of Newlyn East in the County of Cornwall had died on the 1st August 1927 in a private nursing home at Newquay. He left his entire estate to his brother Ferdinando Wallis Bennet but as appears from his letter dated 8th August 1927 to Leonard Darwin, Ferdinando refused to go and live at Tresillian and suggested that Leonard should live at Tresillian with the further idea that Leonard's unmarried sister, Mary, should keep house for him until he married.

Early in 1928, and at the time of his father's painful illness, Leonard Bennet became engaged to Miss Betty Wynter a Cornish girl whose family's long domicile in the County of Cornwall matched that of the Bennet family.

Captain Leonard Wallis Bennet, R.A., married Miss Armenell Betty Wynter at Liskeard on Tuesday 5th September 1928. The *Cornish Times* of

Friday 7th September 1928 devoted more than half a page to the wedding. Under the heading Popular Liskeard Bride the report read as follows:

> Seldom has more general interest been shown in any social event in Liskeard than on Tuesday in the wedding of Miss Armenell Betty Wynter to Captain Bennet of Tresillian. So much kindly interest was only to be expected at the marriage of a young lady whose vivacity and charm had made her a popular figure in the borough and throughout East Cornwall. A niece of Mr G.N. Glencross, J.P. and Mrs Glencross of Luxstowe, with whom she has resided in recent years. Miss Wynter is a noted sportswoman of varied interests. A follower of the East Cornwall Hounds and the Trethill Harriers as well as the Dartmoor Otter Hounds on their visits to the locality, she is also a keen motorist, and her clever and fearless driving in Cornish motor trials has earned the unstinted praise of competitors. She has also achieved distinction as a successful dog breeder specialising in bloodhounds, sealyhams and collies for which she has won prizes at many of the important

Parish Church of Saint Martin: Liskeard.

shows. A keen supporter of the Girl Guide movement, she has been the enthusiastic captain of No. 1 (Open) Company which has spacious headquarters at Luxstowe, and in many other directions she has been prominent in the social and sporting life of the town and district.

The bridegroom, Captain Leonard Wallis Bennet, a member of a well-known North Devon family, is the sole surviving son of Colonel F.W. Bennet and Mrs Bennet, Fairlea, Northam, and is strongly connected with Cornwall as a grandson of the late Mr R.G. Bennet, J.P., and a nephew of the late Colonel E.G. Bennet, both formerly of Tresillian House, Summercourt, to which property he has succeeded. Destined for the regular Army, he was a cadet at Woolwich when war was declared against Germany. He received his commission in the Royal Artillery in February 1915 and in the following year was drafted to France where he served with the 'heavies' for three years, being twice mentioned in despatches. After the Armistice he remained with the Army of Occupation at Brussels and came home in 1919.

Entering the dimness of the fine old Parish Church from the brilliant summer sunshine without, the scene was a memorable one. Every seat was occupied by friends and well-wishers, the nave being reserved for a large number of invited guests. The solemnity and impressiveness of a really beautiful choral service was enhanced by the quiet reverent attitude of the great congregation. Beautiful floral decorations adorned the chancel and altar-rails where tall Harrisii lilies were backed with palms and ferns interspersed with white asters, phlox, marquerites, geraniums and the climbing trails of blue campanula which corresponded to the tints of the bridesmaids' dresses.

A reception followed at Luxstowe, the guests being entertained in a large marquee on the lawn, where bright appropriate music was played. After the reception the bride visited the Cenotaph and laid her bouquet at the foot. Later in the afternoon, amid the good wishes of their many friends, Captain and Mrs Bennet left by motorcar on the first stage of their journey to Scotland where they are hoping for some salmon and trout fishing during the honeymoon. The bride travelled in a frock of reseda satin beaute with fur-felt hat to match, grey lizard shoes and a fur coat. On their return they will take up residence at Tresillian House.

The most detailed account in the *Cornish Times* described the wedding service, the dresses and jewellery of all the principal ladies, and concluded with a long list of wedding presents. Of interest, the principal bridesmaid was Miss Mary Bennet, the groom's elder sister and the bride's train bearer was Penelope Ferguson, the bridegroom's niece. Also present among honoured guests was Captain Guy Vivian, R.N., who had fallen in love with Captain Bennet's sister, Mary, and to whom he was wedded the following year.

As Colonel F.W. Bennet had surmised in a letter to his friend Leonard Darwin dated 8th August 1927, his son, Captain Leonard Bennet, R.A., did decide to retire from the Army and take up residence at Tresillian House following the death of his Uncle, Lt. Col. E Gully Bennet. Leonard Bennet's diary reveals that the estate, as taken over by him, included Tresillian House and grounds and one cottage, Trevarton Farm of some 250 acres, Higher Tresillian Farm with four cottages and about 360 acres, Goonhoskyn Farm with three cottages and about 250 acres in the Parish of St. Enoder; a moiety of Trewinion Farm, Bennallack and Trefullock Farms of about 100 acres situate in the Parish of St. Enoder; a portion of two clay mines behind

Luxstowe: Liskeard. The home of Miss A.B. Wynter.

354

Bennallack, a blacksmith's shop and cottage and another cottage with a few acres of garden all within the Parish of St. Enoder.

Leonard's diary continues:

Arriving home from India I decided to leave the Army and take up my permanent residence at Tresillian House. The house was then surrounded by trees and from the far side of the pond only one window of the house could be seen. In October 1927 I arranged to cut down a large number of trees round the house so that a good view of Chapel Close and the lawn pasture could be obtained, previously neither could be seen. This work was put in hand at once and the major part of it completed by March the following year. In February 1928 I moved into residence with a married couple as staff. The inside of the house was in very bad condition, no water except what came off the roof, no light except oil lamps, entire internal decoration was necessary and eventually carried out and all the furniture was Victorian and very

Tresillian: (from west).

355

uncomfortable at that. Many of the windows on the outside were blank. In April 1928 I started internal work on the house by opening the North Eastern window of the library putting bookshelves on the South Eastern wall, a Devon fireplace and refurnishing the room. The South bedroom over the drawingroom had the window overlooking the pond opened and was repapered and the bedroom over the library had the North window opened and was likewise repapered. A bath was put into the South wing of small size as we were still pumping water required to the roof of the house. Workmen were in the house till the beginning of June. On June 20th 1928 I got engaged so had to have the workmen back again this time to redecorate the drawingroom, inner and outer halls and diningroom. Water put in by ram from the 'House Park'. Electric light with plant in stables and rest of stables converted into garages. This work was finished by the end of September. While the work was in progress the sanitary system was found to be worn out and had to be entirely renewed and 5 modern W.C's with 2 cesspits installed. November 1928 brought gales and about thirty trees on Eastern side of pond came down damaging fence and most of the winter was spent clearing up the mess. Put up a greenhouse near lawn meadow for our own use and built pergola leading down to pond. In April 1929 arrangements were made for the coming child and two rooms in the South West wing were done up as night and day nurseries.

The coming child was Leonard and Armenell's first born who arrived on the 10th August that year.

During the summer the kitchen and scullery floors were taken up and cement put down, the kitchen was also redecorated and the old copper in the scullery which used to boil the water for the bath under my study floor was taken away. The old floor was laid opposite the front door as a crazy paving and the ground in front of the front door where the trees had been was planted with flowering shrubs during the autumn. In the summer the ground between the old lawn and the lower path was turned over and sown with grass. Glasshouses in the garden were painted. December 1929. Gales brought down a number of trees including a puzzle monkey on right of path going up to the garden and a large limb from tree near laundry broke off and damaged chimney and roof.

Leonard Bennet's first child, a daughter, was born in Tresillian House in August of that year and three further daughters followed in 1931, 1934 and 1936. They were the last of the Bennets to be born at Tresillian. Throughout this period Leonard actively farmed the Tresillian Estate but in 1937 he decided to let the home farms and return to Northam, North Devon, where he had spent his childhood. He bought Northam Lodge a property within two miles of his father's old home at Fairlea and there his family settled.

The following year the darkening threat of war brought about mobilisation of the Reserves. After ten years in retirement Leonard Bennet rejoined his Regiment and served throughout the Second World War finally retiring in 1947. On his return to Northam Lodge Major Bennet decided to sell Tresillian and the estates finally passed out of the Bennet family's ownership. Ten years later Leonard Bennet died at the early age of sixty, the last male Bennet in two hundred and fifty years direct succession from the Reverend

Northam Lodge.

357

Thomas Bennet, Vicar of St. Enoder and the last Squire of Tresillian following two hundred and fifty six years' ownership by the family.

EPILOGUE

Major Leonard Bennet's sale of Tresillian in 1947 followed by his death and burial at Northam in 1957 severed the Bennet family's long connection with the Parishes of St. Enoder and St. Newlyn. The baptisms, marriages and burials of all the Bennets of Tresillian are recorded from 1643 in the Parish Registers of Newyln Church commencing with the baptism of John Gully on the 25th July 1643 and concluding with the deaths of Mary Jean Bennet on 2nd June 1906 and her husband Richard Gully Bennet on 11th January 1910.

Without the assistance of Leonard Darwin, devoted friend of Ferdinando Bennet, much of recent Bennet history would have been lost. Who was this man, Darwin? The title Major, Royal Engineers, Retired, discloses little more than he and Ferdinando served in the same Corps. Leonard Darwin was the fourth son of Charles Darwin the pre-eminent English scientist and naturalist. Born in 1850, he attended the Royal Military Academy, Woolwich at the same time as Ferdinando Bennet and together as Lieutenants they entered the Royal Engineers in 1871. After seeing service throughout the world as an Engineer, Darwin, having been promoted to the rank of Major in April 1889, was posted to the Intelligence Branch at the War Office. There he remained until he retired from the Army to enter politics and in 1892 he was elected to Parliament as a Liberal Unionist but lost his seat (Lichfield) at the General Election of 1895. From 1908 to 1911 Darwin was President of the Royal Geographical Society. Throughout the remainder of his long life (he died in his ninety-fourth year on the 26th March 1943) he pursued many other interests and published several scientific books.

As for Ferdinando, a scientist and engineer, he was never accorded the warm citations bestowed upon his illustrious father-in-law, and fellow Engineer, Major General Palmer. Nevertheless Ferdinando's own imaginative thinking was most striking and indicative of his extraordinary aptitude and skill. In 1909 he had written to Darwin of his earlier idea of 'a flying ship skimming over the surface of the water' and his then current idea of 'harnessing the tide' to create electrical power. His flying ship became the hovercraft fifty years later. Harnessing tidal waters to provide electricity became a major study sixty years after he had explained his ideas to Darwin. Unquestionably Ferdinando Wallis Bennet was a gifted intellectual but as his biographer wrote in the *Royal Engineers Journal*: ... Bennet's friends all thought that his abilities warranted a more distinguished career in the Army than that which actually fell to his lot.

One wonders what happened to Ferdinando's sisters Kathleen and Edith. I spoke to their niece, Mrs Evelyn Ferguson, then approaching her 87th birthday, in December 1988. Kathleen Vigor Fox, she told me, had survived her husband for many years and died childless. Edith was known to the next generation of the family as 'the Eagle'. She never married and lived a long life in Newlyn where she was buried.

And as this century draws to a close, what of Tresillian? Some of the fabric from the original Manor House occupied by Sir Robert Tresillian still lies entombed within the present walls seven centuries later. I visited Tresillian House during 1988 and record my gratitude for his kindness to the present owner Mr Rex Davy to whom the barton passed by succession on the death of his father who purchased it from Major Bennet in 1947. The two long drives (Newquay Drive and Truro Drive) lead off from the main Truro Road. They are flanked by elms and oaks as they were sixty years ago. Time has taken its toll of the older trees and acting upon advice from the Forestry Department many have been taken out but all are replaced by thriving saplings. The house is still as it was in Gully Bennet's day, externally a handsome Georgian Mansion. Leading off from the entrance hall the high book-lined study is as Major Bennet improved it in 1928. The nursery wing created by him in the same year for his four daughters has been converted into a flat as also the former laundry, both to accommodate staff employed on the estate. The main house has been modernised within by exceptionally fine interior decorating and is occupied by Mr Davy and his family.

The home farm is now the site of Dairyland, a thriving exhibition and leisure centre comprising a countrylife museum, farm nature trail, farm park and playground. There Mr Davy and his staff attract thousands of visitors throughout each summer, an enterprise which has earned a special commendation from the British Tourist Authority.

But to return to Tresillian House: it is quiet and secluded, distanced from its neighbouring twentieth century activities and still the Manor House. I took a walk past the former stables, around the large pond, through thickets of flowering shrubs to the walled garden created more than a century earlier.

Old green houses have been restored and the present gardener and under-gardener have more than an acre under cultivation within the red brick walls. The graveyard for family dogs started at the turn of this century is maintained beneath majestic trees. Only the lichen covered headstones marking the dog sleeping below record his or her place in the Bennet family's esteem.

A walk across to nearby Goenhoskyn, farmed today by John Richards, completed the Tresillian atmosphere of a bygone age. The fields, meadows, woods and spinneys are the same as those described in Gully Bennet's diaries and upon the yellowing parchments stored in family strongboxes. The signposts in the neighbourhood still point to Nancolleth, Indian Queens, Tregonning, Summercourt, Mitchell and St. Columb. They are part of the history of the Bennets and steeped in the history of Cornwall. Many believe that Cornwall's finest days were those when the County stood firmly behind the King during the darkness of the Civil War. A letter from Charles Stuart reads:

> Carol Rex. To the inhabitants of the County of Cornwall. We are so highly sensible of the merits of our County of Cornwall, of their zeal for the defence of our person and the just rights of our Crown, in a time when we could contribute so little to our own defence or to their assistance, in a time when not only no reward appeared, but great and probable dangers were threatened to obedience and loyalty; of their great eminent courage and patience in their indefatigable prosecution of their great work against so potent an enemy, backed with so strong, rich and popular cities, and so plentifully furnished and supplied with men, arms, money, ammunition and provisions of all kinds; and of the wonderful success with which it pleased Almighty God (though with the loss of some most eminent persons, who shall never be forgotten by us) to reward their loyalty and patience by many strange victories over their and our enemies, in despite of all human probability and all imaginable disadvantages; that, as we cannot but desire to publish it to all the world, and perpetuate to all time the memory of their merits and of our acceptance of the same; and to that end we do hereby render our royal thanks to that our County in the most public and lasting manner we can devise, commanding copies thereof to be printed and published, and one of them to be read in every church and chapel therein, and to be kept for ever as

a record in the same, that as long as the history of these times and of this nation shall continue, the memory of how much that County had merited from us and our Crown, may be derived with it to posterity.

Given at our Camp at Sideley Castle September 10th 1645.

This proud reminder of Cornwall's glorious past occupies a tablet prominent on the wall of the nave of the Church of St. Enoder.

The church, dedicated to St. Enodrus, is part of the fabric of the Bennet's history and conveniently concludes this story almost where it began.

REFERENCES

Deeds, letters, diaries and papers belonging to the Bennet family.

The Parochial History of Cornwall vol. iii, Davies Gilbert.

A Complete Parochial History of the County of Cornwall vol. iii. William Lake.

The Mansions of England and Wales, ed. Edward Twycross.

The Cornish Church Guide, 1925.

The Visitations of the County of Cornwall.

A Handbook of Titled and Official Classes, Kelly & Co.

Dictionary of National Biography.

Western Engineers in the Modernisation of Japan, Teijiro Muramatsu. Hitachi Limited, Tokyo.

Royal Engineers Journal: September 1930 and June 1943.